May 1995

To Good Neighbors
David & Debby Braun
& Kids

Bob McClory

TURNING POINT

TURNING POINT

The Inside Story of the Papal Birth Control
Commission, and How *Humanae Vitae* Changed the
Life of Patty Crowley and the Future of the Church

ROBERT McCLORY

CROSSROAD • NEW YORK

1995

The Crossroad Publishing Company
370 Lexington Avenue, New York, NY 10017

Printed in the United States of America

Library of Congress Cataloging-in-Publication Data

McClory, Robert, 1932–
    Turning point : the inside story of the Papal Birth Control
Commission, and how Humanae vitae changed the life of Patty Crowley
and the future of the church / Robert McClory.
        p. cm.
    Includes bibliographical references and index.
    ISBN: 0-8245-1458-0 (hc)
    1. Birth control—Religious aspects—Catholic Church. 2. Catholic
Church. Papal Birth Control Commission. 3. Catholic Church. Pope
(1963–1978 : Paul VI). Humanae vitae. 4. Crowley, Patricia Caron,
1913–   . I. Title.
HQ766.3.M43   1995
241'.66–dc20   95-3454
                                                                    CIP

Contents

Foreword

By Sidney Callahan

Decisive moments in history shape the lives of individuals and institutions, for good or ill. A gripping account of one such turning point in the twentieth century life of the Roman Catholic Church is found in Robert McClory's story of the rise and fall of the Papal Birth Control Commission. A unique feature of this particular narrative is that Patty Crowley tells the inside story of her experiences on the Commission; as the president couple of the international Christian Family Movement Pat and Patty Crowley had been invited to participate in the meetings held in Rome. Listening to Patty's own words, along with those of other survivors of the Commission, produces a you-are-there immediacy to these pages.

But the tale that unfolds encompasses much more than individual adventures encountered on the road to Rome and back. Looming above, beyond, and within this narrative is the larger question of the appropriate use of Church authority in determining morality for the whole Church. Are the faithful to be consulted, or not? Is the Church to be run like a monarchy, or like a community of believers who constitute the people of God? The sad story of the Commission, how its recommendations were undermined and finally repudiated by Pope Paul VI in *Humanae Vitae*, reveals a disturbing and ongoing crisis in the uses and abuses of Church authority.

Vatican II, we must keep insisting, set forth an inspiring communal and collegial vision of the Church. Those who were not around in those years from 1962 to 1965 may find it hard to comprehend the heady excitement and hope that animated Catholics in that time. Bish-

ops and other delegates from around the world had been summoned to
Rome for a Council, a surprise move by Pope John XXIII, who claimed
he had been inspired by the Holy Spirit. The Council was charged with
the task of renewing the Church's Christian tradition, a renewal that
could throw open the windows of the Church to the modern world
and initiate a new Christian era. During the Council's dramatic deliberations and in its sixteen official documents, the Church would come
to a fresh understanding of its Gospel message and its own nature as
Church.

Concern for marriage and the family, as the basic foundation of the
Christian community, was definitely on the agenda of the Council. But
one specific family issue, the troubling question of the use of artificial
contraception by married couples, was not ever opened up for general
discussion. Although many delegates wished to take it on, the question
was tabled because Pope John XXIII had already established a special
Papal Commission to deal with the question.

When John died in the middle of the Council, Paul VI directed
the Papal Commission to continue its work and even expanded its
membership to include more laity and married couples. The Commission had started as a small interdisciplinary all-male group but grew to
fifty-eight members from all parts of the world; at the end there were
thirty-four laypersons, including five women and three married couples,
among whom were Pat and Patty Crowley from the U.S.A.

The basic question that the Commission addressed throughout its
years of research and debate was whether the Church could and should
change its teaching on the use of artificial birth control. Was contraception truly an intrinsic evil? McClory gives a brief but excellent
summary of the background of this complex issue. He details the ups
and downs of the Church's changing attitudes toward sexuality and
marriage over the centuries; he shows how there gradually evolved a
more positive and personalist perspective on sexuality and marriage.
Indeed the Vatican Council's documents on marriage embody the fruit
of past theological developments; they present a Christian synthesis
that affirms the equal importance of marital unity and procreative
fruitfulness.

Another landmark in the history of the birth control controversy
occurred in 1951 when Pius XII taught that the use of periodic abstinence during the sterile period of the monthly cycle (the so-called
rhythm method) was permitted for couples who had morally valid reasons for avoiding procreation. This was an innovation, yet at the time

of the Council the official teaching remained Pius XI's 1930 encyclical *Casti Connubii*. Pius XI had taught that the use of artificial contraception was an intrinsic evil, always against nature's law, and therefore must be strictly forbidden to married couples no matter what their circumstances. Inspired by the Council's renewal and reform, questions naturally arose about whether the Church should and would change. The struggles of Paul VI are described by McClory, but in 1968 Paul VI returned to the teaching of *Casti Connubii* in *Humanae Vitae*.

It is no secret that in the 1990s the majority of Catholics disagree and dissent in conscience with *Humanae Vitae*'s teaching on contraception. Dissenters include many bishops and the vast majority of theologians and married Catholics. They see *Humanae Vitae* as inconsistent with the Church's evolved position on the goodness of marital sexuality and the importance of responsible family limitation in the modern world. They contend that if rhythm is acceptable, how can artificial contraception practiced for the good of the mother, the good of the married couple, and the good of existing children be an intrinsic evil?

In 1966 an overwhelming majority of the Papal Commission also became convinced that artificial contraception should be accepted. Despite the conservatives' efforts to stem the tide, the members decided that reform in the teaching was not only possible (i.e., it was not an infallible teaching) but also necessary. Whether theologians, physicians, demographers, or Catholic activists like the Crowleys, the majority were persuaded that the use of artificial contraception could be morally acceptable for married couples.

The Crowleys influenced the conclusions of the majority by bringing to the meetings three thousand letters solicited from Catholic married couples from eighteen countries. These letters came from devout members of the international network of the Christian Family Movement and had to be taken seriously as an expression of the sense of the married faithful. Almost all of the testimony reported that couples found the practice of rhythm to be harmful to their marriage and Christian family life. Other physicians on the Commission gave similar testimony. Four of the women members gave strong and moving pleas for a reform in Church teaching. In the end the vote was reported to be 52 to 4 for reform; the majority's report recommending change was sent to Pope Paul VI. The Crowleys went home assured that the Commission's findings would become Church teaching.

By this time, in 1966, the Second Vatican Council had finished its work and the delegates had returned to their dioceses. But conservative Vatican officials such as Cardinal Ottaviani of the Holy Office remained on the scene; they could continue to exercise their powerful obstructive influences on postconciliar events. Such conservatives made no secret of their general opposition to the Council's reforms. And Ottaviani and his four supporters on the Papal Commission were passionately opposed to changes in the teaching on contraception. After the official Commission was disbanded, they met and constructed a minority report, which they then submitted to the Pope.

The machinations and pressure tactics that then ensued as the small group of conservatives sought to destroy and nullify the Commission's report would be material for a farce if the results were not so tragic. Paul VI was torn, but finally gave in to Ottaviani and the arguments of his supporters. Since all this maneuvering was done in secret, there was a great deal of shock when *Humanae Vitae* appeared. The Crowleys could hardly believe it, and like many others reacted with bitter disappointment at the surprising turn of events. Soon widespread protests occurred, with the signed dissent of six hundred theologians, many statements from other Catholic organizations, and outcries from individuals. Statements by many bishops conferences also attempted to soften the teaching and leave room for the dissent of individual conscience.

Controversies and arguments over contraception continue unabated to this day. Pope John Paul II is well known as an ardent advocate of both *Humanae Vitae* and papal authority; he has made every effort to stifle dissent and ensure conformity among the bishops he appoints. Dissenting theologians have found themselves subject to punitive measures. Laypersons, and especially laywomen, who like Patty Crowley continue to voice their dissent, are more or less left alone and ignored. Since many priests and bishops do not assent to *Humanae Vitae* but yet fear to voice their convictions in public, a veil of hypocrisy covers the issue. The married laity, with the backing of theologians and their parish priests, simply accept and practice contraception. Don't ask, don't tell, is the order of the day.

Can we learn any lessons, positive or otherwise, from this story? On a positive note, we can rejoice that the Catholic Church produces such valiant women as Patty Crowley. Woven through the text of this book there is an inspiring, heart-lifting account of Pat and Patty Crowley's life and work. Theirs is a quintessential American saga marked by their extraordinary talent for innovation and practical organization, infused

by an ardent love of God and neighbor. Like some of the other participants in the Commission who come alive in this book, the Crowleys
affect us as being wonderful Catholics struggling to be faithful to the
Holy Spirit.

But what of the victorious villains in this melodrama? Since they
won, at least in the short run, they also have negative lessons to
impart. Yes, they appeared to believe sincerely that artificial contraception was intrinsically evil. But whenever queried, these opponents
of change also admitted that they could not give rational arguments for
their convictions; they held to their position solely because for the past
forty years Roman Church authorities had so taught. Their primary al-
legiance and most passionate belief was that the Church must never
admit to error or even to changes that might look like an admission
of error. The conservatives operated by fear and by instilling fear in
others that reform would endanger the Church's moral authority and
its power to exact obedience.

How ironic that the efforts to protect a pre–Vatican II version of
unbending authority resulted in far greater scandals and more serious
discrediting of Church authority than any change could have done.
The conservatives' efforts to undermine and undo the Council, their
dismissal of lay witness and the process of consultation, their frightened
retreat to unilateral papal power — all have resulted in widespread
alienation within the Church, or at least disaffection with the Vatican.

Inevitably protests and calls for reform mount. *Humanae Vitae* ensured that the old credibility gap would grow into a "credibility chasm,"
as Cardinal Suenens, the great Council leader, had warned that it
would. More to the point, the conservatives ensured that the little
known theological doctrine that a teaching must be *received* in order
to have been successfully taught in the Church becomes ever more
acclaimed and widespread.

Another positive outcome from this painful episode and its disturbing aftermath of repression of dissent is a stronger realization of the
need for structural reform in the exercise of Roman Catholic Church
authority. Vatican II's collegial vision must be put into practice. But
I doubt that we will soon see the formation of a Papal Commission
on the Proper Exercise of Authority in the Church. The bishops conferences and the faithful laity will have to fight the fight for further
renewal and reform in the Church in their diverse ways. Some of the
laity will organize reform movements in the Church, but some, like
Patty Crowley, will turn their energies toward doing the work of God

in the world by helping their neighbors in need. Whichever path is chosen, many Catholics today find themselves longing for Vatican III. Perhaps in the next millennium the Church will get another chance to deal with problems of power that do not fade gently away.

Remember this story and pass it on.

Acknowledgments

I am especially grateful to Patty Crowley, who has long believed the story of the Papal Birth Control Commission deserves to be told and retold. The book was originally her idea, and she generously shared with me her memories of the Commission and the papers of the Crowley Collection, which are in the archives at the University of Notre Dame. I also wish to thank other former members of the Commission, Dr. John Marshall, Laurent and Colette Potvin, Thomas Burch, and Mercedes Concepción, who also shared recollections and documents. Unless otherwise noted, quotations in this book by all the above Commission members are from interviews with me. Similarly, quotations and excerpts from Commission proceedings and related material are from documents supplied by Patty Crowley and other Commission members, except where noted. A special debt of gratitude is owed to Robert Blair Kaiser, whose book *The Politics of Sex and Religion*, exhaustively covers the events of the Commission and its background. Many quotations from speeches and interchanges during the Commission meetings in this book were originally cited in Kaiser's seminal work and are available nowhere else. Other books extremely helpful in setting the scene are John Noonan's *Contraception: A History of Its Treatment by the Catholic Theologians and Canonists*, William Shannon's *The Lively Debate: Response to Humanae Vitae*, Philip Kaufman's *Why You Can Disagree and Remain a Faithful Catholic*, Peter Hebblethwaite's *Paul VI: The First Modern Pope*, and John Kotre's *Simple Gifts: The Lives of Pat and Patty Crowley*. I am also grateful to my wife, Margaret, who liberated me from a wide variety of onerous household tasks to complete the manuscript and who functioned as an invaluable advance editor. Assistance in various aspects of the research was provided by

Rev. Charles Curran, Tom Fox, Yvonne Vanden Avenne, Gabe Huck, Peter Hebblethwaite, and my daughter, Jennifer. The project was also aided by the Davis-Gill Fund through the Medill School of Journalism at Northwestern University.

1

The Confrontation

What then with the millions we have sent to hell, if these norms were not valid?
— MARCELINO ZALBA, S.J.

Father Zalba, do you really believe God has carried out all your orders?
— PATTY CROWLEY

This was a remarkable interchange, coming as it did during the last week of a remarkable process that occurred over a three-year period in the mid-1960s. The process was a unique experiment in open, collegial, almost democratic decision-making. The Pope himself, two popes in fact, had authorized it. The interchange illustrated not only the tension and frustration that existed on both sides of the table but the perception on the part of all participants that they were basically equals. The question on the floor was this: Should the Church change its position that artificial contraception is intrinsically evil and therefore forbidden in all forms and under all circumstances?

Marcelino Zalba, a Spanish Jesuit and recognized expert on Church authority, especially regarding family limitation, viewed the proposed change with undisguised horror — as if the very pillars of creation would topple. Patty Crowley, an American woman, wife, mother, and organizer, saw the change as obvious and necessary — as self-evident as the Church's need to learn from its mistakes.

Along with some four dozen other men, including a sprinkling of cardinals and bishops, and four other women, Patty, fifty-one, and her husband Pat, fifty-three, sat at long tables in a meeting room of the bright, new Spanish College in Rome. They heard the debate, spoke

1

occasionally, and pondered where it all might lead. Careful attention had to be paid at all times because the participants spoke in three or four different languages (mostly French), and by the time the interpreters got through translating a speaker's comment, another person might be talking. It was difficult to listen, and that's what bothered Patty Crowley about Father Zalba. He didn't seem to be listening or thinking about what the people were saying. She thought his mind had been made up from the start. So when he provided a perfect opening, she seized the opportunity to challenge his cosmic convictions. Zalba did not respond. The process continued.

Patty, a mother of five, was a minority of a minority at this gathering. Of the five women in the room, only she and two others were present as married women. And that too bothered her. "It just struck me as ridiculous," she said years later. "How could they be talking about marriage and birth control of all things without a lot more input from the persons most directly involved?"

But the fact that women were there at all was yet another remarkable feature of this meeting. For the Pontifical Commission for the Study of Population, Family and Births (as the body was officially known) departed radically from the traditional male-only, clerical-only membership of papal commissions with its mixed membership of clergy and laity, of men and (a few) women, and of experts from a variety of professions. To be sure, the theologians (all priests) dominated the membership by profession and perhaps would have dominated the discussions if it were not for the open atmosphere and a sizable contingent of people like Pat and Patty Crowley, who came not just to listen but to contribute.

This meeting was technically the fifth of the Pontifical Commission. Six people were invited by the Pope to the first in 1963, thirteen to the second in April 1964, fifteen to the third in June 1964, fifty-eight to the fourth in 1965, and seventy-two to the whole or at least a part of this last meeting beginning in April 1966. The activities of the Commission were supposed to be conducted in total secrecy. The public, in fact, was unaware of its existence until more than a year after its formation. Security was heavy at every session. When Father Theodore Hesburgh, the president of the University of Notre Dame and prominent U.S. churchman, heard of the meeting while in Rome and stopped by to chat with the Crowleys, he asked if he might sit in on a session. Officials said no. No one attended except Commission members, a few appointed consultants, the translators, and a support staff all sworn to secrecy. In 1965 a freelance Italian photographer, a *paparazzo*, sneaked in and sat through part of a meeting until he was spied by the general secretary, who promptly alarmed all present. Several Commission members chased him through the corridors, finally cornered him, snatched his camera, and exposed the film. Before the police arrived, the culprit broke loose and escaped. Commission members were forbidden to take photos even with their own cameras until after the final session on the last day. Pat and Patty snapped some group shots with their Polaroid, producing the only known photographs of this historic gathering.

Most of the reports and records of the Commission turned over to Pope Paul VI at the conclusion have never been released by the Vatican. When some crucial ones were leaked to the *National Catholic Reporter* in 1967, the Pope was so distressed he wrote indignant letters to all the bishops on the Commission. It is possible that the remaining papers, some twelve volumes in all, may meet the same fate as the background papers for Pius XI's precedent-setting encyclical of 1930, *Casti Connubii*. That material simply disappeared in the recesses of the Vatican, as if dropped down a bottomless well.

The meetings had clear schedules and agendas, but there was a lively give-and-take quality through many of the deliberations. The group was not told specifically what conclusions it was supposed to reach, nor how it was supposed to reach them. The Pope wanted this body to follow its own lights. In the end, the overwhelming majority arrived at agreement by cutting a path where one hadn't existed before — a path made possible only because of the group's diverse constituency.

The Commission's Dilemma

Two lightning rods at this series of meetings (as Patty Crowley's mini-dialogue with Father Zalba illustrated) were "mistake" and "change." Throughout its existence the Church has found it difficult to acknowledge mistakes. Yet mistakes there have been. Few would deny that the condemnation of Galileo was a mistake. The Crusades were a mistake. The various Inquisitions were mistakes. The virtual selling of indulgences in the sixteenth century was a mistake. The failure to take any clear stand against human slavery for nineteen hundred years was a mistake. The longstanding opposition to freedom of conscience was a mistake. Each of these represented a stance taken or an approval given by the Church at its highest levels, yet rarely has the Church at its highest levels admitted mistake or error.

To be Catholic is to believe that the Holy Spirit, the Spirit of Jesus, is living with the Church down through the ages protecting it from error. To be sure, no one can say just how far that protection reaches or just how much error the Holy Spirit is willing to tolerate. The record indicates the Spirit leaves a pretty wide margin for human foibles, abysmally bad judgment, and sheer malice. Still, the institutional Church has been reluctant to come right out and make a clean breast of mistakes because that might cause a disastrous loss of confidence and credibility, a diminishing of respect for authority among the members.

In some cases mistakes were simply ignored, allowed to die a natural death. This was the case with the nineteenth-century Syllabus of Errors; it condemned eighty propositions dealing with modern ideas almost all of which have since been quietly accepted by Catholic scholars and the general public. Other mistakes have been explained away as understandable, given the political or social condition of the times in which they occurred. Thus the Crusades were often portrayed as legitimate self-defense against a perceived military threat. The condemnation of usury (demanding interest on a loan) could be seen as a reasonable prohibition against exploitation in the ages when a different economic system prevailed. And so change is allowed to happen in the Church, the sands of history covering old graves.

Sometimes the Church paints itself into a corner, giving the Holy Spirit's protective powers a real challenge. Such was the case with contraception in modern times. In clear, no-nonsense language Pope Pius XI declared in his encyclical *Casti Connubii* that acts of artificial contraception are and always will be "intrinsically evil." "Intrinsically," as unanimously understood by theologians, means "in its very nature" or "in itself." Intrinsically evil acts therefore would never be permitted for any reason whatsoever. The "intrinsically evil" label has not been lightly applied in moral matters. Killing another human being is not considered intrinsically evil — the fifth commandment notwithstanding. Taking another's possessions against that person's will is not regarded as intrinsically evil — the seventh commandment notwithstanding. In these and similar cases, say moralists, circumstances may justify the action: self-defense in the case of killing, for example, or providing food for a starving human being in the case of stealing.

But no circumstance — physical, psychological, eugenic, social, or economic — can be called forth to justify an action that is intrinsically (in its very nature) considered evil. And artificial contraception (which includes every form of birth control but rhythm) was declared intrinsically evil in the encyclical.

Pius XI believed he had good reason to take that position. The Church's tradition of opposition to contraception seemed consistent, yet suddenly Catholics were being drawn away as secular society moved in another direction, embracing birth control as a basic human right. So he took a stand. This doctrine wasn't presented as a mere disciplinary rule obliging only Catholics. It was presented as a universal prohibition, an application of the natural law, a statement of the way things are — for everyone. Non-Catholics, of course, did not take the encyclical seriously, but most Catholics did.

Then came the popularization of the rhythm method, concern over the worldwide population boom, and the pill — all complicating matters for the Pope, the bishops, and the theologians at the speculative level — and for Catholic married couples at the level of daily living. This then was the context for the Pontifical Commission. Could the Church change its unambiguous position on contraception less than forty years after it had been stated so solemnly? No time here for the sands of history to mercifully cover the grave. Could it somehow alter its position so as to allow exceptions without admitting that a mistake had been made? Little room here within the straitjacket of the intrinsically evil category. Small wonder then that tension and frustration would mark the Commission's discussions as it entered its final days.

A decade earlier these weighty matters would have been handled by a specially appointed committee of theologians or a commission of bishops or exclusively by the Pope himself, the Vicar of Christ. But the very nature of the subject — sexual relations between husband and wife — had suggested a different kind of forum, a broader one. So did theological developments in the Church. The Second Vatican Council, which was going on during the same years as the Birth Control Commission, stressed the concept of the Holy Spirit's presence not just in the magisterium (the Church's teaching authority) but in "the faithful of every rank." It spoke of the ancient "sense of the faithful" as an important instrument in determining correct teaching and interpretation. Many theologians even discussed the "consent of the faithful" — that is, the acceptance of a Church teaching by the people — as one of the factors that identify the Church's actual belief. This Commission represented an experiment in some of those ideas — a very tentative, limited experiment — but nevertheless something compatible with the spirit of the Council and with the ideas of the man who created both the Council and the Commission: Pope John XXIII. It was an experiment that might have set a precedent and provided a turning point in the way Church teaching is developed.

Pat and Patty Crowley did not come to this moment totally unprepared. They were president couple of the Christian Family Movement (CFM), a popular program to help couples make the Gospel message relevant to real life. The Crowleys read what the experts were saying about family limitation, and they regularly discussed the challenges of family life with bishops, theologians, and priest chaplains to the more than 150,000 couples involved in CFM all over the world. They had traveled widely — more widely perhaps than any other members of the Commission — to every continent, to numerous world capitals as well as countless backwater villages. They had lived in the homes of the common people, shared their food, and heard their stories. Their ideas reflected — more accurately perhaps than any other members of the Commission — what truly was the sense of the faithful on this subject.

The Forgotten Commission

Today few people have even heard of the Pontifical Commission. It would probably be completely unknown if a few of its members had not chosen to share their recollections, notes, and papers. For the most part, members have been reticent about their involvement, not because the work was difficult and frustrating but because the outcome was so disappointing. One member said, "I don't like to talk about it; I cry every time I have to discuss it because of the way things turned out." In any event, the available material is sporadic, many Commission members have died, and even the youngest are in their sixties. Patty Crowley, whose life moved through a series of upheavals after the Commission, has never been reticent about sharing her views and by sheer will power refuses to let the sands of history cover this grave. Through interviews, speeches, and articles she has written, she has kept the memory of the Commission at least dimly in the public mind.

By contrast, practically everyone has heard of *Humanae Vitae*, Pope Paul VI's 1968 encyclical that upheld the ban on contraception. Its release did indeed mark a turning point in the Catholic Church. Since

Humanae Vitae, the Church has been locked in a kind of sullen stale-mate between those who regard its doctrine as a beautiful, holistic presentation of marriage theology and those who see it as Galileo all over again. Whatever it is, the doctrine is mostly ignored by Catholics, according to twenty-five years of polling by reputable public opinion or-ganizations. The Church's credibility suffered a severe blow from which it has not recovered. At the same time the encyclical has spawned a considerable amount of reflection and creative thinking about the meaning of authority and the limits of responsible dissent.

At the institutional level, nothing has changed. The strictures are still in force, tightened in fact; acceptance of *Humanae Vitae* has even been turned into a kind of litmus test to determine who is worthy to become a bishop and who is not. Thus the problem perpetuates itself.

This book is not so much the story of *Humanae Vitae* but of what came before it and why the great experiment in broad consultation failed. Patty Crowley and other survivors who shared their memo-ries and materials from the Commission are as convinced as ever that change is inevitable, that mistakes should be acknowledged, and that the Church in the end will learn from history — when the people are ready and the Spirit is willing.

2

The Doctrine

*The married laity were a silent group. . . . Women, who might have had
the most to say, were not heard from.*

— JOHN NOONAN

The first speaker the Crowleys heard at their first meeting with the
Birth Control Commission was John T. Noonan, Jr., a thirty-nine-year-
old professor from the University of Notre Dame. Noonan had been
appointed a consultant to the Commission because of his extensive research on birth control. In fact, Harvard University Press was about to
release his book, *Contraception: A History of Its Treatment by the Catholic Theologians and Canonists.* An exhaustive, minutely detailed work,
it remains today the definitive authority on the subject. Noonan wrote
that the Church's teaching against contraception appears to be "clear
and apparently fixed forever." Yet, he pointed out, "A clear examination of the teaching may show that it does not possess an abstract
consistency and independence. It has developed. There has been tension and there has been reaction. Have the options selected made
all further choice unnecessary or impossible?"[1] That was the critical
question the Commission was supposed to answer.

Noonan's historical analysis did not supply one. However, it revealed how uncomfortable churchmen have felt regarding sexual matters through the centuries. It also revealed how the ban on contraception has bounced around like a roller coaster, how it disappeared from
the scene at times, how it's been shaped and reshaped like a ball of
putty under the influence of cultural and theological influences. The
doctrine was anything but clear and consistent.

The Testimony of Scripture

Nowhere in the Old Testament is there a condemnation of contraception. The only Old Testament citation that seemed to condemn it comes from Genesis 38. Onan was killed by Yahweh because he refused to conceive children with the widow of his brother. Though Onan had relations with the woman, said Genesis, "he let the seed be lost on the ground." Scripture scholars have long been convinced that Onan's capital offense was not coitus interruptus but disobedience toward his father, the evasion of an obligation, and a lack of family loyalty. The books of the Old Testament are replete with regulations regarding proper and improper marital activities. Intercourse during pregnancy, for example, was considered a crime on a par with adultery. Yet, Noonan pointed out, "There is no commandment against contraception in any of the codes of the law." Nevertheless, the misinterpretation of the Onan story was destined to become a major Christian argument against contraception — especially after St. Jerome in his Latin translation of the Bible altered the Hebrew text to make it seem that contraception was the real evil.

Roots of the Condemnation: First Century

The notion that sex exists only for procreation came from a pagan philosophy. Jesus left behind no catechism, no code of laws, no specific ethical directions — only the searing example of his life and the command to love one another. In the first century C.E., as the New Testament was being formed, the dominant philosophical system in the Greco-Roman world was Stoicism. The Stoics distrusted emotion, viewed dependence on others with scorn, and spoke in terms of justice, not love. Naturally Stoics had problems with marriage since it tended to make man and woman mutually dependent; they also had trouble with sexual activity because of its emotional (sometimes irrational) overtones. After considerable discussion, orthodox Stoics concluded that marriage is, in the final analysis, an appropriate institution — for one reason and one only: propagation of the race.

Said Seneca, perhaps the best known first-century Stoic, "All love of another's wife is shameful; so too, too much love of your own. A wise man ought to love his wife with judgment, not affection."

Herein lay the seed for the early Christian doctrine on marriage. Sex was valid as a biological mechanism for reproduction, not for pleasure.

Anything that deprived sexual activity of its generative function was by implication illicit and sinful. Seneca's views were echoed almost word for word by the prominent writers of the early Church: Clement of Alexandria in the first century, Origen in the second, Lactantius in the third, St. Jerome in the fourth.

Doubts about Sex: First Century

The threat posed by Gnosticism, an early heresy, left the Church uneasy and distrustful of sex. The Greek word *gnōsis* means knowledge, and Gnostics contended they had access to special, higher information about the real message of Christ and the meaning of his life — information not available to normal Christians. Combining magic, mysticism, and myths with basic Christian belief, Gnostics came in many forms, proselytizing everywhere in the Greek and Roman worlds and winning a multitude of converts. In one extreme form, Gnostics declared that intercourse anywhere, anytime, with anyone was not only permissible but even necessary for salvation. One subgroup recommended 365 acts of intercourse a year, with a different partner every day; another put a special, sacral value on oral sex. At an opposite extreme, other Gnostics declared that intercourse is the ultimate evil and must be avoided by any means necessary, including self-castration. On one point most Gnostics were consistent: marriage was an outmoded institution and the procreation of children should be strictly prevented.

St. Paul has often been accused of having sexual hang-ups because of his injunctions against sensual allurements, wantonness, and actions "of which it is shameful to speak." In fact, Noonan pointed out, Paul's preoccupation probably stemmed from the very real enticements of zealous, free-wheeling Gnostics who were recruiting converts in the churches he had founded.

Though Gnosticism eventually faded, it left behind a legacy of suspicion about sex and considerable confusion about the real meaning of marriage. In such an uncertain environment, Christian writers followed St. Paul's example and developed a theology of virginity as superior to and safer than mere matrimony. St. Justin explained the accepted approach in the second century: "We Christians either marry only to produce children or, if we refuse to marry, are completely continent."

Yet for all this emphasis on the link between sex and procreation, Noonan was unable to find any explicit condemnation of contraception itself in the early centuries. "No one," he wrote, "addresses himself solely to the sinfulness of a single contraceptive act by a married person with reason not to have more children."

The Impact of Augustine: Fourth–Fifth Centuries

Reaction to the Manichees further tainted Christian attitudes. The doctrine on marriage might have broadened in the fourth and fifth centuries if it were not for the threat posed by this Gnostic-like sect, which also opposed procreation but on more elaborate and imaginative grounds. The Manichees claimed sparks of light created by the Father (the good god) had been imprisoned in humans and other worldly creatures formed by the Prince of Darkness (the evil god). Humans, according to the seven sacred Manichee books, could release the trapped light by various methods including sexual intercourse (often in ritual form), but for no reason whatsoever could humans cooperate in the conception of another human being, that is, another creature of the Prince of Darkness.

Much of what is known of the Manichees comes from the voluminous writings of one of their most ardent disciples, Augustine of Hippo. From age eighteen to twenty-nine, he had hurled himself into this system of thought that regarded humans as essentially diabolical and procreation as disaster. On his conversion to orthodoxy, due in large part to the persistence of his mother, Augustine decided to be a perfect Christian. He abandoned his mistress, embraced chastity, and became the most influential theologian in the Church for at least the next thousand years.

The new Augustine attacked the Manichees for their sexual morals and especially for their hatred of procreation. Ironically, he also found them guilty of practicing rhythm. In one of his books he excoriated the heretics for recommending that conception could be prevented by avoiding intercourse during the fertile days of a woman's period as determined by Greek physicians. As a Christian, Augustine found procreation a worthy enterprise and marriage an acceptable, though not ideal, institution.

But due to his Manichean excesses, he held a distinctly jaundiced view toward sex in general and women in particular. His works are replete with comments like this: "I feel that nothing more turns the masculine mind from the heights than female blandishments and that contact of bodies without which a wife may not be had." He regarded virginity as a better state than marriage and extolled Mary as the ideal human because she combined the "impossibles": virginity with the blessing of a child and motherhood without the burden of sex. He maintained that continence within marriage should be preferred over intercourse, telling his disciples, "Insist on the work of the flesh only in such measure as necessary for the procreation of children. Since you cannot beget children in any other way, you must descend to it against your will, for it is the punishment of Adam." He frequently compared sexual activity with the consumption of food: one is necessary for the good of the race, the other for the good of the body; neither activity is especially noble or praiseworthy.

There is in Augustine's analysis no mention of love, noted Noonan. Marriage is instead seen as a legal contract designed for procreation — a conception that has colored the Church's marriage legislation ever since. As Christianity settled in as the official religion of the old, fading Roman empire, the teachings of Augustine acquired an almost infallible character.

Mistaken Biology: Sixth–Eleventh Centuries

Given the limited understanding of the human reproductive system, the distinction between contraception and abortion was not clear for many centuries. Condemnations in old Church documents are usually unspecific. The earliest refer to the taking of drugs or herbs to induce sterility; later there are frequent references to "onanism," which meant coitus interruptus (male withdrawal and ejaculation outside the vagina of his wife). By contrast, abortion is derided repeatedly as a grave sin. Offenders were prohibited from receiving communion for periods ranging from ten years to life. Concluded Noonan, "If abortion is so often castigated, and contraception so little, contraception cannot have been regarded generally as a major offense against God."

During the Dark Ages from 700 to 1100, there was little development. The Stoic-Augustinian foundation remained firm and unchallenged. For a time all contraceptive acts were regarded as murder. One text formulated during this era acquired a kind of immortality. Called *Si Aliquis*, it declared, "If someone . . . does something to a man or woman so that no children be born of him or her, or gives them to drink so that he cannot generate or she conceive, let it be held as homicide." Incorporated into early canon law in the thirteenth century, *Si Aliquis* remained part of official Church law until 1917.

A Harsh Doctrine: Twelfth Century

The exaggerated link between sex and procreative intention stiffened in the twelfth century as Catharism (or Albigensianism), yet another heretical movement, showed itself in Europe. Cathars claimed that coitus, even in marriage, amounted to adultery. In a short time Cathar congregations headed by a hierarchy of bishops and priests contended with traditional Christian churches for the loyalty of the faithful. The movement occasioned an ecumenical council, the Fourth Lateran, which condemned the heresy. As before, the authorities relied on Augustine, arguing that carnal intercourse in marriage is licit, though only for reproductive purposes. Conjugal relations solely to avoid adultery or for the satisfaction of lust were regarded by some commentators as venial sins and by many as mortal. In the Canterbury Tales, Chaucer's parson advises the faithful that marital relations not for children but "only for amorous love" constitute a mortal sin. This is not to suggest that married persons always followed the rule. Secular medical books discussed at length "the use of things preventing conception" though the level of scientific understating left much to be desired. One such volume in the twelfth century listed among acceptable preventatives the eating of iron filings, the rennet of a rabbit, the heart of a deer, black peas, or mint juice. A woman can achieve temporary sterility, suggested another book, by eating a bee.

Glimmerings of Light: Twelfth–Fifteenth Centuries

More balanced attitudes toward marriage and sex gradually developed. The late twelfth century saw the first glimmerings of a more holistic approach. A leading theologian of the time, Peter Abelard, made bold to argue that a couple whose general intention is procreative do not sin in any way should they have intercourse on occasion merely for the sake of amorous love. Abelard's persuasive discourses might have had a deeper effect on Church teaching, noted Noonan, if his personal history had not been so turbulent. Originally a monk, Abelard renounced his vows, married, and fathered a child, only to be punished by Church authority through castration and forcible separation from his wife, Heloise.

The theological giant of the thirteenth century, St. Thomas Aquinas, remained basically faithful to the Augustinian legacy — but with some progressive nuances. He glimpsed something valuable in marriage besides its procreative potential. "For there is something miraculous in a man finding in one woman a pleasingness which he can never find in another, as say the experienced," he noted. And Aquinas prepared the way for later development in his observation that the delight that proceeds from an act shares the moral value of the act itself.

During the fifteenth century more progress occurred. In his book *The Praiseworthy Life of the Married*, Denis the Carthusian (a monk) argued that marriage may not be as great a risk for salvation as many had supposed. And Martin de Maistre, a French academic with a cool, professional style, contended that the traditional doctrine, formulated without any input from married persons, set up unreasonable and intolerable burdens. Citing Aristotle, he wrote, "I say that someone can wish to take pleasure, first for love of that pleasure, secondly to avoid tedium and the ache of melancholy caused by the lack of pleasure." Noonan commented that de Maistre's "appeal to the dilemma of married Christians joined with the most open, penetrating and comprehensive application of Aristotelian reasoning to marriage . . . led to a sweeping legitimation of the non-procreative purposes of intercourse."

The stage appeared to be set at that point, some six hundred years ago, for a major reconsideration of doctrine. If procreation and sex were not inextricably linked, if pleasure was a value in itself, if the need to educate children provided a legitimate reason to limit family size (as some theologians were suggesting), why shouldn't the ban on contraception be reevaluated?

A Road Not Followed: Sixteenth Century

The relaxation of the condemnation of usury provided a precedent, but it was not applied to contraception. Through the centuries usury had been condemned in three different ecumenical councils and in language far stronger and more explicit than ever used against contraception. The doctrine was regarded as fixed and unchangeable. Yet within a relatively short period in the sixteenth century, everything changed. Without acknowledging past error, Church authorities found usury an acceptable, even praiseworthy practice. The development of newer economic systems, they said, required the reevaluation of an ancient doctrine. The shift was not strongly opposed because Church organizations, especially bishops and abbots, had a practical interest in the use of credit. "Centralized financial structures requiring credit were important to a centralized Church," noted Noonan. "The papacy, the bishops, the orders used bankers in the daily conduct of their ordinary business."

Yet these celibates had no such vested, personal interest in the issues of married life. Nor did the theologians who discussed and argued about the morality of various marital activities.

"The married laity were a silent group," said Noonan. "They did not write on birth control. Women, who might have had the most to say, were not heard from." And Noonan added, "The silence is striking in an age when literacy was no longer confined to clerics. It seems accounted for by the strong inhibitions against speaking candidly on sexual behavior stamped as unnatural." And so the ban on contraception was not subjected to the kind of minute scrutiny that might have led to reconsideration. It hung in mid-air, intact and unchallenged.

Rigorism Reborn: Sixteenth–Seventeenth Centuries

The impact of Jansenism muffled new ideas. The founder was Cornelis Jansen, the bishop of Ypres in Belgium and a moral rigorist described by Noonan as "Augustine transported from the fifth century to the seventeenth and restored without allowance for the growth that had occurred in the Church." Jansenism became firmly entrenched in the dominant theological centers at Douai and Louvain. Resurrected were the old links between sin and sex, the repugnance toward pleasure, the insistence that any kind of voluntary sexual stimulation outside marriage whether in deed or thought merited damnation. In the seventeenth and eighteenth centuries the English-speaking clergy received their training principally at Jansenist schools, and in this way the movement was exported to England and Ireland and eventually to America, where it flourished.

An example of neo-Augustinian excess can be seen during the pontificate of Pope Sixtus V in the late sixteenth century. In his bull *Effraenatum*, Sixtus invoked all the penalties of homicide from both canon and secular laws against those who "proffer potions and poisons of sterility to women and offer an impediment to the conception of a fetus." This amounted to the strongest sanction ever against contraception, and it might well have resulted in massive prosecution were it not for the fact that Church and civil authorities refused to impose it and Church members declined to take it seriously. *Effraenatum* thus became a prime case of a doctrine "not received" by the Church, even though enjoined by its highest authority. Within three years of Sixtus's death, his successor repealed most of the penalties, saying the bull should be regarded "as if it had never been issued."

The Permissive Approach:
Eighteenth–Nineteenth Centuries

In the eighteenth century a "don't ask — don't tell" trend developed. The predominant voice on marital morality was St. Alphonsus Ligouri. A civil lawyer before he became priest, bishop and founder of the Redemptorist religious order, Ligouri strove mightily to temper the severe forms of the Augustinian tradition. He upheld the inherent value of martial coitus even in situations where procreation was not a desired goal, and he counseled confessors to preserve the good faith of penitents by not prying too intently into their marital habits. Such was Ligouri's reputation that he almost single-handedly moved the emphasis in marital morality away from the mechanics of the act and toward the concerns and needs of the persons involved in the act. The trend grew stronger in the nineteenth century. When a bishop in 1842 asked the Sacred Penitentiary of the Vatican whether spouses who did not accuse themselves of contraception in confession should be considered in good faith and therefore not subject to explicit interrogation, the response was that confessors "would do well to follow the advice of Alphonsus Ligouri."

When Pope Leo XIII in 1880 issued a major encyclical on marriage, he did not even mention coitus interruptus or any other form of contraception. "Not a sentence indicated directly that it was a major problem," said Noonan. "Under 'duties' of spouses it was not mentioned. Even when the Pope turned to the bishops to urge them to instruct the faithful on the nature of marriage, nothing specific was said against it." Instead Leo stressed the holiness and sacramentality of marriage.

Explicit Condemnations:
Nineteenth–Twentieth Centuries

Concern about a declining birth rate in the nineteenth century prompted Church authorities to move aggressively against contraception. The decline, first observed in France in the early eighteenth century, was due, in the view of most observers, to an increase in contraceptive activity. The condom had become readily available, though coitus interruptus seemed the preferred practice. Vatican officials made sporadic attempts to impose stricter policies against contraception, but with little consistency.

In 1886, for example, the Vatican Sacred Penitentiary said confessors who have "founded suspicions" should regularly interrogate penitents, instruct those found to be practicing birth control on the seriousness of their sin, and refuse absolution unless they promised to cease the practice. It remained unclear what "founded suspicions" meant. The order was virtually ignored.

Then in the early 1900s condemnations became explicit when the Jesuit moralist Arthur Vermeersch, who was to have great influence on twentieth-century morality of marriage, entered the scene. Through his writings and growing reputation, he persuaded the Belgian bishops to take the Vatican's strict directives more seriously. Eventually explicit condemnations of contraceptive practices were invoked by Church leaders in France, Germany, and the United States. In some dioceses bishops required their priests to inquire into the practices of every married person coming to confession even if the priest had no foundation for suspicion. A kind of tug-of-war ensued between the proponents of tolerance and those insisting on a more Jansenistic rigor.

In the United States, Monsignor John A. Ryan, a professor at the Catholic University of America, well respected as a pioneer on Catholic social teaching, tried to develop a middle course. He acknowledged a widespread use of birth control by Catholic Americans but doubted they perceived the practice as mortal sin. He recommended their good faith be not too hastily disturbed. Vermeersch and the Vatican would not let that attitude prevail for long.

The Challenge

From within their human experience of marriage . . . the married couple, and they alone, can answer the question of what God requires of them concretely in their vocation.

— BISHOP WILLIAM BEKKERS

To understand their task, the Commission members had to realize how profoundly public attitudes toward contraception had changed during the twentieth century. What the Church regarded as pariah and perversion, secular society (and other Christian churches) were coming to see as common sense, even salvation. In the United States and in much of the Western world, no one was more active in this reconstruction effort than Margaret Sanger, a New York nurse credited with coining the term "birth control." Struck by the suffering and ill health due to unwanted pregnancies that she encountered in major urban centers, Sanger at the age of thirty-three in 1916 opened in Brooklyn the first birth control clinic in the United States. Nine days later the police closed down the operation, and a judge sentenced her to thirty days in prison for obscenity. She had violated the so-called Comstock law, which forbade, among other things, the dissemination of objects or information for the prevention of conception.

The law had been passed by Congress in 1873, not at the behest of the Catholic Church but through the crusading work of Anthony Comstock, a strict Calvinist and head of the New York Anti-Pornography organization. In his latter years Comstock claimed he had destroyed 160 tons of obscene material and brought about the conviction of "enough persons to fill a passenger train of 61 coaches."[1]

But a lot had changed between 1873 and 1916. The trend from

a predominantly agricultural economy to an industrial one meant that large families were no longer an absolute advantage. Improvements in medicine and health care meant more children survived into adulthood. The need to provide those children with education meant parents had to conserve their limited resources. The first tentative rise in consciousness concerning women's equality meant a rethinking of the traditional motherhood role.

All these factors had been chipping away at the traditional positions ever since a precipitous dip in the birth rate had been observed in France in the early nineteenth century. That dip continued to grow steeper and wider with each new decade. There could be little doubt that couples were taking contraceptive measures largely on their own authority, regardless of the law or the Church.

When Margaret Sanger emerged from jail, she resolved to spend the rest of her life fighting for legal acceptance and popular respectability for birth control. She succeeded in large measure. The Comstock law was rendered impotent by Congress in 1936 and finally laid to rest in 1958. Attitudes regarding contraception gradually shifted from suspicion to tolerance to limited respectability to full acceptance, even advocacy.

Throughout this transition, the Catholic Church at the institutional level never budged. The firm stand that Arthur Vermeersch inspired originally in the Belgian hierarchy was adopted by bishops' organizations all over the world. In a letter read at all Masses on Washington's birthday in 1920, the U.S. bishops said, "It is idealism of the truest and most practical sort that sees in marriage the divinely appointed plan for cooperating with the Creator in perpetuating the race.... The selfishness which leads to race suicide ... is, in God's sight, a detestable thing. It is the crime of individuals for which, eventually, the nation must suffer."[2] Directors and boards at Catholic schools, hospitals, and other institutions felt a steady pressure to resist the contraceptive trend.

Personalist Theology

But even as the Church manned the battlements against the perceived permissiveness and licentiousness, theologians working within the walls were developing a new personalist theology of marriage that would in the long run call all the old assumptions into question. An important pioneer in this was the German philosopher Dietrich von Hildebrand, described by Noonan as "the first married layman to make a substantial contribution to Catholic doctrine on marriage."³ In 1925 he delivered a series of lectures at the University of Munich extolling the concept of sexual pleasure as a good in its own right and sharply disputing the old Augustinian comparison between the appetite for food and the appetite for sex. Of all the appetites in human nature, he argued, the sexual one holds a unique place because of its depth. "De-light in a good dinner, for example, or annoyance at a bad one, belongs of its nature to the superficial zone of human existence." But sexual ex-periences "display a depth and gravity which remove them altogether from the province of other bodily experiences." It is precisely through these experiences, he said, that humans can rise to a realm that is psy-chological and even spiritual. The marital act has not only a function of generation of children; it also possesses a significance for human be-ings as such — namely, to be "the expression and fulfillment of wedded love and community of life." To overlook the union between physical sex and love or its significance and to recognize only the purely unitar-ian bond between sex and the propagation of the race is to "degrade man and to be blind to the meaning of this mysterious domain."

Thus von Hildebrand saw in sexual intercourse an intrinsic impor-tance quite apart from its generative potential. In his later writing on the subject he came close to turning the Augustinian doctrine on its head. Coitus, he said, stands out front as the unique self-giving of hus-band and wife, while the procreation of children should be seen as a kind of "superabundant" bonus. "To this high good (marital inter-course] that has a meaning and value in itself," he wrote, "has been entrusted procreation."⁴

These ideas stimulated a generation of scholarship and investiga-tion. In 1935, ten years after von Hildebrand's Munich lectures, a German priest and theologian, Herbert Doms, enlarged on the insights in his book The Meaning and Ends of Marriage.

Doms said eloquently what had only been hinted at before: not only marriage, but marital intercourse, was a means of achieving holiness. Doms claimed the marital union is not simply or even mainly a physi-cal union; it is rather a union that is metaphysical because it leaves a permanent imprint on the personalities of husband and wife. "The two partners grasp each other reciprocally in intimate love; that is, spiri-tually they reciprocally give themselves in an act which contains the abandonment and enjoyment of the whole person and is not sin," said Doms. Even when the couple really want to conceive through their marital activities, he noted, the intention is personal fulfillment rather than propagation of the species. "The woman says, 'I want to be a mother.' She does not say, 'The species must continue,' or 'It is my duty to have a child.' "[5]

Neither von Hildebrand nor Doms went so far as to find contraception acceptable. Both saw the unitive and procreative ends of intercourse as inseparable. Nevertheless, both challenged at the root level the centuries-old presupposition that marriage could be analyzed (and legislated about) in abstract, categorical terms far removed from the lived experience of couples. Their innovative ideas would be expanded on by later theologians and commentators.

Casti Connubii

In the history of birth control 1930 proved to be a decisive year. First, the Church of England at its triennial Lambeth Conference became the first mainline Christian denomination to officially endorse contraception. By a 3–1 ratio, the bishops provided in their declaration a qualified, almost begrudging assent to the movement for change. "Where there is a clearly felt moral obligation to limit or avoid parenthood, the method must be decided by Christian principles. The primary and obvious method is complete abstinence from intercourse. . . . Nevertheless, where there is a morally sound reason for avoiding complete abstinence, the Conference agrees that other methods may be used, provided that this is done in the light of . . . Christian principles."[6]

This acceptance by the branch of Christianity closer than any other in discipline and theology to the Roman Catholic Church was received as a slap in the face by the Catholic hierarchy. There was more than a little bitterness in the reaction of Cardinal Francis Bourne, archbishop of Westminster. "It is recognized," he said, "that the prelates who have adopted this resolution have abdicated any claim which they may have been thought to possess to be authorized exponents of Christian morality."[7]

In Rome the Jesuit moralist Vermeersch, then seventy-two years old and still teaching at the Gregorian University, believed the Anglican apostasy deserved a definitive, unambiguous response from the highest Catholic authority. It is generally conceded that he was the principal author of the papal document that became, just four months after the Lambeth declaration, the second significant development of 1930. Pius XI's encyclical *Casti Connubii* distilled the teachings of Augustine, Aquinas, and a dozen other classical interpreters of doctrine. Paraphrased were twelfth- and sixteenth-century admonitions against contraception. Omitted was any reference to historical development of the doctrine or the personalist insights of moderns like von Hildebrand. The wording was grave and the judgment seemingly absolute: "Assuredly no reason, even the most serious, can make congruent with nature and decent what is intrinsically against nature. Since the act of the spouses is by its own nature ordered to the generation of offspring, those who, exercising it, deliberately deprive it of its natural force and power, act against nature and effect what is base and intrinsically indecent."[8]

Further on, Pius recapitulated his teaching. "No reason, however grave, can be put forward by which anything intrinsically against nature may become conformable to nature and morally good. Since, therefore, the conjugal act is destined primarily by nature for the begetting of children, those who...deliberately frustrate its power...sin against nature and commit a deed which is...intrinsically vicious."

The tone of the document convinced many theologians, Vermeersch in particular, that here was an infallible pronouncement. Others said it was just a recapitulation of traditional teaching and, though binding on Catholics, subject to future reconsideration. Also disputed was exactly what the encyclical forbade. From the wording it seemed obvious that coitus interruptus and the use of a condom or diaphragm would be forbidden since they deprived the act of its natural power of procreating life. Pius also condemned direct sterilization, that is, having an operation or taking a drug with the intention of avoiding conception. Vermeersch, who provided immediate and authoritative interpretation, explained that although sterilization is acceptable to treat serious health problems, it is so gravely wrong when undertaken for contraceptive purposes that those who obtain an irreversible sterilization may not even engage in marital intercourse unless they repent of their sin.

From 1930 until 1968 *Casti Connubii* stood as the Catholic Church's official marriage document. Those on the Papal Birth Control Commission preferring a wholesale reconsideration or at least a less strict approach would have to confront its seeming finality. It loomed for decades like a great cornerstone, the slightest movement of which might bring down the entire edifice of the Church's marriage doctrine.

Rhythm Approved

The year 1930 also saw a third development that would radically broaden the discussion of birth limitation. In that year the results of two medical researchers were published in Europe and the United States. Working independently, Dr. Kyusaku Ogino in Japan and Dr. Hermann Knaus in Austria established beyond doubt the existence of a "safe period." By avoiding intercourse during the five or six days in the menstrual cycle when ovulation occurs, a couple could prevent conception. In the United States, the findings were popularized by Dr. Leo Latz in his book *The Rhythm of Fertility and Sterility in Women,* which went through seventeen printings within a few years.

Those still reeling from the severity of *Casti Connubii* saw here a ray of hope. In rhythm (or more euphemistically, "periodic continence"), the integrity of the marital act was preserved; couples simply took advantage of nature. Theologians were not so enthusiastic at first. Some called the new development "Oginoism," presumably a first cousin of Onanism. Vermeersch insisted rhythm would certainly spawn a contraceptive mentality among Catholics, leading ultimately to "the heresy of the empty crib." Others, including Monsignor John Ryan, could find no intrinsic evil in rhythm. Gerald Kelly, a leading Jesuit moralist, gave this cautious approbation: "Only exceptional couples can take up the practice of the 'rhythm-theory' without exposing their married lives to grave dangers; and even these couples usually need the special grace of God."[9]

The discussion continued from 1930 to 1951, when Pope Pius XII provided some clarity in an allocution on the subject. Speaking before the Italian Catholic Society of Midwives, he gave explicit approval of the rhythm method — with certain qualifications. Its legitimate use depended, he said, on whether or not adequate grounds existed to limit offspring. He declared, however, that "serious motives" of a "medical, eugenic, economic and social" nature are "not rarely present" [meaning are *often* present], and they may persist "for a long time, even for the duration of a marriage."[10] These motives, he declared, make "the observance" of the sterile period licit on moral grounds.

The statement, with its recognition of "economic" and "social" reasons for family limitation, seemed a departure from the restrictive and crabbed interpretation of some moral theologians; rhythm was not to be seen as an emergency measure justified only in extraordinary situations. Henceforth Catholics were free to make judgments within a relatively wide range of "serious motives." The two statements of doctrine — Pius XI's *Casti Connubii* and Pius XII's talk to the midwives — became the Yin and Yang of twentieth-century Catholic marital teaching: on the one hand, contraceptive birth control was ruled immoral; on the other, rhythm and it alone was found permissible.

Lest anyone miss the point, the Pope went on record one month later before a meeting (ironically) of the Italian Association of Large Families. "We have affirmed," he said, "the legitimacy and ... the limits — in truth very broad — of a regulation of offspring which, unlike so-called birth control, is compatible with the law of God."[11]

The implications of the statement were fascinating. While most moralists tried to categorize the sort of "serious motives" that would justify long-term use of rhythm, others began to ponder (at least in private) harder questions: By approving rhythm, wasn't the Holy Father really saying that it is lawful to separate sexual intercourse from its procreative purpose? And wasn't he urging scientists to find easier and better ways for couples to enjoy marital relations and at the same time avoid pregnancy? In effect, Pius XII seemed to be opening a line of reasoning not far removed from that of von Hildebrand and Doms.

The Pill

But before these matters could be adequately addressed, the coming of the birth control pill complicated everything. It arrived in 1952 just one year after Pius's speech to the midwives. A Boston physician, Benjamin Sieve, reported that the drug hesperidin had produced temporary sterility in a test group of three hundred couples. Moralists were quick to condemn: as a sterilizing agent, the drug was considered a form of self-mutilation and therefore a violation of the fifth commandment; as a contraceptive it barred reproduction and therefore violated the sixth commandment. Hesperidin discussion was short-lived because in just the next year, 1953, a different, apparently more effective oral contraceptive was developed using a synthetic form of progesterone. Progesterone is produced naturally by a woman's body when she is pregnant, and it halts ovulation. The new synthetic variety essentially fooled the ovaries into believing pregnancy had occurred, thus rendering a woman sterile as long as she took the pill.

This drug would have met the same unwelcome reception as its predecessor if it were not for the fact that it had other effects besides sterility. Experiments showed that the progesterone pill could help regulate irregular and unpredictable menstrual cycles. It also proved useful in correcting certain menstrual disorders such as abnormal bleeding. According to the time-honored principle of the double effect, an action that has several effects is morally permissible if the good effect flows directly from the action (and not as a secondary result of the bad effect), if the person intends only the good effect, and if the resulting good is greater than the permitted evil. In the case of the pill, it seemed the first two conditions could easily be met. For example, a woman using the pill might intend only to regularize her cycle and not the concomitant sterilization. But some debate ensued among theologians over whether regularizing a woman's cycle or curing menstrual problems constituted a "sufficient reason" to allow the bad effect. Several said female irregularity should not be considered a malady meriting such an extreme remedy. It is noteworthy that the discussion on this important point involving women's health was carried on in the 1950s exclusively by men, virtually all of whom were celibates.

In 1958 Pope Pius XII offered guidance when he spoke at a conference of hematologists. If a woman takes "such medicine, not to prevent conception, but only on the advice of a doctor as a necessary remedy because of the condition of the uterus or the organism, she produces indirect sterilization, which is permitted according to the general principles governing acts with a double effect."[12]

Still, the pill continued to raise fascinating questions. Would it be permissible for a woman to take the pill during the time she is breast feeding her infant in order to guarantee that she does not become pregnant? Some said yes, since she would be only making certain that nature did its job in providing a period of normal sterility. Others said no, since she seemed to be directly intending sterilization. Might a woman who wanted to become pregnant use to pill in order to experience its "ovulation rebound" benefits? Research had shown that fertility potential increased dramatically if the pill was taken regularly for several months and then discontinued. Most commentators favored such a use, but some saw a problem because the good effect (pregnancy) might be produced through the bad effect (sterility).

By the 1960s, the pill was widely used by couples, and it was just as widely discussed, not just by specialists but by average lay people, especially those of childbearing age. One reason for its popularity, at least among Catholics, was a growing disillusion with rhythm. It did not work nearly as well in practice as in theory. Lighthearted references to "rhythm babies" were not so funny to couples who found another pregnancy a severe hardship.

Calls for Change

In 1961 a dramatic call for the Church to reconsider its restrictive approach to the pill appeared in an unlikely place: *Good Housekeeping* magazine. John Rock, a Boston physician who helped develop the pill, argued that synthetic progesterone only makes it possible for humans to do predictably and by the use of reason what nature does in an unpredictable manner through the non-rational organs of the body. Expanding the idea in his later book *The Time Has Come,* Rock said the pill merely modifies time sequences in the body and therefore does not deserve the label of sterilization. He preferred terms like "a deferment of the reproductive system" or even a "conservation" of the system. While a woman is on the pill, he noted, "the ova, instead of maturing to a condition where they must die if they are not fertilized, will rest in the ovary to become available when, on omission of medication, nature calls them forth."[13]

Rock's reasoning stirred a cavalcade of reaction from official Church sources, most of it negative. Yet it stimulated further thought in some quarters. In Louvain, Belgium, theologian Louis Janssens, a veteran commentator on marital morality, declared he could find no essential difference between the use of the pill and the practice of rhythm. In rhythm, he noted, the couple intends to suppress reproduction and does so by carefully calculating the time of ovulation and the time required for the disintegration of the ovum. "All these calculations show quite well that a temporal obstacle is intentionally being placed in the way of the ovum's performing its reproductive function (just as the use of mechanical methods or of coitus interruptus places a spatial obstacle for the same purpose)."[14] Use of the pill also involves the use of a temporal obstacle, he said, and like rhythm it preserves intact the structure of the act of intercourse. Following Rock's thought, he said, the pill should not be considered sterilization as that word had been generally understood, since it doesn't destroy any organ or diminish its health; it only delays its activity.

In 1963 for the first time, a Catholic bishop publicly broke ranks with his peers over the question of birth control. William Bekkers, bishop of 's-Hertogenbosch, Holland, spoke on national television and said the Church does not have answers on these complicated issues and should stop pretending it does; in the meanwhile, couples must rely on their faith and common sense: "From within their human experience of marriage, that is, out of their lives and responsibility for each other, for their reproductive powers, and for the family that already exists, the married couple — and they alone — can answer the question of what God requires of them concretely in their vocation. They must decide how large their family should be and how their children should be spaced. . . . This is a matter for their own consciences with which nobody should interfere. . . . The Church does not judge situations from a prejudiced, aloof point of view. . . . It knows that what may be attainable for one person is not necessarily so for another."

Bekkers suggested that official Church pronouncements ought to contain qualifiers like "as far as we can judge now." A few months later, the Dutch bishops in the first statement ever on the pill by a national hierarchy, agreed with Bekkers. Scientific advances, they noted, present problems for which the Church "has no immediately appropriate answers ready that meet all situations."

It was in the midst of so many challenging and contradictory positions that Pope John XXIII appointed the Pontifical Birth Control Commission.

4

The Awakening

For the first time in our experience with the Church, our ideas were respected.

— PATTY CROWLEY

When Patricia Crowley was born in 1913, Pius X was the Pope in Rome, and the distinction between clergy and laity was clear and apparently fixed forever. As Pius put it: "The Church is essentially an unequal society...comprising two categories of persons, the pastors and the flock." Since the pastors alone possess authority, "the one duty of the multitudes is to allow themselves to be led and, like a docile flock, to follow the pastors."[1]

The Church's unyielding stand on contraception was one part of a larger picture: a Church that felt itself threatened on all sides by expanding technologies, new materialistic philosophies, and the surge of European nationalism. The siege mentality prompted a whole battery of laws and condemnations, the violations of which meant mortal sin and possibly eternal hellfire. In his book *The Catholic Experience*, historian Jay Dolan observed, "Catholicism was clearly a religion of authority, and people learned not only to pray but also to obey. Being a Catholic meant to submit to the authority of God as mediated through the Church — its bishops and pastors. In such a culture, the rights of the individual conscience were de-emphasized, as each person was conditioned to submit to the external authority."[2]

Church was seen as essentially a vertical structure with the truth coming down from above: from God to the Pope, from the Pope to the bishops, bishops to pastors, and pastors to laity. In the United States and Canada, especially, with long traditions of Jansenistic conformity, Pope Pius X's definition of Church came close to reality.

Patricia (always known as Patty) was the daughter of Ovidas Joseph Caron (more familiarly referred to as O.J.). He was born in Quebec but moved to the United States with his father and brother after a diphtheria epidemic killed his mother and his other siblings. O.J. was only six at the time. He was raised in the strict, no-nonsense, unquestioning style that Pius would have found exemplary. He started working at nine emptying cuspidors in a textile factory and never got beyond the sixth grade. As an adult O.J. Caron settled in the Midwest, and, with the aid of two partners, bought a textile mill in Rochelle, Illinois, near Chicago. It would become the Caron Spinning Company, a highly successful operation.

Patty's mother, Marietta Higman, was from a socially prominent and quite affluent family in St. Joseph, Michigan. She was a devout Baptist and member of the Daughters of the American Revolution, so her marriage to O.J., a French Canadian Catholic, in 1912 was not especially welcomed by her parents. It wasn't welcomed by the Catholic Church either, which resisted mixed marriages in those days, but the necessary dispensations were obtained, and the ceremony was performed before a priest.

Catholic marriage doctrine was honored in O.J. and Marietta's home: she bore three children in a little more than three years: Patty in 1913, Richard in 1914, and Marietta in 1915. Two more, Joan and John, would come a few years later. The burden of caring for these first three, born in such quick succession, taxed Marietta to the limit. She appeared close to a nervous breakdown in 1921 when it was decided to send Patty, then eight, to the boarding school of the Sacred Heart convent in Lake Forest, Illinois. The school was a favorite with the socially elite families along Chicago's North Shore, and the sisters who ran it, known as the Madames of the Sacred Heart, were renowned for educating girls in the fundamentals of Catholicism and social propriety. The sisters so impressed Marietta with their care and concern that she herself became a Catholic a year after Patty's first communion.

Observed John Kotre in his book *Simple Gifts: the Lives of Pat and Patty Crowley*, "The elite Catholicism that Marietta drew from the Sacred Heart nuns merged in the Caron family with the strict Jansenism of her husband and left strong impressions on their daughter." Recalled Patty, "I always remember when we were little, Daddy would never go to communion unless he went to confession right before. My father always kept the rules. We went to church every Sunday, ate fish on Friday (although Daddy hated fish), and went to Catholic schools. That was our religion, really. We usually said grace only on Christmas and special occasions."[3] In the Caron home religious ideas were never subjects for debate or even discussion.

When the family settled in Chicago, Patty, often ill as a child, was transferred to the Chicago school run by the Sacred Heart religious order. It was, she later recalled, "really very exclusive. They made you feel you were better than everybody else because you were going there and getting special training." Patty was not entirely comfortable in this rarefied atmosphere. After graduation from eighth grade, her mother let her attend a neighborhood Catholic high school, Immaculata, where, she said, "I was nobody and had to make my own way. I discovered another world besides people with money. That was the best thing that ever happened to me."

The experience was short-lived. Still in awe of the sisters, Patty's mother sent her back to the Sacred Heart school for her junior and senior years. Patty attended Trinity College in Washington, D.C., majoring in French and history, which allowed her to have a junior year abroad at the Sorbonne in Paris. At Trinity she had a class with Monsignor John Ryan, the veteran commentator on birth control but better known for his social justice advocacy. "We took the class because we heard it was easy," said Patty, "and it seemed pretty boring. But when we found a way to get him off his book and start talking to us about justice in society and labor unions, he was fascinating. I think he opened my mind to another side of things."

Patrick Crowley was born in 1911, two years before Patty, the second son of Jerome Crowley, a successful Chicago lawyer who had defended Shoeless Joe Jackson in the notorious Black Sox baseball scandal, and Henrietta O'Brien, whose family owned the expanding O'Brien Paint and Varnish Company of South Bend, Indiana. Both parents were of mostly Irish ancestry and committed to the rule-keeping variety of their faith, though a bit more relaxed about it than the Carons. They were members of a circle of similar Irish-descent, affluent Chicagoans who played bridge, golfed, and vacationed together. Patrick was provided a full Catholic education, including Loyola Academy and the University of Notre Dame. He was a handsome, outgoing young man with a great sense of humor and a lot of self-confidence, but he was not an outstanding student. After college, with the Great Depression in full swing, the Crowley family felt the pinch. Pat worked days at his father's law office and attended evening classes at the Loyola School of Law.

Pat and Patty met at a party in 1934 and dated regularly for several years. The Crowleys regarded the well-bred Patty as quite acceptable. The Carons, on the other hand, were not pleased at first with the budding relationship. They regarded the good-natured, easygoing Patrick as just "another lazy Irishman" and refused to give their consent for the marriage until Pat was making at least $55 a week. The couple lied to the Carons, assuring them Pat was earning that and more, although the real figure was only $45. Pat, twenty-six, and Patty, twenty-four, were married at Our Lady of Mount Carmel Church in Chicago in 1937 and settled down, as biographer Kotre noted, "to a marriage indistinguishable from others of that time and place. They did what their friends did. He went to work and she stayed home. They went to church. They went to cocktail parties."[4] They attended the football games at Notre Dame and fell in easily with other young marrieds, delighted with an economy finally emerging from the depths of the Great Depression.

One of their social outlets was a regular gathering of couples that started out as a poker club but became better known as "the stork club" when the wives had babies in quick succession. The men tended to gather in one area and talk about politics and world affairs, while the women congregated in another and discussed child care and recipes. Patty found herself resenting the enforced segregation, so she and some women friends studied up on a bill pending in Congress, then dazzled their spouses with their awareness of the larger world. "I think it helped the men realize that we had something to offer," said Patty.

Mrs. Caron, recalling her own experiences as an overstressed young mother, urged the newlyweds to delay having children for a while. And they did try. "We used the rhythm method," said Patty. "It never occurred to us to try anything else. Pat never liked it, checking the calendar for safe days. He always said it was so unnatural it just seemed ridiculous. Besides, everyone we knew was having children — five, six, ten, even more. That's just the way things were in those days."

Pat graduated from law school and went to work with his father's law office. Through a series of coincidences, he quickly became legal counsel to his in-laws' business, the Caron Spinning Company, and an officer and counsel to the paint and varnish company owned by his mother's family. Thus was settled early his lifelong position as a corporation lawyer. Their first child, Patricia (known as Patsy), was born in 1939, another, Mary Ann, in 1943 — following a miscarriage and an infant death — and a son, Patrick, in 1944. Pat was not drafted during the Second World War because of his family responsibilities though he provided legal counsel to a government agency. With the war over and career prospects secure, they built a rambling house in affluent Wilmette, Illinois (at a bargain price of only $15,000). There was little to suggest Pat and Patty's life would be notably different from that of their comfortable, successful neighbors.

An Idea Whose Time Had Come

While Patty Caron and Pat Crowley were growing up in the Chicago area, a new breed of Catholic layperson, far different from that idealized by Pius X, was just beginning to emerge in Europe. The person most often credited with the transformation was a determined Belgian priest, Canon Joseph Cardijn. As a young man, he had witnessed the death of friends and relatives, including his own father, in the horrendous factories of Antwerp and Brussels. He had also witnessed a great exodus from the Church on the part of working-class Belgian Catholics, who were finding the vision of Karl Marx far more sympathetic to their plight. Cardijn vowed to spend his life reclaiming the lost workers.

In theory the Church fully supported the rights of employees to unionize and demand better conditions; Pope Leo XIII had been explicit on that in his encyclical *Rerum Novarum*. But no one had been able to translate the dynamic message into practical terms — until Joseph Cardijn arrived. He did so by borrowing a formation tool effectively used by the communists: the cell system. He persuaded small groups of young workers to meet regularly and report what was going on in the factories. After a while, he got them to make judgments on what was occurring in the light of Christian principles. And eventually he encouraged them to determine practical actions on the basis of those judgments. The method was simple: observe, judge, act. These cells of peer groups spread more quickly through Europe than Cardijn ever imagined — from Belgium to Holland to France to Germany. The *Jeunesse Ouvrière Chrétienne* (JOC), or Young Christian Worker movement, saw lay Catholics speaking out for the first time on issues of economic and social justice, quoting the Gospels and the papal encyclicals.

In 1924 conservative Catholics, especially factory owners, persuaded Cardinal Desiré Mercier of Malines-Brussels to condemn the movement as an insidious form of Marxism. But Cardijn found refuge in

Pope Pius XI, who endorsed the Jocist system of Catholic Action in 1925 and advocated its use internationally. The Pope made it clear, however, that the clergy were still in charge, since the Christianizing of the world was mainly their responsibility. He defined "Catholic Action" as "the participation of the laity in the apostolic mission of the hierarchy" — a definition that would remain unquestioned for more than forty years.

The Jocist style of organization, known as the Young Christian Workers (YCW) in English, crossed the Atlantic in the person of a German priest and veteran Jocist organizer, Louis Putz, who migrated to the United States in 1939 at the beginning of World War II. Putz, who settled at the University of Notre Dame, found social and economic conditions different in this country, but adaptations were made to YCW, and a new variation, Young Christian Students (YCS), began to sprout in Catholic parishes and universities.

In 1941 Putz and Donald Kanaly, an Oklahoma priest who had studied the Jocist movement in Belgium, presented their ideas at Chicago's major seminary in Mundelein, Illinois, at the invitation of the rector, Monsignor Reynold Hillenbrand. As rector Hillenbrand had already inspired hundreds of young Chicago priests with his vision of an energized laity, supported by a dedicated clergy, carrying the Gospel message into the secular world. In fact under Hillenbrand, Chicago was experiencing a virtual renaissance — with liturgy, doctrine, and social action combined in a synthesis that spawned organizations like the Catholic Interracial Conference and the Catholic Labor Alliance.

Putz's observe-judge-act approach appealed to Chicago seminarian Paul Hazard. After he left the seminary he and a friend thought Jocist ideas might be useful for Catholic businessmen and in 1943 decided to form a group. The first person they invited to join was young Chicago lawyer Patrick Crowley. According to Kotre, "Within a few weeks, six men, all in their thirties and all married, were meeting with a chaplain in Pat's office in downtown Chicago — where the boss (in this case Pat's father) would allow them to get together after hours. Soon Father Putz was meeting with them and explaining the Jocist technique, and Monsignor Hillenbrand was instructing them in the liturgy."[5]

Years later Pat Crowley acknowledged he joined the group because neither he nor Patty was fully satisfied with their comfortable, suburban lifestyle. "The hunger to do something positive and permanent gnawed deep inside," he said, "though perhaps it didn't show much."

When Pope Pius XII issued the encyclical *Mystici Corporis* within a year after the group was formed, Pat took it as a sign of divine approbation. The encyclical echoed the ideas Hillenbrand had been indoctrinating in them: the Church, the whole Church, is the living Body of Christ, its parts interrelated so intimately that any member who fails to make a proper contribution is helpful neither to self nor to the Church. The laity, declared *Mystici Corporis*, have their own distinct function in the mission of the Church and in the world. Said Pat, "We learned that we had a role to play, that we were the Church.... I had gone to Notre Dame, but they didn't know about it when I was there. Nobody else knew about it, but we did and the Pope did. So he wrote about our group."

There was one problem. The Jocist method was based on peer groups, with like ministering to like, yet this new group included a variety of professions. According to Pat, "There were all kinds of different jobs; lawyers, insurance salesmen — others who worked for a living. One night a guy came along and said, 'Well, everybody in the group is married.' Now that wasn't very remarkable, because if you weren't married in 1943, you weren't home. But we decided anyhow that we'd straighten out marriage and move on to something serious."

A Proliferation of Cells

Though marriage proved difficult to "straighten out," it provided a gold mine for the inquiry method. In those post-war days the divorce rate was rising as traditional family values yielded to new ideas of sexual freedom, self-expression, and unlimited mobility. By 1946 the original men's group had grown to six Chicago-area groups, all using the Cardijn method to ponder how the Christian message related to modern marriage. (From the original men's group was born the Cana Conference, a marriage renewal program that eventually became national.)

Patty Crowley found the male-only character of the groups "ridiculous," and when the wives decided to form their own group, she at first refused to join, then relented. The women's group met weekly with the assistance of a priest chaplain, discussed articles, and became as fascinated with the observe-judge-act format as were the men. This group launched the first Pre-Cana conferences for engaged couples, which also grew into a national program. After some months Pat and Patty formed the first husband-wife Catholic Action cell ever in the Chicago area, at their parish in Wilmette, and others came in quick succession.

In Patty's view, the groups, whether mixed or single-sex, worked well because, according to the Cardijn format, the priest chaplain was absolutely prohibited from commenting until the end of each meeting. He was, after all, not a peer, and thus unequipped to observe, judge, or act on marital and family issues. "For the first time in our experience with the Church, our ideas were respected," said Patty. We were becoming independent, thinking for ourselves; it was a great feeling."

In 1947 after Patty gave birth to her fourth child, Catherine Ann, she hemorrhaged seriously and required emergency surgery, which left her permanently sterile at the age of thirty-three. The experience touched both of them deeply. "It was a traumatic thing for Pat," said Patty. "Everything was happening so fast. Everyone was around my bed doing something, but all I had to do was think. I thought I was going to die. When you are there, and conscious, and you think you're almost gone, you really do think about the life you have led and I knew I hadn't done much. You think that, well you haven't got much time, there are so many things to be done. If I lived, I had better start. I think after that it was our gratitude that I didn't die. I always say people should almost die once."[6]

It was at this time the Crowleys began to accept into their family foster children from the Catholic Charities organization. Over the years they would eventually house fourteen. The first, Algis Augustine, a refugee from Lithuania, arrived at the age of three; the last, Theresa, who came at three months, they later adopted. They also began to house foreign students in their home for extended periods, more than sixty in the next twenty years. The untroubled suburban life slipped into the past as their home became the scene of ceaseless comings and goings, sometimes bordering on chaos. Author Kotre, who interviewed the Crowley children, wrote, "The foster children [who] came from broken homes ... were emotionally wearing. With them came periodic visits from social workers to make sure the Crowleys weren't mistreating their wards. (Patty never understood why they worked on her instead of on the children's parents.) When parents wanted to visit their children, they had to be entertained — sometimes fended off. There was constant worry that the older children, the hardest to handle, would run away. On occasion they did, and Pat and Patty took off in pursuit. In such an atmosphere the Crowley children came to value time alone with their mother and father."[7]

Equally absorbing was the Crowley's work with the Catholic Action cells, as their numbers increased at an almost geometric rate. In 1947 the organization, which included the Cana and Pre-Cana operations as well as the couples' groups, was named the Catholic Action Federation, with chaplains appointed by Chicago's Cardinal Samuel Stritch and with Pat Crowley as federation president. Together with some friends the Crowleys financed the publication of a booklet, *For Happier Families,* which sold (at thirty-five cents each) twenty-three hundred copies in its first edition and became famous over the next twelve years as "The Yellow Book," the official manual for first-year groups. In 1949 a national convention of Catholic Action delegates was held at a Chicago area retreat house and the organization was officially named the Christian Family Movement (CFM). It was decided that a committee would develop yearly inquiry books for ongoing groups. In the decades to come, under Hillenbrand's guidance, an orderly cycle of inquiries was established; couples wrestled in successive years with the implications of Christianity in various aspects of life: family, political, parish, international, economic, and cultural. The Church's position on birth control was never questioned in these inquiries.

A Worldwide Movement

The Crowley's relationship with Monsignor Hillenbrand, the national CFM chaplain, was always a bit ambiguous. Hillenbrand was a charismatic figure who would lecture about liturgy and social justice in a kind of dull monotone that was nevertheless so commanding and compelling that he came across like Moses delivering the Ten Commandments. But he had an autocratic side and was not easily persuaded to change his mind on anything. Also, despite his openness to the laity, he was uncomfortable in the presence of women. "We learned so much about the Church from him," said Patty, "but he had limits and in the end I guess we tested them."

As CFM spread across the nation in the 1950s, the Crowleys got in the habit of traveling around, often combining Pat's trips on legal business with CFM recruiting efforts. Sometimes they took the children along, always staying with the families they visited and eating what the family ate. Said Patty, "Oh, we had a lot of nerve. We'd use any excuse to meet with couples. And a lot of the meetings were not successes, believe me. We didn't make a big hit in some of the places."[8]

The unique relationship between Pat and Patty themselves was unquestionably a factor in CFM's phenomenal growth. Noted Kotre, "Those who saw Pat and Patty live and work together say she was the energizer, the organizer, the 'motor.' 'More efficient,' they say, 'more intense,' 'far shrewder,' 'more profound,' 'more abrasive' even. Pat had the wide-eyed curiosity of a college freshman sitting at a bar, willing to try anything, if only for a lark. 'Oh boy, let's have a convention,' he would say with glee, and Patty would coordinate the incredible detail that made the convention happen.... Hers was the animus, his the anima."[9]

By 1956 CFM had spread to twenty-six foreign countries and the Crowleys went on a six-week world tour, with stops in the Far East, Middle East, India, Egypt and Europe. Studying Pat's detailed diary of that trip, Kotre found "unabashed religious sentiment, irrepressible boyish enthusiasm, reports telling of speeches to Catholic college students, seminarians, businessmen, connection after connection with Catholic couples, workers, clerics, cardinals."[10]

The following year the Crowleys and their four children attended the first convention of the Latin American branch of CFM, with delegates from most South American countries and Cuba. By then suspicion about the Cardijn method had been resolved: CFM was almost universally regarded as a loyal, orthodox arm of the institutional Church — a model of "lay participation in the apostolic mission of the hierarchy." In October 1957 Pope Pius XII awarded Pat and Patty Crowley the *Pro Ecclesia and Pontifice* medal, a kind of ecclesiastical distinguished service cross, during the World Congress of the Laity in Rome.

What Church officials may not have realized was that CFM and its cousins, YCW and YCS, were training great numbers Catholics, especially young Catholics, to critically scrutinize the institutions of society, including the Church. It was teaching them as members of the One Body of Christ to observe, judge, and act — to value and trust their own experiences and insights on everything relevant to their lives. The Church as conceived by Pius X was fading into the past, perhaps never to return.

5

The Commission Created

The First Meeting, 1963

I don't think any of us felt the old doctrine could or should be changed.
— JOHN MARSHALL

The person most responsible for the creation of the Birth Control
Commission was Leo Joseph Suenens, the archbishop of Malines-
Brussels, Belgium. An extremely pastoral man, Suenens had long been
concerned about the prohibition against "unnatural birth control" (the
Vatican's preferred term covering everything except rhythm) and the
distress it created among Catholics of child-bearing age. In 1956 Suenens wrote a book called *Love and Control*, in which he strove mightily
to reconcile the Church position with common sense, natural law
theory, and the experience of the people in the pews. He cited the
traditional arguments and took note of some newer, more existen-
tial ones (including the claim that marriages with one or no children
have a substantially greater likelihood of failure than those with two or
more children). Wrote Suenens, "Contraception is an essential denial
of conjugal communion, which it secretly disintegrates and turns into
self-seeking."[1]

However, when he began examining some of the subtleties of the
prohibition, he became troubled and unsure. For example, priests were
supposed to explain that wives whose husbands insisted on coitus interruptus would not sin themselves if they remained "passive" during
intercourse. Suenens said wives found it meaningless and "repug-
nant" to define something as passivity that necessarily involves a
certain amount of activity. The difficulty of communicating to ordi-

nary, good-willed Catholics such moral nuances raised in Suenens's mind the thought that there might be something wrong, not with Belgian parishioners, but with the traditional doctrine itself.

In the late 1950s, Suenens launched a series of yearly informal conferences at the University of Louvain, inviting doctors, economists, theologians, and other specialists to wrestle with the Church's position on the basis of their experience and study. Among those participating from the beginning was Dr. John Marshall, a British neurologist, then in his mid-thirties, associated with the National Hospital for Neurology and Neurosurgery in London. Marshall, a married man and father, was also working with the London-based Catholic Marriage Advisory Council, which was attempting to scientifically validate the effectiveness of rhythm. He found an ideal locale to test the new temperature method of rhythm: the heavily Catholic, relatively isolated Isle of Mauritius off the coast of Africa, where the population was booming. This pioneering study, which Marshall oversaw, provided some fairly encouraging results for temperature-style rhythm, he said. "It certainly was not the Vatican roulette its critics claimed, nor was it as good as its enthusiasts would have wanted it to be." Marshall's expertise in this area and his balanced assessment made him a valued colleague at the Louvain gatherings.

He found the conferences stimulating — a group of experts dialoguing and exchanging ideas with no obligation to draw any conclusions. It was there he became acquainted with the other invitees, most of whom were Belgian associates of Archbishop Suenens, including demographer Clement Mertens, physician Pierre von Rossum, and economist Jacques de Wilmars. Theologians were in the minority; Suenens knew what most of them thought. He wanted a different, more diverse perspective. Another regular at the conferences was a Swiss Dominican priest, Henri de Riedmatten, a kind of roving ambassador and observer on behalf of the Holy See in a variety of venues including the United Nations headquarters in Geneva.

The Suenens Intervention

The Louvain conferences might have continued indefinitely as exploratory, academic exercises were it not for the preparations for the Second Vatican Council in 1962. Suenens in those days was unquestionably a rising star among the world's hierarchy and a favorite of

Pope John XIII. His organizational skills would be critical in getting the Council off the ground and moving it forward.

According to Suenens, he approached Pope John in March 1962, six months before the scheduled opening, and asked, "Who is working on an overall plan for the Council?"

"Nobody," said Pope John.

"But there will be total chaos. How do you imagine we can discuss seventy-two schemata [draft texts] . . . about all that is known and a few other things besides?"

"Yes," John agreed, "we need a plan. . . . Would you like to do one?"[2]

Suenens consented, with the stipulation that the Council must not get bogged down trying to do everything. Later that same month Pope John named Suenens a cardinal.

Suenens and his associates made a noble effort to incorporate the draft material, most of which had been submitted by the Curia, into a coherent two-layered plan. As it turned out, the plan did not work out as he hoped. But he would remain the critical organizer and a central figure throughout the Vatican Council. One of the drafts submitted for early consideration especially caught Suenens's eye and left him aghast. It was the one on Christian marriage, De Castitate, and it had been authored by Franciscan theologian Ermenegildo Lio. In the document Lio simply reaffirmed almost word for word Pius XI's 1930 doctrine in Casti Connubii and Pius XII's 1951 guarded approval of rhythm in the midwives' talk. Completely ignored was any reference to the newer personalist approaches to marriage or any recognition of the ferment occurring in the Church over birth control.

Suenens feared this dated, simplistic document might slip through the screening committees and attain a kind of immortality as Vatican II doctrine, so he approached Pope John and urged the pontiff to form a small commission of his own to study the whole birth control issue in detail. Suenens later told a reporter he argued that the time was ripe to submit "an intelligent position on responsible parenthood and at least try to reform the old idea, the more children the better."[3]

John consented, and the Commission — the Pontifical Commission for the Study of Population, Family and Births — was born in March 1963, three months after the conclusion of the first session of the Vatican Council. The formation of the Commission was not announced publicly. It would, in fact, hold three meetings before anyone outside an inner circle knew of its existence.

(As it turned out, the Lio marriage draft, which stimulated the Commission's creation, was rejected for Council consideration, but it would not stay buried. It rose again in a new form during the third session of the Council only to be essentially quashed again. In 1969, however, it would find a permanent home at last — as part of Paul VI's encyclical *Humanae Vitae*.)

Another reason existed for establishing the Commission — one perhaps that had more persuasive power with Pope John. The United Nations and the World Health Organization had announced its first ever conference on world population problems. It was slated for mid-1964 in New Delhi, India. The Vatican feared the sort of sweeping recommendations for population control that might come from such an event. Up until 1963 the Holy See had been part of a symbiotic alliance that managed to keep population growth off the UN agenda. The alliance consisted of the communist bloc, which contended that a Marxist economic system could support unlimited growth; the Third World nations, which saw population control as part of a Western plot to hold them in subjection; and predominantly Catholic nations, which objected to most forms of birth control on moral grounds. With the conference pending, the Pope needed suggestions on strategy.

The six members of the new Commission, all personally known by Suenens and presumably suggested to the Pope by Suenens himself, included medical doctors Marshall and von Rossum, demographer Mertens, and economist de Wilmars, along with diplomat de Riedmatten and Stanislas de Lestapis, a French Jesuit sociologist. Four were laymen, all married; two were priests; none was a professional theologian.

Marshall first discovered he was a member when he was quietly taken aside by de Riedmatten at Suenens's 1963 conference in Louvain. Always cautious and proper, de Riedmatten, already appointed the Commission's general secretary, told him that the "Higher Authority" (his habitual euphemism for the Pope) had set up a small commission to look at "specific questions with relation to population" and would like him to serve on it. Marshall agreed.

The First Gathering

Pope John died in June 1963, and the Commission he established held its first meeting four months later on October 12–13. The place was a scenic hotel near Louvain called Hof Ter Bank (House in the Woods), and the discussion was quite general and very cordial, partly because there was no clear agenda. Marshall said de Riedmatten, whose language and leadership style were equally vague, told the members the Higher Authority needed advice on the UN meeting and hoped they could provide some. Accordingly, demographic discussion consumed much of the time. But given the membership, it was inevitable that specific birth control methods would come up. Dr. von Rossum, personal physician to the queen of Belgium, made a case for accepting the pill as a contraceptive. Borrowing from the ideas already widely circulated by Dr. John Rock and Canon Janssens, he argued that the pill does not place any barrier between sperm and ovum and ought not be labeled sterilization since its effects are temporary and controllable.

"We knew," said Marshall, "that von Rossum reflected views that were common among theologians at Louvain. We saw his point and it was an interesting thesis. But we remained doubtful." To Marshall and others, this approach seemed a kind of gimmick, a casuistic loophole to get around the traditional doctrine without challenging it to its face. Besides, it was unclear at that point whether the pill might actually work by preventing a fertilized ovum from being implanted in the womb, and thus prove objectionable as a form of abortion.

The group's recommendations, contained in a twenty-two-page report prepared by de Riedmatten, were quite orthodox and lacked even a hint of disagreement or dissent:

- Rhythm is unquestionably "the Christian position" on family limitation, and it is hoped that modern science will develop methods "that could be harmonized with the needs of human love and human morality."

- Rather than wait for the Vatican Council to issue a statement on birth control, the Pope should provide "light and order" as soon as possible for those who are disturbed and thus help clear up the confusion caused by promoters of "the most adventuresome methods."

- Earlier papal statements on the evils of contraception, especially those by Pius XII, constitute "luminous teachings" and should be widely promulgated to deter overpopulated nations from promoting sterilization, contraception, and abortion. If the Church remains silent, it will fail in its role as "defender of the natural moral law."

- More study is needed to determine the mechanics and side effects of the pill. It would be "preferable" for the Pope not to take an absolutely definitive position on the pill at this time.

When the group broke up, said Marshall, it was clear that the participants needed a lot more input if they were going to contribute anything substantive — on the scope of the world population problem, on the great variety of contraceptives becoming available, on medicine and eugenics and theology. "But I don't think any of us felt at that point that the old doctrine could or should be changed. We didn't see ourselves as the sort of group that would move in that direction." Their first and most important task, as Marshall saw it, was to help the Pope interpret teachings, basically accepted by most Catholics, to the diverse nations and cultures that would be gathered at the United Nations. At least, that was the impression they were getting from de Riedmatten.

The Growing Reevaluation

Within three months of that first session, Commission members and the general public would discover that Catholic acceptance was not nearly as basic as they imagined. Robert Blair Kaiser, a correspondent in Europe for *Time* magazine, learned through a series of interviews how widespread dissatisfaction and, in fact, popular dissent from the old doctrine had become.[4] In Amsterdam Father Leo Alting von Geusau, director of the Dutch Documentation Center, reported on a survey by the Dutch bishops that showed a high rate of rejection of Church teaching on the part of ordinary Catholics. It also revealed that eighteen of twenty theologians consulted rated the pill as morally "tolerable" or "good" as a contraceptive. In parishes, said von Geusau, priests were telling their people that "anti-conception is not good but that birth control pills are licit in particular instances because theologians are divided on the matter."

William Bekkers, the bishop who first called for reconsideration during a nationally televised speech, met Kaiser in his diocesan office and defended his position. In his book on the controversy, *The Politics of Sex and Religion*, Kaiser wrote, "Bekkers said reevaluation would have to come, 'no matter whether one takes it as a disciplinary document or a doctrinal statement. In the first place, an encyclical is not infallible. Some may object and say, "Yes, but when a teaching gets the consensus of all the bishops, then you have to regard it as authentic teaching.'"

Bekkers said he wasn't quite sure there had ever been, or was now, a real consensus of the bishops: 'What may seem like a consensus may be a mere slavish and subservient parroting of the pope's words.' "

In Nijmegen, the internationally known Dominican theologian Edward Schillebeeckx said he saw a "ladder of values in marriage with love at the top and biology at the bottom. Since the biological value is secondary, or lower, its exclusion can be justified by reason of the highest value." When pressed about the argument that contraception violates the nature of the sexual relationship, Schillebeeckx replied, "It is necessary to put the stress, not on the concept of 'nature' but on 'the person.' Nature is based on *some* absolute, but we are only coming to a gradual understanding of this idea." He maintained that "man's nature is itself in evolution. Nature is essentially dynamic. For example, there was a time when love did not belong to the essence of marriage. Now it does."

Schillebeeckx said he favored the pill as an ideal contraceptive because it doesn't interfere with the act itself. In fact, he explained, if a couple ought not to have any more children because of physical, economic, or other solid reasons, they might be "morally obliged" to use the pill in preference to rhythm simply because the pill is the "more efficacious" and effective means of preventing pregnancy.

Kaiser expressed his genuine surprise at hearing a Catholic theologian speak of contraception as a "moral obligation."

In Louvain the *Time* correspondent interviewed Canon Janssens, who was happy to expound on the position he took publicly earlier in 1963. Mechanical means of contraception act to destroy the meaning of conjugal love, he said. But the pill, like rhythm, places no barriers between "the organs of husband and wife. . . . It doesn't destroy anything. The pill works more like rhythm." He concluded that conscientious and responsible use of the pill can be a morally good act, possibly even better than the rhythm method.

In Kaiser's excursions, only a handful of the experts he encountered seemed less than enthusiastic about the pill. Two of these were Clement Mertens and Stanislas de Lestapis. Both were members of the Birth Control Commission, which had just had its first meeting, but Kaiser was unaware of this at the time and neither informed him of his participation. In Louvain Mertens, a demographic specialist, said he could not see the pill as a practical solution for population growth in underdeveloped countries, and besides, he had problems with Janssens and Schillebeeckx's emphasis on the "interpersonal, gift-giving" aspect of intercourse. "To love each other," he said, quoting French author Antoine de Saint-Exupéry, "it is not enough to look at each other, but the couple must look out to something else."

In Paris economist de Lestapis said he considered rhythm as the only moral form of birth control. Church studies, such as those conducted by Dr. Marshall on the Isle of Mauritius, indicated it could work, he noted, even among relatively uneducated people. A wide-open pill culture, de Lestapis explained, "would make things too easy. In such a culture, men would not learn to master themselves."

Clearly at this early date, many members of the Commission were not in a frame of mind to start a revolution and appeared somewhat critical of what was going on around them.

Kaiser's *Time* magazine article, published in February 1964, was among the first from a major secular source to document the changing scene. "In Rome, in all of Holland, in Belgium, in France (where I have taken my soundings), in Germany (where I understand the same depths are being reached), the theologians are daring to talk about their new insights," he wrote. "Their bishops are adding up the insights and some have already given their private assent to the revisionist thinking."

Reactions came quickly. The American Jesuit theologian John Ford, who would play an extremely important role in the fate of the Birth Control Commission, told the Catholic News Service that Pius XII's censure of the pill was still in force. "Consequently, unless and until the Holy See gives its approval to some other teaching (a highly unlikely eventuality), no lesser authority in the Church, and least of all a private theologian, is at liberty to teach a different doctrine or to free Catholics from their obligation to accept papal teaching."

The Los Angeles archdiocese director of public information blamed the messenger. "The richest source of confusion is the oversimplified and thus misleading treatments which [theological opinions are] ... bound to get in popular journals like *Time*," wrote John T. Sheridan in the archdiocesan weekly, *The Tidings*. "The Church's position on contraception has not changed, is not changing and gives no indications that it will change."

"A Mass of People"

While the Crowleys had no idea a Commission had been created, they were growing familiar with the problem the Commission would tackle.

In March 1963 Pat, representing CFM, was among fifteen lay leaders invited to Rome to discuss the Church's role in the modern world and the work of the Second Vatican Council. Pat was proud of the honor, especially the opportunity to meet Pope John himself (as it turned out, only five weeks before his death). In his family newsletter, Pat dropped the names of progressive theologians and bishops he met, then mentioned one "who seemed to have just returned from the Council of Trent: Father Lio." He did not realize, of course, that this was the very Ermenegildo Lio whose reactionary writings on marriage had prompted Cardinal Suenens to press for the Commission.

In July of that year, Pat and Patty attended the congress of the Latin American Christian Family Movement in Rio de Janeiro, attended by some two thousand couples. With its emphasis on the dignity of women and the importance of addressing societal issues, the movement was growing rapidly in Mexico and South America. Confronted with staggering rates of illegitimacy and throngs of uncared-for street children in the large cities, the congress passed a resolution asking the Association of Catholic Doctors for a clear statement on "the morality of various methods of birth limitation." The extent of this crisis was not lost on Patty, who toured some of the favelas with unpaved streets, corrugated tin huts, and raw sewage running through the ditches. "A mass of people," she said, "you couldn't help but be shocked and wonder what the answer was." In their newsletter home, the Crowleys said, "Let's hope the Church and the wealthy find effective ways to deal with the common good."

That summer the CFM newsmagazine ACT, with a circulation of forty thousand, printed in its entirety the statement of the Dutch bishop William Bekkers, in which he said the married couple "and they alone ... must decide what God requires of them concretely ... how large the family should be and how the children should be spaced."[5] The reprint was not intended to challenge Church law, said Patty, only to alert CFMers about the ongoing discussion and its implications. A principal speaker at the CFM national convention in August was the Redemptorist theologian Bernard Häring, an expert (peritus) at the Council, whose pastoral approach to marriage problems was growing in popularity and creating some controversy. Häring did not mention family limitation in this talk.

Confronting Fundamental Issues

The Second and Third Meetings, 1964

I found myself asking, how much are we supposed to sacrifice to protect the integrity of the marriage act?

— THOMAS BURCH

Since the Birth Control Commission was not Pope Paul's idea, he could have simply let it lapse after its first, inconclusive meeting. But there is evidence he sincerely wanted its guidance. Like Pope John before him, Paul hoped the Church could reach out to the larger world and therefore felt it needed a broader base of input than that supplied by cardinals, bishops, and Curia officials. Shortly after his election in 1963, he took the unprecedented step of bringing lay people into the subcommittee drafting the Vatican Council's document *The Pastoral Constitution of the Church in the Modern World.*

The Pope approved a second session for the Commission for April 1964, with seven new members added to the original six. The additions included five theologians, all priests: Redemptorists Bernard Häring, a German, and Jan Visser, from Holland, both teaching at Rome's Pontifical University; Jesuits Joseph Fuchs from Germany and Marcelino Zalba from Spain; and Pierre de Locht, a Belgian teaching at Louvain. Also named were two laymen, both sociologists: Bernard Colombo of Italy and Thomas Burch of Washington, D.C.'s Georgetown University, the first American representative.

Häring, then fifty-one, perhaps the best known Catholic moral theologian in the world, was invited personally to join the Commission by

Paul himself when Häring preached a retreat for the Pope and top Curia officials in early 1964. His liberal tendencies were no secret, but in the formal invitation he received later, Commission secretary de Riedmatten wrote, "It is the High Authority who has wanted diverse currents of opinion to be represented in the group. Yours are well known." A similar caveat appeared in the invitation to de Locht, an adviser and close associate of Archbishop Suenens. "The Authority demands that the group be surrounded with the greatest reserve and the greatest discretion," said the secretary.[1] The other three priests were regarded as quite conservative on marital issues.

Layman Colombo was the brother of Carlo Colombo, the Pope's personal theologian. Burch, at twenty-nine, the youngest of the Commission members, was the demographic director of the Population Study Center at Georgetown. He was one of the very few Catholic demographers in the United States who had written articles on the physiological effects of the pill.

Burch said the invitation, which came to him directly from de Riedmatten, was written in French and veiled in "vague, diplomatic" language: The Pope needed advisers to help him deal with "certain issues" in the international forum, provided "such intervention would be deemed necessary." Curious, Burch accepted.

The meeting took place on April 3–5 in Rome in the Pio Latino, a drafty, unheated building — which left the thirteen Commission members shivering through the sessions. Asked about his own specialty, population researcher Burch declared that growth rates had to be curbed some way. He noted that 150 years ago the odds were fifty-fifty that a newborn baby would die before reaching the age of twenty; a couple would need to have eight children if they expected three or four to survive into adulthood. Now, said Burch, it is likely all eight will survive, especially in the developed nations. The implications of human reproduction have changed drastically, he said. But Burch was in no frame of mind to overthrow conventional values.

"As an orthodox, indoctrinated Catholic, I came in convinced the use of the pill as a contraceptive was wrong," he recalled. Burch was familiar with Louis Janssens's contention that the pill is not a sterilizer, but he was not impressed. It seemed, he said, like an attempt to "treat moral theology like a kind of applied biology."

The Theologians' Debate

The most magnetic presence at this meeting was Bernard Häring, who shared his own growing concerns and ideas in a wide-ranging presentation. To say the "end of intercourse" is procreation (the union of sperm and egg) when most of the time such a union is physiologically impossible, declared Häring, seems to be an illogical position. The real task of the Christian is "to discern the will of God regarding parenthood within existing conditions and in an environment of love"; it is not important that each and "every marital act be procreative but that the marriage in its totality should be." Häring took issue with theologians who claim that couples who commit a single contraceptive act sin mortally, while those who use natural family planning selfishly and have no children or very few do not sin — or do so only venially. That mentality, said Häring is "simply absurd." He emphasized that the virtual disappearance of arranged marriages in the developed, industrial world had altered the nature of the institution, pushing the importance of mutual, sustained love into the foreground.

In any event, said Häring, he could not see how the use of the pill could be considered intrinsically evil and thus always and everywhere forbidden regardless of circumstances.

Jesuit Fuchs took issue with Häring. Since an "ordination to procreation" is inherent in each sexual union (even though physiologically speaking procreation may be impossible), Fuchs said, "the integrity of the act itself" is destroyed when contraceptive measures are taken. Furthermore, said Fuchs, this new emphasis on love, however well intentioned, seems to distort the time-honored Christian doctrine. After all, he noted, the essence of marital consent is the mutual "exchange by man and woman of their rights to sexual activities apt for procreation." This was precisely the position of the Vatican. But Häring's comments about the critical importance of love were affirmed by others in the group, so much so that several Commission members felt the old distinction between primary and secondary ends of marriage should be scrapped. A vigorous though restrained exchange followed concerning what is natural, and therefore inviolable, and what isn't. Famine and disease are natural, someone pointed out, yet no one questions the validity of scientific intervention to stem the consequences. The question wasn't asked but seemed to be implied: Why does the marriage act merit such extraordinary immunity from interference even when the gravest reasons for interference seem to be present?

De Riedmatten refrained from going into these difficult matters in the points he stressed in his nineteen-page summary of the Pio Latino experience:

- "The group unanimously affirms that love is at the heart of marriage, and a majority of the members agree that the love of husband and wife would not, in any way, be ranked among the secondary ends of marriage."

- However, the members recognize that the Church cannot change the traditional teaching on the primary end at this time since the pronouncements of the magisterium on the subject are "too recent to be questioned."

- Though some members are reluctant to condemn the pill, they are in accord that rhythm is still "the most desirable means of exercising responsible parenthood."

- The members concur that "the natural law alone cannot provide a good answer" to the perplexities presented by the birth control dilemma. A better approach might be to view marriage from a more Biblical point of view, as a "community of salvation" rather than in technical, natural law terms.

Burch left the meeting somewhat confused about where all this was headed. "We weren't a democratically constituted group," he said, "we certainly weren't following Robert's *Rules of Order,* and no votes were taken." He hoped for some clarification at the next meeting, expected to take place in about six months, in the fall of 1964.

"Disturbing" Opinions

But two weeks after the members went home, the long simmering dispute over marital morality made the front pages of most newspapers in the Western world. British Jesuit Thomas D. Roberts, the retired archbishop of Bombay, India, declared in an interview in the *Times* of London that he could find no rational argument to prove that contraception is wrong He threatened to argue his case during the next session of the Vatican Council. "If I were an Anglican," he was quoted as saying, "I would accept the position taken by the Lambeth Conference [the Anglican meeting in 1930 that approved contraception]. How you can destroy that position by reason alone is not clear to me."[2]

In an expansion of his thesis, Roberts said, "On the grounds of reason alone, one can conceive of many cases in which a husband and wife might, after having examined their consciences, decide that contraception was the only means for preserving the health of one or the other spouse, or for preserving the marriage itself. If that is so, then with the most spiritual of motives such a husband and wife might be convinced that contraception was necessary for the growth of holiness which is the aim of the sacrament of matrimony."[3]

If his was an erroneous position, Roberts challenged Church officials to provide rational arguments to refute it. The Church has always claimed that the intrinsic evil of contraception was evident from reason and was not a matter of divine revelation; so, said Roberts in effect: prove the point or abandon it.

Roberts, not an easy man to ignore, possessed a certain gritty authenticity. Long involved in peace and justice causes, he had devoted himself in extraordinary ways to the poor of India, then resigned his post so that a native Indian could take over. The *Times* quoted several persons, including Roberts's Jesuit superior, who declined to contradict him.

John Heenan, the archbishop of Westminster, could not ignore this break in the ranks, however. In a terse statement in early May "in the name of the hierarchy of England and Wales," he appealed to papal statements going back to *Casti Connubii* and quoted St. Augustine as the voice of tradition. "It has been suggested that the council could approve the practice of contraception," he said. "But the Church, while free to revise her own positive laws, has no power of any kind to alter the laws of God."[4]

The uproar continued when a reporter for the British newspaper the *Guardian,* interviewed Bernard Häring in Rome and asked about Heenan's rebuttal. Häring did not adopt Roberts's ideas in full but was quoted as saying, "I think the British bishops erred...in their statement."[5] Progesterone pills, he explained, do not interfere with the act of conjugal intercourse and cannot therefore be lumped with other contraceptives.

Further reactions, including a rebuttal by Roberts of Heenan's rebuttal, kept the fire aglow through May, and it flared up again at the end of the month when Cardinal Alfredo Ottaviani, the pro-prefect of the Holy Office, entered the fray. In an interview in the Italian magazine *Vita,* he said the Vatican "doesn't like this or that local authority to express doctrinal views on debated questions which call rather for a central directive.... It is necessary to preserve unity of thought and policy. The supreme magisterium [that is, the Pope] must speak on grave and debatable questions, which should not be left to a single opinion whether that of a bishop or a cardinal." All hope that the Church could ever swallow the pill should be abandoned, said Otta- viani, because it violates the integrity of the sex act and, in any event, its widespread use could lead to "hedonism."[6]

Pope Paul, who had wanted the birth control issue handled with the "greatest discretion" and in a highly "confidential manner," had to be alarmed at what was becoming an international media circus. And so in early June cables were sent to the members of the Commission, summoning them to an emergency session set for June 13–14, scarcely five weeks after the one they had just attended. The invitations came this time from Amleto Cicognani, the Vatican secretary of state and de Riedmatten's immediate superior. The Holy Father "begs you to do the impossible," he said: return on short notice to help quell the con- troversy resulting from "opinions which are disturbing the children of the Church."

Cries for Help

Disturbing opinions were circulating in the United States as well, though often in more muted form than in Europe. Particularly intrigu- ing was a 1964 article that ran in the Crowley's CFM newsmagazine ACT. It was a reprint from the *Ligourian* magazine entitled, "Mother of 12 Appeals for Realistic Spiritual Guides." In it an anonymous woman upbraided "my friend the theologian" for failure to respond to real-life situations. "If I am married to a man who might find it difficult to save for the children's education and buy five pairs of shoes at one time," she wrote, "the rhythm method might be justified. Ha! We memorized that book in our first year of married life. We use it now to replace a lost caster on the baby's crib.... I am the one surrounded by wild, scrappy, noisy, dirty little boys, carrying a runny-nosed baby. Vom- iting at intervals with my next pregnancy; overwhelmed with noise, dirt, spilled foods, overflowing diaper pails, broken furniture and un- paid bills. I am Job, robbed of everything and seated on a dunghill." She took issue with the theologian's "boss." "He leaves no doubt about who runs things, does He? Offer Him an inch and He takes a mile. I tried offering Him my days and they became so difficult I wept with frustration.... He snatched away my offering and gave me nothing." In the end, the harassed woman said she came to terms with her life by simply accepting the way things are, "by grasping the cross more firmly the heavier it becomes."[7]

The mother of twelve thereby dodged the issue, but CFM respondents did not. "For God's sake and in his name," wrote one woman, "would the Church please review its attitudes on marriage, childbearing and related areas. We need help now or an awful lot of us will fall down under our cross."[8]

Recalling those days, Patty said loyalty to the Church was always a given: "Yet we wanted people to think about things like this with open eyes and make some judgments in the light of what the Gospels said. That's what CFM was supposed to do, and I think it was doing it."

A Turning Point

When the Commission members reassembled in June, this time at the Domus Mariae house in Rome, they learned that two new priest members were resent: Tullo Goffi, an Italian and personal friend of Paul VI, and Fernando Lambruschini, a theologian at the Lateran University. The Commission at this point was constituted of fifteen members, all male: ten priests and five laymen. De Riedmatten informed them that the Authority wished to quiet further speculation by making a "pronouncement" on June 23, the first anniversary of his papal coronation. He hoped for answers on three questions: What is the relationship of the primary and secondary ends of marriage? What are the major responsibilities of married couples? How do rhythm and the pill relate to responsible parenthood? Given the gigantic scope of those questions and the meager results of the first two Commission meetings, Paul's hope was not well founded.

Nevertheless, the Commission approached the task manfully, with the same sort of non-confrontative discussion that characterized the earlier gatherings. And progress occurred, though not perhaps the sort Paul VI envisioned. Until that June 1964 meeting, the members had seen themselves as court advisers to the Holy See, operating more or less strictly within the limits of the relevant encyclicals and traditional theology. Häring had suggested moving beyond that, but their recommendations from the first two sessions indicated that caution prevailed. Now the Pope was pleading for advice and Häring (for reasons never explained) was not present at this emergency session.

The Belgian theologian Pierre de Locht accepted the challenge. He suggested that in order to move forward, the old terminology about the ends of marriage and acts "apt for procreation" and the demands of natural law had to go in favor of new terms and new understandings. The newcomer Lambruschini protested that new terminology would cause confusion among the faithful. Economist de Wilmars interjected that terminology is not the real problem but the ideas behind the terminology.

Someone then asked de Locht, "Aren't you really raising questions of fundamental theology? Are we supposed to be raising such questions?"

"Yes," said de Locht, "why not?"

The discussion came to a dead stop. Said Dr. Marshall later, "It seemed like we were seeing the real task for the first time. I believe that moment was a turning point."

During a coffee break, the members shuffled around in unaccustomed silence, said Marshall, while de Locht himself stood on a balcony fingering his rosary. "We were thinking and praying about what lay ahead."

Marshall had gotten into the habit of taking walks during session breaks with the German moral theologian Joseph Fuchs, who appeared to be a Vatican hardliner but a thoughtful man nonetheless. "I wasn't much enamored myself with the casuistry of trying to fit the pill in somewhere," said Marshall, "and I respected Fuchs' solid grounding in tradition. But as the sessions continued, I could see a kind of evolution going on in his thinking — a sense that our understanding of the nature of intercourse was plainly inadequate. Others, I believe, were moving the same way."

After three days though, all was still in a state of flux, and the Pope's questions remained unanswered. De Riedmatten needed something, so he concentrated on the pill and put two questions to a vote, the first votes since the Commission was formed: Is the pill morally acceptable for contraceptive use? Nine said no and five said they were unsure. (Two of those in doubt, de Locht and Dr. von Rossum, indicated they were leaning in favor of the pill.)[9] Should the Pope approve of the pill at this point? All fourteen present said he should not, and six suggested that he say nothing whatsoever on birth control at this point.

The lone American, Thomas Burch, married and the father of three young children, the last of whom had arrived despite the use of rhythm, was growing impatient. "The more we engaged in rational discussion," he said, the more we looked at world poverty, the more we recognized that procreation also includes the responsibility to educate, the more we talked of marriage as a total blending of two lives — our attempts to operate out of the old theology looked silly. The questions shouldn't any longer be about sperm meeting egg or whether somebody has good enough reason to take the pill to regularize her period. What about the life of the husband and wife and the kids they've already got. I found myself asking, how much are we supposed to sacrifice to protect the integrity of the act?"

The Pope Speaks

The members returned home, and nine days later, on June 23, in a speech before the college of cardinals at the Vatican Paul revealed for the first time the existence of the Commission. The birth control problem, "which everyone is talking about," is "extremely serious," he said, and poses "extremely complex and delicate questions." The Pope appeared to be opening a door for development when he said that the Church has a duty to proclaim the law of God but must do this "in the light of scientific, social and psychological truths" which require "very ample study and documentation." "The question is being subjected to study, as wide and profound as possible.... It is under study, which ... we hope will soon be concluded with the cooperation of many and outstanding experts."

Then came the word of caution: "But in the meantime we must say openly that up to now we have not sufficient reason to consider the rules laid down by Pope Pius XII ... to be out of date and therefore not binding. These therefore must be considered valid, at least so long as we do not feel obliged in conscience to change them. In such a serious matter it seems good that Catholics would want to follow one rule only, that which the Church propounds with authority.... For the moment no one should take it upon himself to make pronouncements differing in terms from the present regulations."

Some have speculated that the Pope had decided by this time that contraception was indeed intrinsically evil — pill or no pill — and in his own mind the book on the subject was closed. If that was the case, why did he place such much hope (and pressure) on the Birth Control Commission and why in the months ahead would he expand the group, more than tripling it in size so that laypeople would constitute the majority? Perhaps he genuinely believed the Holy Spirit would provide wisdom through this unique assembly. On the other hand, the ongoing existence of the Commission — his personal and very private Commission — would justify keeping the volatile issue of birth control out of the unpredictable hands of the bishops during the very public proceedings of the Vatican Council — which was scheduled to take up the subject at its next session in four months.

An Expanding Dialogue

The Council and Commission, 1964

I beg you, my brother bishops, let us avoid a new Galileo affair.

— CARDINAL SUENENS

After the conclusion of the third meeting, Canon de Locht, who started everyone thinking about fundamental change in the birth control discussion, wrote to de Riedmatten and said it was time for fundamental change in the Commission's membership as well. The group needed the insights of a broader range of theologians, he contended, and more importantly, it needed the input of those touched most deeply by the Church's marriage doctrine — married people themselves. To drive home this latter point, de Locht persuaded a Belgian couple, Herman and Lena Beulens, to draft a statement that was then signed by some 120 Catholic laity, including 55 physicians and 30 university professors. Copies were sent to the Pope and the bishops attending the Council. The statement declared that the traditional view of the natural law needs reinterpretation in light of the possibility of more intelligent intervention in nature due to scientific discoveries. There are times, the statement said, when the greater good of a couple or of the human race itself would seem to justify intervention in the biological order.[1]

Indeed, 1964 was marked by a remarkable sustained rise in the lay voice on the subject of birth control. The book *What Modern Catholics Think about Birth Control,* presented the insights of twelve lay Catholics, all professionals in a variety of disciplines, most of whom argued that marital sexuality stood at a threshold requiring development of the old doctrine. In a second book, *The Experience of Marriage,* thirteen couples expressed their views and made at least two clear points: a majority of couples find rhythm frustrating and not very effective; and many couples resent the narrow interpretation of marital relations presented by celibate theologians who formulate doctrine by talking to one another. Several cited Cardinal John Henry Newman's pioneer essay *On Consulting the Faithful about Doctrine.* In it Newman showed how the laity on more than one occasion had prevented the whole Church from lapsing into heresy, even when the majority of bishops seemed fully prepared to lapse.

Four Potent Speeches

During the third session of the Vatican Council in October 1964, it became evident that some prominent members of the world's hierarchy had been reading and listening to the lay voice. The twenty-two hundred assembled bishops were scheduled to discuss the latest draft (or schema) for the text of *The Pastoral Constitution on the Church in the Modern World.* — better known later by its opening words *Gaudium et Spes* (Joy and Hope). It had already gone through four drafts, largely because the chapter on Christian marriage was considered so delicate. The Council president solemnly informed the bishops that, at the Holy Father's request, they were not to concern themselves with birth control morality in the document, since the Pope's special Commission would handle that subject. But this withdrawal of the topic only served to inject a certain tension into the discussion of the schema. The Council could hardly produce a meaningful document on marriage without coming very close to the delicate subject. Besides, none other than moral theologian Bernard Häring was a principal expert on the Council Commission formulating the text, and his reformist tendencies were apparent in the latest draft. In addition, there was his very recent altercation with Cardinal Heenan over Archbishop Roberts's defense of contraception.

Heenan attempted a preemptive strike early in the session. In a long, vehement speech, he said, "Between sessions of this council, the Church of God has suffered a great deal from the writing and speeches of some of the experts. They are few in number but their sound has gone forth to the ends of the earth. These few specialists care nothing for the ordinary teaching authority of the bishops, nor, I regret to say, for the pope. It is idle to show them a papal encyclical in which a point of Catholic doctrine is clearly laid down.... We must protect the authority of the teaching Church. It is of no avail to talk about a college of bishops if, in articles, books, and speeches, specialists contradict and pour scorn on what a body of bishops teaches." The latest schema, he said, seems to suggest that married couples and they alone must decide what is right and wrong.[2]

Better, suggested Heenan, that the whole chapter on marriage be tabled and given to a post-council committee of theologians and pastoral specialists to produce an orthodox text.

On October 28 and 29, four bishops stood up and spoke, one after the other, to declare their disagreement with Heenan, their genuine sympathy toward the hardships of married couples, and their own ideas on marital morality. A great deal of what these four said went beyond anything Häring, Roberts, or the other "specialists" excoriated by Heenan had uttered in public.

The first was Cardinal Émile Leger, archbishop of Montreal: "Many theologians think that our present difficulties derive from an inadequate presentation of the goals of marriage. We have had a pessimistic, negative attitude toward love. This schema is intended to amend these conceptions and clarify love and its purposes." In fact, he said, the schema should go further. "Love is a good in itself. It makes its own demands and has its own laws.... Let us be clear. Otherwise the fear of conjugal love that has so long paralyzed our theology will persist. We must affirm that the intimate union of the couple finds its legitimate end in itself, even when it is not directed toward procreation."[3]

Next came Cardinal Suenens, who was simmering over the Pope's removal of birth control from the Council agenda. He hadn't envisioned that the subject would be stripped from the Council agenda entirely just because of the Commission's existence. Suenens suggested that perhaps the Birth Control Commission and the Council commission working on the schema could work together to produce a coordinated doctrine. Then Suenens asked if thus far "we have given sufficient emphasis to all aspects of the teaching of the Church on marriage, [if] we have opened our hearts completely to the Spirit in order to understand the divine truth. The Bible is always the same. But hasn't there been too much emphasis on the passage from Genesis, 'Increase and multiply,' and not enough on another phrase which says, 'And they shall be two in one flesh'? These two truths are central and both are scriptural." Does classical Church doctrine, he wondered, take into account "the complexity with which the real or the biological interferes with the psychological, the conscious with the unconscious? We have made progress since Aristotle — and even St. Augustine. Let us have done with Manichean pessimism. In this way we will understand better what is against love and what is not against love. I beg you, my brother bishops, let us avoid a new Galileo affair. One is enough for the Church."

Then was delivered one of the most remarkable speeches in the entire course of the Council. The eighty-seven-year-old tall, bearded patriarch of Antioch, Maximos IV Saigh, approached the microphone and declared, "Among the anguishing and sorrowful problems which agitate the human masses today, there emerges the problem of birth regulation, a problem most urgent since it is at the bottom of a grave crisis of the Catholic conscience. There is here a conflict between the official doctrine of the Church and the contrary practice of the vast majority of Catholic families. The authority of the Church is once more questioned on a large scale. The faithful are reduced to loving outside the law of the Church, far from the sacraments, in constant anguish."

Maximos then stated his own convictions and asked some hard questions: "In marriage the development of personality and its integration into the creative plan of God are one. Thus, the end of marriage should not be divided into primary and secondary. . . .

"And are we not entitled to ask if certain positions are not the outcome of outmoded ideas and perhaps a celibate psychosis on the part of those unacquainted with this sector of life? Are we not perhaps unwittingly setting up a Manichean conception of man and the world, in which the work of the flesh, vitiated in itself, is tolerated only in view of children. Is the external biological rectitude of an act the only criterion of morality? . . . . Isn't it the duty of the Church to educate the moral sense of her children . . . rather than to envelop [them] in a net of prescriptions and commandments and to demand that they purely and simply conform to these with their eyes closed?" He concluded, "Let us see things as they are and not as we would like them to be. Otherwise we risk speaking in a desert."

Finally Cardinal Bernard Alfrink of Utrecht, Holland, spoke of the "anxieties" of loyal, married Catholics. Though the Church is the guardian of divine law, he said, it cannot ignore "the growing recognition of the essential distinction between mere biological sexuality and human sexuality. . . . An honest doubt is rising among many married people and also scientists and some theologians regarding the arguments used to prove that the only efficacious moral and Christian solution to...conflicts in married life...is complete or periodic continence....Only if there is real certainty regarding the knowledge of the true content of divine law can and must the Church bind or free the consciences of her faithful."

The thunderous applause that followed each of these talks showed the ideas had resonated with many bishops. Bernard Häring later commented on the reaction of the assembled bishops. "The moderators were told not to allow any more talks in this direction, especially since these men had received the applause of the majority of the council."[4] It is interesting to speculate what might have happened if a vote concerning the intrinsic evil of contraception had been taken at that juncture. But it was not taken, nor would such a vote ever be taken at the Second Vatican Council.

Cardinal Ottaviani, the head of the Holy Office and defender of the faith, arose and spoke of his deepest convictions: "I am not pleased with the statement...that married couples can determine the number of the children they are to have. This is unheard of, from previous centuries up to our own times. The priest who speaks to you is the eleventh of twelve children, whose father was a laborer in a bakery — a laborer, not the owner of a bakery, a laborer. He never doubted Providence, never thought about limiting his family, even though there were difficulties."[5]

When Häring (ironically, also the eleventh of twelve children) was asked if Ottaviani had not also received strong applause for his remarks, he said, "Yes, he did, only with the difference that he received a strong applause from very few hands. But [for the others] there was applause and manifestation from many hands."[6]

Discussion of the schema on marriage continued for several days. A decision was reached to send it back to the Council for yet another revision. Its final form would be settled — amid yet more turmoil — at the Council's final session more than a year later, in late 1965. Meanwhile, Pope Paul summoned Cardinal Suenens and personally admonished him for his outspoken statements on the Council floor. A mortified Suenens was moved by this chastisement to interrupt a debate on a totally different topic later and declare that he never meant to question authentic Church teaching or to suggest that the Birth Control Commission ought to operate differently from the way the Holy Father intended.[7]

The Growing Commission

Meanwhile, de Riedmatten received word from the Vatican to expand the Commission on a large scale. How the new names were selected has never been revealed, but it is likely all were approved by the Vatican Secretary of State's office and possibly by the Pope himself. The net result was an increase of forty-three members, raising the total from fifteen to fifty-eight, and changing the whole operation from a discussion group to a mini-congress. It appears the goal was to broaden membership professionally, ideologically, geographically, racially, and philosophically — and to include at least a few women. The new makeup included thirty-four laypersons, five of whom were women; twenty-two were priests and two were bishops. Thirty-four members came from Europe, eleven from North America, five from Asia, five from Africa, and three from Latin America.

In its expanded format the United States had the largest national contingent with nine members; Belgium and France had eight each, Germany and Italy five each, and Spain three. The Third World was represented by a sprinkling of individuals from countries including India, Senegal, the Philippines, and Chile. Professionally, theologians still predominated with sixteen on the Commission; but there were thirteen medical doctors now, including three gynecologists and two psychiatrists. And there were demographers, sociologists, economists, and even an acupuncturist. Many were academics from Catholic institutions like the Gregorian and Lateran universities in Rome and Louvain in Belgium; a few were associated with secular schools like Oxford and the University of Paris. Only a handful were well known outside their own disciplines: German theologian Bernard Häring, British economist Colin Clark, U.S. theologian John Ford, U.S. psychiatrist John Cavanagh. The two bishops were Leo Binz, the conservative archbishop of St. Paul-Minneapolis, who was to serve as the Commission's president, and Joseph Reuss, an auxiliary bishop of Mainz, Germany, and an outspoken, progressive voice at the Vatican Council.

Attracting considerable notice was the presence on the expanded Commission of three married couples, all named *as couples* rather than for their competence in some scientific discipline: Dr. Laurent and Colette Potvin, of Ottawa, Canada; Dr. Charles and Marie Rendu of Paris; and Patrick and Patty Crowley of Chicago. However, Doctors Potvin and Rendu were both physicians, both involved in rhythm clinics, so their presence served a double purpose. Only the Crowleys would serve on the Commission exclusively as a married couple. To prepare for the forthcoming expanded meeting, an executive committee of the Commission, including de Riedmatten, de Locht, and Dr. Marshall, held two sessions in Brussels, in December 1964 and early March 1965.

The word came to the Crowleys unexpectedly in early December 1964 in the form of a letter from Cardinal Amleto Cicognani. "I have the pleasure of informing you that the Holy Father has deigned to appoint you members of the special Committee for studies on problems of population and birth control. The Committee, formed at the beginning by a small group of experts, has been subsequently enlarged.... Please accept my congratulations on this appointment, and the sentiments of my high regard." The letter had come through the Vatican pipeline: from Cicognani to the Vatican's apostolic delegate in the United States, to Cardinal Albert Meyer, archbishop of Chicago, to the Crowleys. Meyer included a letter of his own with congratulations and a suggestion that the appointment be kept confidential.

"We didn't know how to react," said Patty, "and we never did find out how we were selected. We just assumed it was because of our work with the Christian Family Movement."

Laurent and Colette Potvin were similarly surprised by a letter from Cicognani. Laurent, forty-four, was an internist in private practice in Ottawa. Concerned about the family limitation questions of his patients, he had established a small clinic where trained volunteers helped couples learn the temperature method of natural family planning. He and Colette, forty-two, were also involved in a Catholic-sponsored marriage preparation program. "I had no idea who suggested us," said Laurent, "but of course we were honored." The Potvins had five children and would have no more. Colette, like Patty, had been forced to have a hysterectomy after her last delivery. When they got to Rome, the Potvins discovered that the other married couple invited, the Rendus of France, were also unable to have more children.

Pat and Patty visited Cardinal Meyer, who encouraged them to accept the appointment, though he (just back from the Vatican Council's third session) offered little hope the Commission would achieve anything significant. They also talked to their mentor, Father Hillenbrand, and to Jesuit Scripture scholar John McKenzie, a longtime friend who shared what he knew of the Commission's activities to that point.

Further instructions came in the mail from de Riedmatten, who said the next meeting would be held the following March in Rome and provided the names of the other members. He promised a detailed report

on the previous meetings but the Crowleys never got one. They began conferring by phone with other members and thinking about what
they could do to make a contribution during the Commission's deliberations. "I think we felt a little intimidated," said Patty. "It seemed like
everyone else had some speciality, while we were just married people.
And since I couldn't have any more children, birth control wasn't a
personal problem for us."

After a discussion with another of the new members, Dr. André
Hellegers, a gynecologist with the medical school at Johns Hopkins
University in Baltimore, the Crowleys decided to seek input through
their CFM connections. In early January they sent letters to members
of the CFM national executive and coordinating committees, informing them of their appointment and asking them to solicit opinions and
comments on family limitation, especially rhythm, from the group leaders and CFM members in their area. They also sought comments from
their wide range of personal contacts. Within a few weeks they began
amassing a pile of notes and letters from all over the country. And
they were shocked.

"Pat and I read everything," Patty said, "and we both cried. We
couldn't believe the hardships people were going through to follow
Church teaching. With just a little encouragement these couples were
pouring their hearts out. That was the beginning of a real eye opener
for us." They would bring more than a hundred letters with them to
the March meeting in Rome.

The Caucus

In mid-January, eight members of the North American delegation to
the Commission met in Baltimore to get acquainted and plan strategy. Besides the Crowleys and Potvins, the attendees included Thomas
Burch, the sole veteran of the Commission; Donald Barrett, a sociologist from Notre Dame; Father John Ford, from Catholic University
of America; Dr. John Cavanagh from Washington, and Dr. Hellegers.
When Burch told the group that the sessions had been conducted in
French and that a certain amount of confusion prevailed, the group
attempted to draft a letter to the Holy Father. Feeling expansive, they
suggested, among other things, that simultaneous translations be provided at all sessions, that all proceedings be recorded and transcribed,
with copies made available to all participants, and that a larger bud-
get be provided for support services. If money was a problem for the

Vatican, some suggested that the Americans could raise a substantial amount through their contacts. They also advised the Pope to reaffirm his own teaching authority so that the conclusions of the Commission, *his Commission*, would have more weight when promulgated.

After thinking about all this, the North Americans decided not to send the letter after all. "We felt it would be presumptuous to tell the Pope at our first meeting what he should do," said Patty, "so we decided to back off."

Laurent Potvin found the whole enterprise confusing. "As Catholics we thought it would be absolutely impossible to change what Pius XI taught," he said. "I think the rest did too. So I wondered, why are they calling us together?"

Even as the Crowleys and the other newly appointed Commission members were preparing to assist the Holy Father, members of the U.S. hierarchy were growing concerned: too much talk about birth control, too many controversial opinions in the air. In late 1964 the National Council of Catholic Men (NCCM) produced a four-part television series entitled "The Church and Marriage."[8] The series, written by John Leo, then an editor at *Commonweal* magazine, was apparently quite straightforward and non-controversial, tracing the history of Catholic marriage doctrine through the ages and ending with a balanced presentation of the present dilemma. The script contained nothing that had not already been publicly aired in the media. The program was scheduled for showing in January 1965 on NBC's Catholic Hour. But Archbishop Leo Binz, the bishop in charge of the National Council of Catholic Men, informed the NCCM director in December that the bishops did not want the program to run — and it didn't. Binz, a new member of the Birth Control Commission, passed the word under orders from the chairman of the National Conference of Catholic Bishops. He had not himself seen the series but noted that while the Commission studied birth control, the Pope did not wish public discussion of the subject.

The NCCM producers were furious at this, the first cancellation in their thirty-five years in Church-related radio and television. A note from the bishops' conference censor revealed just how delicate the birth control subject had become and how determined the bishops were to keep it under wraps. "I do not believe it is possible to discuss these issues before millions of people who are unable to make the distinctions and qualifications demanded," said Father Louis Arand of the Catholic University of America. "If there is no authoritative guidance and teaching, then everyone will and must feel free to come to his own conclusions. And mere private judgment in matters of morals will be at least as pernicious as private judgment in matters of dogma."

There was no suggestion here that an informed laity might have anything to contribute on a subject so close to their lives or that they would even benefit from hearing what the acknowledged experts had to say.

Seeking "Immediate Action"

The Fourth Meeting, 1965

Listen to the anxiety of so many souls and work diligently without worrying about criticism or difficulties.

— POPE PAUL VI

The fourth meeting of the Commission was held on March 25 through March 28, 1965, at the newly constructed Spanish College, a semi-nary on the outskirts of Rome. The unusual presence of women at a top-level Vatican meeting resulted initially in an awkward situation. When the Crowleys, Rendus, and Potvins arrived, they were informed by de Riedmatten that husbands would have their living quarters at the college, while the three wives, along with two unaccompanied women on the Commission, would stay at a sisters' convent a mile down the road. The couples took the enforced separation in stride, and Pat's quip, "I guess that's one way to solve the problem," was later quoted in a range of publications from the *Ladies Home Journal* to the Paris *Match*.

The tone of this meeting was all business. Commission veterans were now fully prepared to take on the "fundamental issues" only touched on at previous sessions. Everyone had heard of the outspoken, tone-setting views of Cardinal Suenens, Patriarch Maximos, and others at the Vatican Council; there was a sense that this assembly had a man-date from Pope and bishops to speak honestly and clearly. The schedule allowed little time for dissipation: Mass of the Holy Spirit at 7:30 A.M., followed by breakfast; presentation of papers and discussion beginning at 9:00 and continuing almost all day except for a brief lunch and two

coffee breaks; dinner at 8:00 P.M., followed by more formal presenta-
tions until 10:00 when the women were driven to the convent and the
doors of the college were locked.

The members were broken into three working sections: theologians
and historians in one group, doctors and psychologists in another,
demographers, sociologists, and economists in a third. While this
new format limited the interdisciplinary give-and-take of earlier meetings, it allowed for more concentrated work. Also scheduled were
general sessions of the full assembly to discuss a list of questions
posed by de Riedmatten for "immediate action." A coterie of multi-
lingual seminarians provided simultaneous translations for those who
required them.

The always gregarious Pat Crowley attempted to inject some in-
formality into the proceedings. On the eve of the first work day, he
suggested a community sing-along, but no one else seemed interested.
Undeterred, he then pressed for group singing at the morning Masses,
and this was agreed on though not too enthusiastically. "People tried,"
said Patty. "The problem was that the only songs everyone knew were
Tantum Ergo and Salve Regina." Pat and Patty urged members to
sit at different tables for each meal so the fifty-eight could become
acquainted, and this proposal proved quite successful. Others found
different ways to avoid tedium. Dr. Marshall was among those who
bribed the doorkeeper to let them out after 10:00 so they could relax
and talk informally at a nearby cafe.

As the newcomers got acquainted, the Crowleys discovered that
one member, Mercedes Concepción, had met them before when she
visited their home in the late 1950s as one of the scores of foreign
students to receive their hospitality. She had been studying sociology
at the University of Chicago. Concepción, now thirty-seven and director of the Population Institute at the University of the Philippines,
was quite certain why she had been named to the Commission. "I
came from a developing country, I had a doctorate in sociology, and I
was a woman," she said. Concepción had strong convictions about the
Church position. "I thought change should come and could come," she
said later. "The Church would simply have to bend in the face of the
growth rate in our part of the world."

Meetings of the full assembly were held in a long, narrow room, with
the members sitting along the walls and the speaker in front. Here they
heard John Noonan's two-hour summary of the history of contraception the first day. Nearly every published account of the Commission

mentions that talk as stimulating and extremely helpful — particularly his revelation of how differently love, sex, and marriage were understood in different times. Regardless of the present situation, it established that marriage doctrine had surely been susceptible to significant change through the ages. Noonan's talk, said Patty, though long and academic, was "extremely enlightening to us; we started to see for the first time what we were dealing with."

Tom Burch called the Noonan talk "a major intellectual influence" on the assembly, since it put the issue "in perspective and revealed how the understanding of reproduction had changed."

Said Laurent Potvin, "When we saw how the doctrine changed, I began to get a little enthusiastic."

De Riedmatten was at first uncertain in which of the three specialized sections to place the Crowleys. Doctors Rendu and Potvin, along with their wives, fit nicely into the medical group, but the Crowleys did not. "I don't think they knew what to do with us," said Patty, "so we ended up most of the time in with the theologians. Since we weren't really sure what the Church wanted, we tended to hang back and listen a lot."

The "immediate action" questions showed that the Pope expected the group to go deeply into the contraception issue and was almost desperate for advice on what he himself should do. But they were so overwhelming in scope as to paralyze even the most capable body of experts. Among them: Has sufficient doctrinal progress been made for a pronouncement by the Church (that is, the Pope)? If a pronouncement is made modifying some aspects of current teaching, how should the changes be explained to the people? Is the doctrine of Pius XI's *Casti Connubii* and Pius XII's approval of rhythm (the Yin and Yang of modern marriage teaching) reformable? Are some forms of birth control intrinsically evil and should Catholics be warned about using them? Should the magisterium speak out about rhythm and legitimate uses of the pill? If no pronouncement is deemed appropriate, what advice should be given to pastors and confessors?

In his usual diplomatic but circumlocutious style, de Riedmatten said the purpose of the questions was to help the Commission "formulate its views on the possibility of considering that certain points seem today to be sufficiently settled so that the commissioning Authority can intervene, in the manner it considers preferable, this intervention to be of such a nature as to permit as a consequence the solution of several difficulties pending."

A Vote on Reformability

Perhaps the most basic among the questions was whether the current doctrine is reformable — that is, subject to change. If not, then the game would be essentially over, with the Holy Father compelled to re-iterate the statements of the past, though possibly with a more modern, personalist spin. The theology section responded by producing considerable heat — and some light — as they debated reformability and related matters in eight separate meetings over the four days, introducing twenty-six reports. The case for tradition was spelled out by the Spanish Jesuit Zalba, who insisted current doctrine is not only ir-reformable but infallible. He cited the centuries-old condemnation of coitus interruptus, the teaching of procreation as marriage's primary end, and the prohibition of direct sterilization, all constituting part of a universal pattern. "We stand before a practically uninterrupted tradition," he said. American Jesuit John Ford concurred, quoting strong language from *Casti Connubii*: "This prescription [against contraception] is in full force now as it was before, and so it will be tomorrow and forever, because it is not a mere human enactment but the expression of a natural and divine law." Said Ford, "If that isn't infallible language, what is?"[1] Zalba and Ford were joined by Father de Lestapis, Archbishop Binz and others in a firm stand on this.

Canon Philip Delhaye, a theologian at the University of Lisle in France, disagreed. *Casti Connubii* and other authoritative documents should be regarded, he said, not as doctrine strictly speaking but as "pastoral guidance" — that is, explanations or updates on earlier decrees and therefore subject to modification in the light of changed circumstances. Moral matters do not lend themselves well to ultimate, unchangeable judgments, others in the group agreed. Infallibility and irreformability pertain only to matters of divine revelation, argued Bernard Häring, and not to interpretations of the natural law. Dominican Michel Labourdette from France took up the same theme. "A document concerning very precise moral conduct loses its force because it presupposes situations in which many of the elements have changed," he said. "Did not Pius XII already start an evolution? His acceptance of regulating births and his approval of periodic continence already strike a new note."

Jesuit Joseph Fuchs surprised some by stating his view that the doctrine can indeed be reformed. He had been regarded as a hard-line conservative and an advocate of rhythm as the only acceptable birth control method when he came on the Commission one year before. As he interacted with his peers and learned about the fallibility of rhythm methods from Dr. Marshall — he would soon learn more from the Crowleys — his convictions shifted. "I think it was hard for Fuchs," said Laurent Potvin. "Here was a man teaching one way for twenty years or more, and it's not easy to see the other side after that."

De Riedmatten, growing eager for some conclusions, called for a vote by the theologians. Twelve, including Canon Pierre de Locht and Bishop Joseph Reuss, said the present teaching can be reformed (though Fuchs noted that doesn't mean it should be). Seven, led by Zalba and Ford, said it could not be changed. Though the vote hardly told Pope Paul what to tell the public, it presented a fairly clear picture of the direction in which the experts were moving. Patty Crowley, who witnessed much of the interchange, found herself siding almost instinctively with Häring. "Both Pat and I saw him as so caring and sympathetic with real people," she said. "Some of those men seemed to live only in a world of ideas." Zalba she regarded as habitually "sour and negative — he saw contraception as intrinsically evil from the start and he would not budge an inch." Colette Potvin was impressed with Häring, and Canon de Locht as well. "These were men looking beyond what popes had given us," she said. "They seemed concerned with the problems of living a marriage today."

The morality of the pill was also discussed amid disagreement by the theologians. Here Fuchs's lingering conservatism showed; he could not see how it might be acceptable as a contraceptive, and besides, he argued, approval of the pill could open the door to the condom, coitus interruptus, and other contraceptive methods. Others, including de Locht and Häring, seemed almost ready to let that door open. With the exception of abortion, said de Locht, "no method can be called intrinsically bad or good. They are all unimportant in themselves and their moral significance lies in the life of the husband and wife. Obviously, some methods are theoretically more efficient than others.... It is not fertility that decides the moral value of methods; it is the way in which these methods, with greater or lesser merit, preserve the significance and authenticity of conjugal intimacies." Häring reiterated his own conviction that marriage as a whole ought to be open to new life, but that doesn't mean every single sexual encounter between husband and wife must be. No formal votes were taken on this issue, and as the days passed, it became obvious that few "immediate action" questions would be answered.

The Crowley Survey

In their presentation to the full group, the Crowleys came armed with copies of the correspondence they had gathered. Pat provided the rationale for their approach after giving a history of their own family and explaining what the Christian Family Movement is and how it works.

"CFM is known to be a sympathetic setting for large families. Since being told of our appointment and being authorized to consult our contemporaries, we have been shocked into a realization that even the most dedicated, committed Catholics are deeply troubled by this problem. We have gathered hundreds of statements from many parts of the United States and Canada and have been overwhelmed by the strong consensus in favor of change. Most expressed a hope that the positive values in love and marriage need to be stressed and that an expanded theology of marriage needs to be developed. Most say they think there must be a change in the teaching on birth control. Very few know what this change should be; they are puzzled but hopeful.

"We understand that when the Church was considering the problem of what to do about reviewing the teaching on usury, the testimony of business people was heard and considered. If there is any parallel between the teaching of usury and the teaching on family limitation, then possibly there is a precedent for the testimony of those most affected by the doctrine.... Many of the couples have large families — six to thirteen children. Most are able to educate and support the children. Some have intermittent financial, physical, and in a few cases, psychological problems.... Most expressed dissatisfaction over the rhythm method for a variety of reasons, running from the fact that it was ineffective, hard to follow; and some had psychological and physiological objections."

Pat then shared the collective views of six "exceptionally active" Chicago area CFMers, including Matt and Margie Ahmann and John and Mary Ann McCudden: "We believe the end of marriage, considered in its natural as well as sacramental aspects, is both personal and social.... The bearing and raising of children are normally the means by which this end is reached; the intention of fruitfulness is normally part of the marriage union.... The number of children by which a couple can best reach this end can be determined — should be determined — by the couple alone; if the decision is made to limit the number of children, this should be done on the basis of Christian charity; i.e., unselfishly, out of a love that sees some larger good to be accomplished by the limitation. Discussions of the morality of sex in marriage should be based on considerations such as these, not on analysis of the isolated act of intercourse."

The Commission members who sifted through copies of the Crowley survey could not but be moved by the sincerity of the respondents. By definition, CFMers were not Church fallen-aways, lukewarm parishioners, or cafeteria Catholics, accepting what pleased them and rejecting whatever demanded commitment. They were the couples who took religion seriously enough to meet with like-minded friends at least every other week to discuss their faith and its implications in their lives. They were often the superactive minority in their parishes, the ones priests and nuns depended on to hold everything together — and pay the bills. What did it mean, the Crowleys wondered when they first read the replies, that this nucleus had been quietly growing frustrated — even hostile — at what they regarded as an unreasonable burden? "We began to ask ourselves," said Patty, "does God really demand this of people who are trying to live a full, generous Christian life?"

The replies seemed especially poignant because the doctrine was not taken so seriously elsewhere. Said Patty, "People at the meeting told us the only places where the ban on contraception was obeyed were the United States, Ireland and wherever the Irish missionaries went."

One father of six wrote: "Rhythm destroys the meaning of the sex act; it turns it from a spontaneous expression of spiritual and physical love into a mere bodily sexual relief; it makes me obsessed with sex throughout the month. It seriously endangers my chastity; it has a noticeable effect upon my disposition; it makes necessary my complete avoidance of all affection toward my wife for three weeks at a time. . . . Rhythm seems to be immoral and deeply unnatural. It seems to me diabolical."

A mother who used both the basal temperature and calendar methods, said: "I find myself sullen and resentful of my husband when the time for sexual relations finally arrives. I resent his necessarily guarded affection during the month and I find I cannot respond suddenly. I find also that my subconscious dreams and unguarded thoughts are inevitably sexual. . . . All this in spite of a . . . generally beautiful marriage and home life."

A couple, both thirty-three, wrote: "As busy parents raising children,

we know few moments of complete harmony and personal communion. Our physical and spiritual union, when it does occur, is just such
a moment. It should not be subjected to scientific and metaphysical
scrutiny. We do not believe that every time a man and wife feel a
need to express their love to each other that it is a 'call from God'
to raise more kids. Neither is it a resurgence of the base and selfish
sex drive.... We are frail and lonely people holding to the only mutual
concern and affection we really know."

In an earlier era the letters might have been dismissed out of hand
by Church authorities as irrelevant: doctrine is not determined by opinion polls; people tend to blame the lawgiver rather than admit their
own sinfulness; just because something is difficult doesn't mean it's unnatural or unjust. But at this meeting the Crowley report was received
with extraordinary respect by the assembly. It was not definitive, yet for
some it seemed closer to Newman's notion of "consulting the faithful"
than anything they had heard at the session. For Laurent Potvin, who
had long experience teaching the temperature method of rhythm, the
reports confirmed what he believed — that rhythm was not a universal
answer for every couple and may not be a total answer for any couple
through the entire child-bearing years.

Before the March meeting adjourned, the Potvins were asked to
survey the opinions of Catholics regarding birth control in French-
speaking Quebec, and the Rendus agreed to undertake a similar study
in France. Pat and Patty were asked to prepare for the next session
a larger and more scientific survey through their CFM connections
on how married Catholics throughout the world regarded the rhythm
method. Said Patty, "We knew we had just touched the surface and we
were anxious to find out what people really thought."

"Continue Your Deliberations"

Meanwhile, the medical professionals discussed every known form of
contraception along with its benefits, liabilities, and probable moral
implications. They produced seventeen reports. The social science
section labored over dimensions of the world population boom but
was loath to suggest how responsible parenthood could be promoted
in a uniform way in diverse cultures. They came up with sixteen
reports.

Toward the end votes were taken — not binding, just to measure the direction of thinking, said de Riedmatten. There was general

agreement that the Pope should not at this time reiterate past condemnations. He should, however, the body concurred, issue a "basic
document" on marriage containing four major points: parenthood
should be responsible (that is, a couple should consider a range of factors in deciding how many children to have); conjugal love is at the
heart of marriage (not a subordinate component); sex has a positive
value independent of procreation; and young people need better education about the nature of marriage and its responsibilities. Agreement
was also expressed that the natural family planning method should be
more widely encouraged, though enthusiasm for rhythm was less ardent
than at earlier meetings.

On the last day the Commission went to the Vatican for its only
face-to-face meeting with the Holy Father. Either ignoring or forget-
ting the mixed nature of the group before him, Paul twice addressed
them as "dear sons." But his message displayed unbounded confidence
and support in the work. Said Paul: "We ask you urgently not to lose
sight of the pressing need of a situation which asks of the Church and
of her Supreme Authority to give guidance without ambiguity. Consciences of men cannot be left exposed to uncertainties which today
very often prevent married life from developing according to the Lord's
plan."

He urged the Commission to continue its deliberations "in complete
objectivity and liberty of spirit.... You are at a new and decisive stage
in your work.... Give yourselves to your task wholeheartedly, let that
which needs it ripen, but listen to the anxiety of so many souls and
work diligently without worrying about criticism or difficulties."

The Pope even went out of his way to state that the scope and com-
position of the Commission was his own by personal choice and design.
"It is our wish that the basis of your investigations should become
broader, that the different currents of theological thought be better
represented in it, that the countries which know ... serious difficulties
... should raise their voice among you, and that laymen, and especially
married couples, should have their qualified representatives in such a
serious undertaking."

Pat and Patty were convinced change was coming. All signs pointed
that way: the theologians' strong vote on reformability; the mellow-
ing of some conservatives; the eagerness of the members to hear the
voice of the people; the Pope's encouraging words. They were not
alone in that assessment. In his fifty-eight-page report to the Holy
Father (along with fifty-nine section reports), the usually cautious de

Riedmatten wrote, "Everybody, conservative or progressive, theologians or laymen, all are convinced of the necessity for the Church to
make a fresh move in order to face up to the distress of conscience
and the needs arising from the facts that cannot be denied." Then
he added a cautionary note just to be on the safe side: "Any move
could only be within the framework of the teaching of Christ and of
the Church."[2]

Dodging the Bullet

The Council, 1965

I was always in the minority.
— CARDINAL ALFREDO OTTAVIANI

The Commission members may have been committed to change, but Cardinal Alfredo Ottaviani was not. He never wanted the Second Vatican Council, and he did not want the Birth Control Commission either. In the view of the aged head of the Holy Office, the Roman Catholic Church was "a perfect society," sufficient unto itself, impervious to cultural shifts and other outside influences. The motto on his coat of arms was *semper idem* (always the same). Dr. John Marshall, who served on the Commission from the beginning and for a time on its executive committee, believed the Commission would have been constantly interfered with, dictated to, driven to distraction, and probably disbanded by mid-1965 if Ottaviani had had his way.

But the Commission was not under his direct jurisdiction. It had been assigned to the Vatican Secretary of State's office headed by Cardinal Amleto Cicognani. This was done because its original mandate was to aid the Pope in responding to the United Nations regarding population policy, a matter of international diplomacy. While hardly a progressive force himself, Cicognani had been the apostolic delegate to the United States for twenty-five years and was therefore a bit more tolerant of open discussion and decisions by vote rather than by authoritative fiat. Besides, Commission Secretary Henri de Riedmatten had direct access to the Pope and did not have to maneuver his way through a heavily bureaucratic operation. Whenever de Riedmatten approached the Holy Father, said Marshall, he was invariably told to go ahead, take the next step — don't be afraid.

"I think all of us on the Commission felt our ideas were respected," said Marshall. "There was no sense we were being driven down some predetermined road. Openness and frankness prevailed — almost to the end."

Nevertheless, during the nine months from the fourth Commission meeting in March 1965 to the closing of the Vatican Council's fourth and final session in December, considerable pressure was being applied from several sides, though most lay members of the Commission were only dimly aware of the mounting tension. The Commission would not hold its final sessions in Rome until the spring of 1966, long after the Vatican Council had finished its business.

Cardinal Ottaviani, the defender of the faith, and his like-minded cohorts realized that if the momentum for change (specifically the doctrine on marital morality) were to be halted, it should be stopped at the level of the Council *and* the Commission. But he had been repeatedly thwarted so far because the progressives, personified by Belgium's Cardinal Suenens, outstrategized and outvoted him.

Indeed, the link joining Suenens, the Vatican Council, the Birth Control Commission, and Ottaviani remained as firm as it was antagonistic throughout the mid-1960s; it had much to do with what occurred and did not occur in those momentous years. It was Suenens who had persuaded the Pope to create the Commission in the first place after Suenens had seen the original chapter on marriage proposed for the Council by Ottaviani's theologian, Lio. And it was Suenens who subsequently got Lio removed from the Council's Mixed Commission (composed of bishops and experts from several other commissions), which radically revised and re-revised the statement. On the other hand, Ottaviani, a member of the Holy Office for thirty-five years, never took kindly to defeat; he had a well-justified reputation for getting his way in the end.

It is tempting to contrast the two as extremes of the forces at work in the Church at that point. Suenens, in his early sixties, tall, erect, stately, seemingly at ease in any situation, experienced in public relations, available to the media — the quintessential progressive. Ottaviani, in his eighties and described as multi-joweled and almost completely blind, stubborn, demanding, imperious, suspicious, ill at ease with the press — the unconditional reactionary. And between them Pope Paul VI, intellectual, fully aware that the Church's belated entry into the twentieth century should not be derailed, yet extremely respectful of the demands of tradition, worried about how to bring orthodoxy out of a tangle of competing, often contradictory ideas. In addition, he knew, as Pope John knew before him, that he needed the wily old Ottaviani and the whole Roman Curia if he ever expected the reforms of Vatican II to become practical realities.

The Pope Struggles

In a remarkable interview with Italian journalist Alberto Cavallari at this time, Paul groaned about his fate: "So many problems! How many problems there are, and how many answers we have to give! We want to be open to the world, and every day we have to make decisions that will have consequences for centuries to come.... There are some questions that are particularly difficult for us, such as those connected with the problem of the Christian family.

"Take birth control, for example. The world asks what we think and we find ourselves trying to give an answer. But what answer? We can't keep silent. And yet to speak is a real problem. But what? The Church has never in her history confronted such a problem." Then, said Cavallari, the Pope started to say something, hesitated, then blurted out, "This is a strange subject for men of the Church to be discussing. Even humanly embarrassing.... So the commissions meet, the reports pile up, the studies are published. Oh, they study a lot, you know. But then we will have to make the final decision.... We have to say something. But what? God will simply have to enlighten us."[1]

Ottaviani tried to help him along. Presumably with the Pope's consent, he told de Riedmatten in June to produce immediately a statement reflecting the points thus far agreed on by the Birth Control Commission. If approved, the document would be made available to the world's priests as a "pastoral instruction." Alarmed, since areas of agreement were few and still vague, de Riedmatten called together a subcommittee of the Commission theologians to assist him (de Locht, Häring, de Lestapis, and Labourdette). Ottaviani added a more conservative editorial board; before they were finished, a further body of four priests and four physicians, including Marshall, Hellegers, and von Rossum, was summoned. De Riedmatten himself wrote the text, which he submitted to Ottaviani, who, in turn, circulated it among various Vatican congregations where alterations were made. The final product, known as "the Green Book" and bearing the fingerprints of so many hands, was not well received when review copies made the rounds. The reason was obvious. Wrote de Riedmatten, "The document represents a total collaboration on the given points. . . . As soon as a question or a formula statement provoked any controversy, it was systematically omitted."[2]

Bishop Reuss, Archbishop Binz, and even principal author de Riedmatten, urged the Pope to withdraw it, arguing that it was hopelessly bland and, in addition, somehow misrepresented where the Commission stood on several key points. The Green Book was never distributed.

Pope Paul then turned in the other direction — to his friend Suenens, asking for a simple, intelligible statement that would allow him to endorse change without undermining his own authority or that of his predecessors. This, it seemed, would allow him to bypass both Council and Commission. Nevertheless, Suenens obediently produced a five-page paper that claimed doctrinal development was an integral part of the Christian tradition. The Pope reportedly said, "A very good text, but I must read it with a peaceful mind," then turned it over to Ottaviani for his consideration.[3] Though the head of the Holy office no doubt liked the idea of settling the whole thing with a single stroke of the pen from the High Authority, he could never endure the theology of Cardinal Suenens. Like the Green Book, the statement perished. A Suenens adviser commented sadly, "The Pope can't seem to stay away from the Holy Office."[4]

Even when Paul visited the United Nations headquarters in New York City on October 4 for his memorable "War never again, war never again!" speech, the subject of birth control was still on his mind. "The life of man is sacred," he told the delegates. "Respect for life, in regard to the great problem of natality, should find here in your assembly its highest affirmation and its most reasoned defense. Your task is to improve food production that there will be enough for all the tables of mankind, and not press for an artificial control of births, which would be irrational, so as to cut down the number of guests at the banquet of life."[5]

The Ford Intervention

Meanwhile in Rome the Vatican Council was putting the finishing touches on the long-disputed text of the chapter on marriage (schema 13) of *The Pastoral Constitution on the Church in the Modern*

World (*Gaudium et Spes*). Repeatedly the Ottaviani forces had been routed. Their attempts to restate in the text the old distinction be-tween primary and secondary ends of marriage failed. So also did the effort to incorporate a juridical definition of marriage as "the right over the body for acts apt for generating children." Far from reviving distinc-tions, rating relative values, or relying on textbook definitions, the final draft called conjugal love "eminently human" and involving "the good of the whole person." This love, "merging the human with the divine, leads the spouses to a free and mutual gift of themselves, a gift proving itself by a gentle affection and by deed. Such love pervades the whole of their lives.... This love is uniquely expressed and perfected through the marital act. The actions within marriage by which the couple are united intimately and chastely are noble and worthy ones. Expressed in a manner which is truly human, these actions signify and promote that mutual self-giving by which spouses enrich each other with a joyful and thankful will."[6]

Still, the possibility remained that a carefully crafted, last-minute in-tervention might turn the text into a defense of *Casti Connubii* and thereby render any further deliberations of the Birth Control Com-mission moot. As described by Robert Blair Kaiser in *The Politics of Sex and Religion,* the story of that effort has all the elements of a fast-paced ecclesiastical who-done-it with Father John Ford in the lead and Cardinal Ottaviani pulling the strings behind the scenes.

On November 9, while schema 13 discussions progressed, Ford, from his residence in Washington, D.C., wrote to Archbishop Egidio Vagnozzi, the apostolic delegate to the United States, saying he had to see the Pope immediately. He had in his possession incontrovertible evidence that at least one member of the Birth Control Commis-sion, namely, Canon Pierre de Locht, "has taught contraception to the priests and people of Belgium for some years; he professes a type of situation morality which is clearly opposed to the decree of the Holy Office.... And judging by his writings I cannot help but conclude that he is one of those who does not believe that the Church has any right to bind the consciences of individuals in moral matters."[7] Ford was one of the best known Catholic moralists in the United States and had been for many years. Together with his colleague and fel-low Jesuit Gerald Kelly, he had authored manuals in use in dozens of major seminaries; their commentaries on moral questions appeared regularly in *Theological Studies* and other journals. As a new mem-ber of the Birth Control Commission at its most recent meeting, Ford

had been enraged at the seeming ease with which a heavy majority of
the theologians determined that *Casti Connubii* contained reformable,
non-infallible positions. No one at the meetings argued more strongly
for the opposite view. Now, said Ford, he believed he could help the
Holy Father find a way to stem the tide.

When Vagnozzi did not reply quickly, Ford flew to Rome and went
immediately to Ottaviani's office. In a memo to the cardinal, he explained his concerns, insisted he must see Pope Paul himself, and
wondered if de Riedmatten had tried to block his efforts to get through.
Ottaviani, said Kaiser, liked Ford's feisty spirit and probably had him
meet with other similarly obstructionist theologians. These included
papal theological adviser Carlo Colombo and Birth Control Commission members Visser and Zalba. Buoyed by Ford's sense of mission,
the group developed a strategy to wrest victory out of the jaws of
defeat.

On November 16, it appeared they failed: the Council assembly, by
a 4–1 ratio, approved a second reading of the latest draft on marriage.
All that remained was for the Council's Mixed Commission (a combination of bishops and experts serving on several other commissions) to
discuss certain amendments that had been proposed to the text. According to the rules, any such amendments had to be consistent with
the spirit and sense of the text.

Before that discussion got underway, Bishop Colombo on November 19 arose at a Council session and said he did not like the text
(implying that the Pope didn't either); he thought a Council subcommittee should meet with certain members of the Birth Control
Commission (particularly theologians like Visser, Ford, and Zalba)
to determine if the approved marriage text should be scuttled and
whether the Birth Control Commission had any future. Sensing an assassination attempt in progress, Bishop Reuss objected strongly, and
the Council majority rejected Colombo's suggestion.

Three days later, on November 22, Ford obtained his audience with
the Pope and claimed the Council's marriage text implicitly denied the
intrinsic evil of contraception (even though it did not touch on birth
control methods) and would shake the faith of the strong and encourage gross immorality among the weak. Evidently, the Pope was moved
by Ford's fervor and arguments.

The Papal *Modi*

Two days after that meeting, when the Council's Mixed Commission met to go over amendments, the members were surprised to find two new appointees in their midst: Ford and Ermenegildo Lio, author of the long since discredited version of the marriage chapter. Both had been added through the intercession of Cardinal Ottaviani, chair of the Mixed Commission. Late in the afternoon, a shock went through the group when Cardinal Ottaviani warned everyone they were under an oath of secrecy and introduced a letter from the Vatican Secretary of State directing the Mixed Commission "in the name of the Higher Authority" to make explicit reference to Pius XI's *Casti Connubii* and Pius XII's allocution to the midwives in the chapter on marriage. Also they were to add four *modi* (insertions) to the text. Council observer Xavier Rynne wrote, "When the *modi* were read ... there was a look of triumph on the faces of the American Jesuit Father John Ford and the Franciscan Father Ermenegildo Lio, advocates of an intransigent position on the subject of birth control, while Cardinal Browne is alleged to have said, *Christus ipse locutus est* — Christ himself has spoken." As presented, the *modi* would reestablish procreation as the principal end of marriage and give the authority of the ecumenical council to a ban on all and every type of artificial contraception. "At one fell swoop," said Rynne, "not only would the work of the Council so far be compromised, but the Special Papal Commission entrusted with the whole matter of demographic study and family planning by the Pope himself would have been rendered useless." The stunned members of the Mixed Commission adjourned to plan their response. De Riedmatten said the whole thing was a surprise to him, and de Locht saw it as a return "pure and simple" to *Casti Connubii*.[8]

The next day several high-level members of the Mixed Commission spoke out. Archbishop John Dearden of Detroit said there was great resentment of the way the group was being "bulldozed" into violating Council rules barring changes in text, and Cardinal Leger of Canada said the interference could irreparably damage the reputation of the Holy See. Ottaviani was furious that somehow word of the *modi* had been leaked to the press and was getting prominent play in the Italian dailies. There followed a great scurrying back and forth to the Pope's apartment by representatives of both sides.

Paul then offered a bit of clarification in a letter to the Mixed Commission. First, he said, the *modi* were a matter "of great importance" to him, but second, the method of formulation was "not obligatory," and third, changes could be made in the wording provided the sense was retained. He reserved to himself a decision on accepting or rejecting their alterations. Theoretically, the Pope was putting himself on both sides of the fence; practically, he was leaving the door open for the Council's Mixed Commission to disarm the *modi*. And that is what they did, though not without a fight from the right.

The first of the *modi* called for the words "anti-conceptual arts" to be inserted in a sentence listing misuses of married love. The Mixed Commission changed the words to the more generic "illicit practices against human generation." The second called for the omission of one word ("also) in another passage, the effect of which would have been to make the procreation and education of children "the whole meaning of family life." By altering the original text a bit, the members asserted that the other purposes of matrimony "are of no less account" than procreation. The third called for the insertion of the phrase "sons of the Church, who must sincerely cultivate the virtue of chastity, may not undertake methods of birth control which have been or shall be found blameworthy by the magisterium." After considerable discussion, it was decided to alter this passage and to include in a footnote that while the Special Birth Control Commission is in existence, "this holy synod does not intend to propose immediately concrete solutions." The fourth of the *modi* was similarly disarmed by placing it in a different context than that requested by the Pope. As to *Casti Connubii* and Pius XII's acceptance of rhythm, a brief mention of these was placed in another footnote where it appeared more as a reference to past history than a guiding light for the present or future.

In their altered form, the *modi* were presented to the Pope and he accepted them without comment, though they had been rendered essentially toothless. The whole *modi* affair seemed to illustrate Paul's ambivalence — his willingness to be pulled first one way then another.

Ford was livid. He complained to Pope Paul personally and repeated dire warnings about the future. The Pope reportedly answered, "You, a moral theologian, tell me there is only one way to look at this matter. On the other hand, Bishop Reuss is also a moral theologian and he tells just the opposite. Go to him and argue the matter out. When you two moralists reach an agreement, come back to me with an answer." In a note to the Holy Father, Cardinal Ottaviani said, "I did all possible to have the Commission accept the modifications of Your Holiness, but was always in the minority."[9] Yet as far as Ottaviani,

Ford, Lio, and others were concerned, the battle over birth control was not over.

Most lay members of the Birth Control Commission were only vaguely aware of these thrusts and counterthrusts in Rome. Several from the American delegation met in Washington, D.C., and wrote a four-page letter to de Riedmatten suggesting a need for the addition of "systematic, speculative theologians" to the Commission. More and more clearly, they could see their deliberations raising questions of how authority works in the Church and to what extent change is possible — questions going deeper than the morality of contraception. Suggested were three well-known European figures, Yves Congar, Hans Küng, and Karl Rahner, and two Americans, Jesuits John Courtney Murray and Robert Drinan. None was named to the Commission.

The Survey, 1965 - 66

Is contraceptive sex irresponsible when I have already borne ten little responsibilities?

— A CATHOLIC MOTHER

When the Crowleys returned home from the 1965 meeting in Rome, the birth control issue was already under wide discussion within the Christian Family Movement. The CFM publication ACT stirred the waters with a series of hard-hitting articles. The most analytical, written by Father Walter Imbiorski, director of the Chicago Cana Conference, presented tough questions:

- "If contraception is forbidden by the natural law, why is that in Western society only Catholics ... recognize and acknowledge this prohibition?"

- "If one were to permit contraception in marriage ... what kind of compelling argumentation could be developed for premarital chastity?"

- "Is frequent and continued physical expression of love in marriage truly a necessity for the fostering and deepening of love and for the good of the marriage?"

- "If a wider use of contraceptive means is ever permitted, will this do anything significant to make marriages better?"

- "Is 'how many children can I rear well?' a question that must get more attention?"[1]

A flurry of reader response followed. Yes, said one couple, frequent sexual union is necessary for fostering love, and no, a change should not undermine the Catholic position on premarital chastity if marriage is seen as the "responsible context" for mutual love and service. "We are convinced," they said, "this stated law is not the last best word. We hope for a change — especially for a change of emphasis."

Wrote a young woman, "There is nothing more artificial about any form of mechanical contraception than there is about iron lungs, artificial limbs, or synthetic larynxes and heart valves. All of these are considered perfectly legitimate means of correcting or nullifying defects in the 'natural' man.... The 'natural value' to be considered here is the totality of the human being's tendency toward monogamous mating for life, including reproduction, rearing and educating offspring.... At present our entire morality of marriage is a negative eleventh commandment: 'Thou Shalt Not Commit Contraception.'"

Other respondents, however, reacted far more conservatively. "The old teaching is still official," said a priest from Missouri. "And that is true no matter how much evidence we gather for a change.... The fact that dedicated Catholics disobey is no excuse."

"If God intended to have an essentially unitive act broken up into parts, then he would certainly have put marriage on a less than a sacramental footing," wrote a priest from Wisconsin.

"Does CFM mean Christian Family Movement or 'Contraception for Me?'" asked a California couple.

"Please put our particular CFM group down as being in favor of adherence to the teaching of Holy Mother Church," wrote four couples from Louisiana.[2]

The Crowleys saw the debate as healthy — an indication that CFMers were applying two of the movement's three commandments to the problem: they were observing, and they were definitely making judgments. With their mandate from the Commission, Pat and Patty set about producing a broad, more scholarly look at the effects of rhythm among their members. In this they were aided by Donald Barrett, a University of Notre Dame sociologist and also a member of the Birth Control Commission. Questionnaires were sent to lead couples of Christian Family Movement groups in the United States and Canada for distribution among their members. Some also went to CFM groups in England, New Zealand, and other English-speaking countries. The members were asked basic biographical information and then queried (with assurances of anonymity) about whether they used the rhythm method, whether it worked, and if it failed why it failed. They were also asked if rhythm proved harmful or helpful to their marriage relationship (regardless of whether or not it succeeded in limiting family size). Slightly different questionnaires were circulated in Spain, Mexico, and several South American countries.

The quick replies confirmed what the Crowleys already knew — they were touching a sensitive nerve. Besides the fourteen hundred returned questionnaires from English-speaking countries, they received summary reports from Spanish surveys, as well as a swatch of reports from far locales such as India and Tanzania. Two California CFM organizations sent the results of their own survey of almost four hundred couples. In addition, an August 1965 article about the Crowleys and the Commission in *St. Anthony's Messenger* magazine, entitled "The Church Calls for the Facts," elicited some two hundred personal responses and letters. In the end, the Crowleys had amassed replies from approximately three thousand couples in eighteen countries.[3]

Aided by the Notre Dame sociology staff, Barrett crunched the hard numbers, analyzed the letters, and produced a twenty-three-page report for distribution to all the Commission members at the upcoming 1966 meeting. Giving the document a special punch was the inclusion of excerpts from scores of the couples' comments.

Scientific studies of the rhythm method under its various names (periodic continence, natural family planning, use of the safe period, etc.) had been going on since the mid-1930s, with reported success rates ranging from highs of 86 percent to lows of 14 percent, depending on who was being researched and where the research was done. The Crowley-Barrett survey, however, was no random sample of the child-bearing population, and that gave it a unique value in Barrett's judgment. "From the sources of the responses ... and also from the tone and specific content of their responses, they have a special devotion to the Church, which could not be said of all in a representative sample of Catholics," noted Barrett. "In a real sense, this is a 'known' population, a committed number of Catholics, most evidently more active than others.... These couples are seriously concerned about the religious, moral, psychological, and sociological features of their family situation."

The average age for husbands was thirty-six, for wives thirty-four, married eleven years, with an average of 4.9 children. Only 5 percent had never attempted rhythm, and 10 percent had used it less than a year; 50 percent had been using rhythm seven years or more. The methods varied from calendar only to temperature only, to a combination of both, to calendar, temperature, and tape (for measuring cervical mucous), to a mix of other combinations.

Divided Views

On the surface the results seemed to confirm that for many of these committed Catholics the rhythm method did work and sometimes provided other benefits — but often at a high cost. For others it didn't work and the cost was even higher. Some basic findings of the survey along with typical comments:

- When asked if it was "helpful" in spacing children, some 43 percent said it was, while another 21 percent found it "partly helpful."

"Rhythm has worked," wrote one couple, "and we must work at it, however, and pray together.... Now we have great respect for one another and believe God wants it."

"Rhythm works well," said another couple. "We use the temperature system. Wives need rest, exercise, good diet for regular cycles.... Was Christianity meant to be easy? ...

"Rhythm may be hard, but with Mass, rosary and grace over time, the learning is easy," wrote a couple. "We should desire to have all the children God wants us to have, not our selfish selves."

- About 32 percent said the rhythm method did not work for them despite efforts. Among those who failed, 65 percent reported unpredictable menstrual cycles as the problem.

"My husband is thirty-six and I am twenty-six, and we have four children," said a wife. "My temperature charts are unreadable by my doctor. Also the tape was always green. We used the pill for six months, and then my periods became as irregular as before (thirty-eight to seventy-six days)."

- Twenty percent ascribed the failure to carelessness in keeping track of the calendar, inadequate information on the mechanics of rhythm, or an overwhelming need to express love.

- A sizable 64 percent asserted that rhythm was positively helpful in some ways to their marriage.

"From a spiritual viewpoint, it was good self-discipline and a definite sacrifice," commented a husband with six children who had been married fourteen years.

"Since the birth of our fifth child my husband has been very faithful in checking the calendar," said a wife, married eleven years. "Consequently no fear of 'am I pregnant again?' We are both much more relaxed and enjoy each other more than ever."

"We feel it was a great teacher of self-discipline," wrote a couple married twenty-six years. "Christmas every day would lose some of its pleasure. Anticipation building toward an event that requires some cooperative effort always seems to satisfy better."

- Only 28 percent claimed it was helpful in absolutely no way.

A couple married fifteen years with six children wrote, "I feel any priest or bishop who advocates rhythm should take his rectal temperature for a few weeks. It is our opinion that if the clergy took rectal temperatures that Catholic marrieds would not still be waiting for an answer on contraception."

To insure balance in such a sensitive area, the couples were also asked if rhythm was in any way harmful to their marriage relationship, and a surprisingly different picture emerged.

- Some 78 percent (including therefore a great number who had found rhythm at least somewhat helpful) claimed it had also harmed their relationship due to tension, loss of spontaneity, fear of pregnancy, etc.

"We found the practice of rhythm very frustrating, artificial, and distasteful," said a young couple married six years with two children and three miscarriages. "It removes the natural spontaneity from marriage and generally distracts from or inhibits the intimate communication which is essential."

"I felt like a human thermometer," wrote a woman married eighteen years with two children. "My husband and I are very close and I felt like love was put on a business schedule. Instead of 'I love you,' I began to hear, 'How's your temperature?'"

Rhythm "makes a mockery of love," wrote a couple married fourteen years with four children. "No free giving of oneself, no joy in the union. The constant reference to the chart to determine safety takes on an aura of grudging obedience to Church law, with rebellion in the heart."

- Only 22 percent could cite no harmful effects.

"Awful Stories"

In other words, the most prevalent reaction seemed to be one of controlled frustration. These couples were struggling to find something positive in what had struck them as basically negative. Some found it, some did not. For Patty Crowley reading the letters provided further conviction that Catholic marital doctrine needed a major overhaul. Reinforcing her misgivings were the simply "awful stories" of those struggling to live their lives under incredible burdens.

"I am a mother of five expecting my sixth in September," said a woman in Virginia. "My veins rupture due to pregnancy. In the past year eight veins have ruptured, which is a danger to me. My Christian doctor told us no more after the fifth. Our income makes it a struggle with children so close. We did write the Pope in October, asking for help for us women and told of my veins rupturing. We did receive a Papal blessing, the formal card type."

Due to irregularities of the menstrual cycle, wrote a couple married thirteen years with six children, "we have been restricted to a system — if you could call it that — of utilizing only the last six or seven days of the cycle. This has a stifling effect on the rapport and spontaneity that should mark a good marriage."

A wife of fourteen years with seven children wrote, "The slightest upset, mental or physical, appears to change the cycle and thereby renders this method of family planning useless. Our marriage problem is not financial.... But my husband has a terrible weakness when it comes to self-control in sex and unless his demands are met in every way when he feels this way, he is a very dangerous man to me and my daughters. Apart from these times he is completely normal and tries in every way he knows, such as morning Mass, sacraments, prayers, etc., to accumulate grace."

"Following my third pregnancy in two years I almost smothered the baby with a pillow because I couldn't stand its crying," wrote a wife in her forties. "Now in a few years we will have to abstain entirely, perhaps for years when I become irregular due to menopause. I am very depressed and becoming more so. What will another baby do to me at this age? Mental illness on both sides of the family. I devoutly hope the Council will devise some method soon, more reliable for middle-aged women."

For many in the survey, the rhythm experience produced a crisis of faith in God or, more commonly, of faith in the Church.

"Which is more pleasing to God," asked a mother of ten, "trusting in the miscalculations of rhythm or making a full, generous decision in holiness to have a child? Rhythm leads to self-seeking, promotes excess in infertile times and strain in fertile times. Is contraceptive sex irresponsible when I have already borne ten little responsibilities? The epistemology of priests is different from the sources of truth of the laity. The former is unreal."

"A wife cannot go on being a baby machine," said a young mother, "and the Church leaves her in a desperate state. We have three sick kids at home, another kicking in my stomach, and a husband full of booze. I have lived on hope, hope in God, hope in taking a long time for the next pregnancy, hope that somebody understands my problem. Do the bishops really love their flocks?"

"My husband is a convert and we use rhythm with fairly good success, but only out of obedience to the Church," said another young mother. "It results in biological control but produces emotional extremes of anger, impatience, despair, even infidelity. How can we imitate God's love by rationing ours?"

Wrote a forty-three-year-old mother of four from New Zealand, "Why is it so difficult for husband and wife to love God and each other at the same time? Why is there always this conflict, this choice between God and spouse? We have no intention of practicing birth control unless it is allowed by the Church. . . . After all, what is rhythm? Call it self-control if you like, but when you analyze it, it's really birth control."

Conflicting Advice

The survey revealed the varied and often arbitrary advice married couples were receiving from priests. However, the fact that so many had sought such advice showed that here was an especially sincere, respectful group, their doubts in the Church and hierarchy notwithstanding. Some responses:

• "Before marriage the priest told us it would be a sin to use rhythm right after marriage. After the first child he gave permission, but we had seven babies in a row. The tape failed. The priest permitted the pill to regularize the cycle. After a year we went off pills and immediately had our eighth pregnancy. Ow! Back on pills for a year, but after that what — our ninth?"

- "Although I had three children in diapers, the priest permitted rhythm only for six months. Other women were told differently... but rhythm love-making is nerve-wracking, feast or famine. My husband became angry when I avoided him in fertile times. It is a scandal to shop around for a pill priest!"

- "After our second child the doctor said I should have no more for five years or so. My priest said he had no right to say that. Our third pregnancy died and I almost died too. Rhythm is too hard on us all."

- "Abstinence in rhythm hurt us terribly. All we did failed to help. One priest's advice was silly though kind. Another called us animals, and I cried for weeks. Now we take pills. We do not feel this is a mortal sin, but I cannot bring myself to go to Communion. My husband and I love God and the Church. There must be another way."

- "We used birth control but the priest refused absolution without a promise to stop. I'll find a more lenient priest. I want to be a good Catholic, but the Church gives us no choice."

- "My psychiatrist said the Church has no right to tell us to have children by practicing rhythm if anyone's nerves and attacks were as bad as mine. My priest said we shouldn't even use rhythm. We tried rhythm, but my husband has threatened to leave and he is very angry. I'm panicky with this pregnancy. We need compassionate help."

Evidence also emerged in the survey that some Catholic couples were using the pill, not just to regularize periods but as a contraceptive, and were using it in clear conscience. Some typical responses:

- "We have eleven children, the last two being rhythm babies, although we abstained from day five to day twenty-five. Yet my husband needed me during the fertile days....I met a Catholic psychologist who has helped three hundred priests and he has worked wonders. I'm now on pills. I feel good and believe we now have the graces of the Sacrament of Matrimony."

- "I am very irregular. We had two quick births, and with the last I became very ill and my nerves are gone. We used the pills to regulate the cycle, but afterward the cycles went as high as forty-three days. I take the pill; I don't feel birth control is wrong in our case. I went against abstinence because it is impossible. We may stop birth control later."

Sociologist Barrett noted, "There is confusion about what the Church and the priests have developed to rationalize the pills, and most cannot appreciate why their use must be limited in a moral context. But once a couple takes the pills, then a more secure and positive view of self, conjugal relations, and family life tends to arise. Very few couples report feeling that use of the pills is immoral. On the other hand, there are feelings of indignation and of being unjustifiably discriminated against when priests say that pills are morally not warranted in their cases, especially when they know so many other couples have been approved for the pills on grounds . . . similar to their own."

Hoping for Change

The respondents in the survey had plenty of advice on what the Church (and the Pope in particular) should say on the subject of birth control, most of it based on the same logic and reasoning that had been circulating in the Birth Control Commission. Examples:

• "We believe that the Church can develop a change in its position. It should state that this change is based on a greater knowledge of the marital relationship, the emotional and physiological nature of man and woman. The new position should state the primary functions of marriage are both conjugal love and procreation and that the prudent use of contraception is permitted, according to the dictates of the individual conscience."

• "God has created us to develop our talents to govern the universe and ourselves. Since medical research has learned a method of intelligently controlling ovulation, it would seem reasonable for men to use this knowledge for the good of their own family. Other functions are intelligently controlled with no question as to the morality of the use of a drug."

• "If then matrimony is a lifetime commitment of love, the commitment to cooperate with God in the birth, training, and education of children should also be viewed from the standpoint of a lifetime. The Church should ask only that the spouses love each other for the lifetime of the marriage and should not seek to indicate that any act of sexual intercourse should or should not be directed toward parenthood. To do otherwise is ultimately for the Church to develop a theology of the sperm and egg — both of which are parts of the whole and are not the whole human being himself."

• "The statements on this subject therefore must come from those who live in the situation on a daily basis. Secondhand knowledge is not adequate to serve as the foundation upon which this important area can be discussed. . . . The Church, working together with married couples and listening to suggestions with an open mind, can prove to be the leading force in this matter. Strict laws, however, seem inappropriate and detrimental to marriage."

Patty Crowley could not have said it better herself, and at the 1966 meeting of the Commission she and a few others would arise in the mostly male, celibate bastion and try to articulate what all these anonymous voices were trying to say.

The Rise of the Laity

The Final Meeting I, 1966

We think it is time that this Commission recommend that the sacred-ness of conjugal love not be violated by thermometers and calendars.
— PATTY CROWLEY

The first four meetings of the Birth Control Commission were brief, three- or four-day affairs. The final meeting, held at the Spanish College in Rome, would last almost three months, beginning in early April 1966 and finally concluding at the end of June. This was the meeting when decisions had to be made, and the Vatican spared no expense in supplying photocopying machines, secretarial services, and professional translators borrowed from the United Nations office in Rome. Only de Riedmatten, some members of the executive committee, and most of the theologians were present the entire time. The schedule was set up so that theologians, physicians, and social scientists would meet during various weeks and in various combinations, with occasional general sessions interspersed. Also planned was a "pastoral" week, with the spotlight on the laypeople on the Commission, especially the women. The Commission would reach its climax in the final week of June at a plenary session.

Not everyone realized it, but the rules had changed. The Commission's members, according to the official schedule in Latin, were no longer members but "experts" (*periti*). The real members were sixteen cardinals and bishops named by the Holy Father. Most would be attending only the final plenary meeting, and it would be this new body — not the full Commission — that would make the final determination of what advice to give the Pope. It would be logical to see the hand of Cardinal Ottaviani in this unexplained procedural shift. He was well aware of the overwhelming consensus for change. With the hierarchy functioning as an intermediary buffer between the Pope and the Commission, the recommendations might be softened, even eviscerated.

Among those named were Cardinals Ottaviani, Suenens, Heenan, Julius Doepfner of Munich, Valerian Gracias of Bombay, Lawrence Shehan of Baltimore, and Joseph Lefebvre of Bourges, France (not the Lefebvre who would later lead the Traditionalist Movement). The new bishops included Carlo Colombo (the Pope's theologian), John Dearden of Detroit, Claude Dupuy of France, Thomas Morris of Ireland, José Rafael Pulido-Méndez of Venezuela, Jean Baptiste Zoa of Cameroon, and Karol Wojtyla of Poland. Wojtyla, the future Pope John Paul II, declined to attend out of a sense of solidarity with the Polish primate, Cardinal Stefan Wyszynski, who had been denied a travel visa by the Polish government. Bishops Reuss and Binz were already on the Commission.

Realizing the importance of this climactic meeting, Pat and Patty Crowley wrote to John Cody, recently named archbishop of Chicago, seeking his advice and input. Cody did not respond. The Crowleys planned to arrive at the meeting in May, climaxing a two-month round-the-world tour of their far-flung CFM family, a duplication of their trip ten years before. On that journey, they were astonished at the crowds that came to hear them and the intense interest of the media. Word had gotten out that this couple had an inside line on immanent change in the Church's stand on contraception. The Crowleys noted in their newsletter that on their arrival in Sydney, Australia, "a delegation met us at the airport, including two photographers and six newspaper fellows. What a grilling we had in the press room! The subject: pills, pills, pills. Our response was CFM, etc., etc. The newspaper accounts of our interviews were always amazing." In Tasmania between meetings with CFM groups, the local bishop invited them to his house to share his own views on what they and the Commission should do. At another airport, they reported, their hosts stood around "while we answered questions about the Birth Control Commission. The reporters always want to know if we're for contraception and ask when the Pope will speak. We observe that he and we haven't made a decision. After a few stabs the interview is finished and the reporters leave, thinking we might compete with Dean Rusk for double talk."

When they got to Rome, Pat and Patty were delighted to find that they and the other two married couples would be housed in a three-bedroom apartment near the college instead of in segregated quarters, as at the previous meeting.

The Theologians Vote

The April sessions of the Commission focused on theology and showed how the tone had moved to "fundamental questions." Debates over the pill gave way to discussion of natural law, the limits of Church authority, and especially just what constitutes intrinsic evil. Was the prohibition against contraception an ideal which Christians should aim for but not be overly alarmed about when they fell short? Or was it an absolute — like the law of gravity — for which a deliberate violation merited automatic punishment? Progressives like Häring stressed latitude in interpreting laws and spoke about *epikeia* — exceptions to the law for special circumstances. Conservatives like Zalba preferred the hard line: neither Pope, Council, Commission, nor compassionate pastor may tolerate exceptions to the law.

In the midst of the debate, French theologian Philip Delhaye tried to offer a compromise. The reaction revealed the deep division among the theologians. Since there is clearly a doubt about the intrinsic evil of contraception, said Delhaye, and since the doubt isn't going to be settled soon, why couldn't the Catholic Church make a disciplinary law forbidding contraception to its members, just as it made laws requiring Mass attendance on Sundays and abstinence from meat on Friday? In one fell swoop, he said, the question would be wrested from the natural law debate, compassion would be shown to the faithful (since a disciplinary law doesn't oblige when there is a serious problem), and the Church would be free to drop or modify the law later when better information became available.

Pierre de Locht objected that applying a Church law remedy to a natural law problem would be absurd. "You can't legislate morality by just laying down some rules," he said. "It is necessary to inculcate a moral sense by emphasizing the fundamental virtues: charity, justice, prudence, responsibility, the essential values of love and marriage."[1] The German Redemptorist Visser interjected that the presence of doubt is no reason to alter the obligation of an old law: "It is imprudent to toss aside the observance of a norm because of doubt alone. The burden of proof falls on the one who doubts.... If we rejected the traditional doctrine on the basis of doubt... there would be few moral truths which could not be called into question."

But Jesuit John Ford insisted doubt shouldn't even be discussed because on the matter of birth control there is no doubt. The magisterium has spoken; obedience is the only appropriate response.

His fellow Jesuit Joseph Fuchs disagreed, contending that such a literal line of thought would take everyone down a blind alley: "Continuity of a teaching doesn't consist in repeating what has been said before in other circumstances but in continuing to see if these earlier pronouncements actually took permanent values into account. We are not talking about fidelity or infidelity to prior teachings; we are trying to see if there are some truly new perspectives which would require new responses."

Then Fernando Lambruschini, an official in the Roman Curia, said the bottom line is that people will not obey a law they don't understand; and that is precisely the Catholic response to the ban on contraception: the people don't get it.

The prolonged theological debates reached a kind of summit on May 6. De Riedmatten asked each of the nineteen theologians to give a six-minute presentation of his position, after which a vote would be taken on two questions: Is the doctrine of *Casti Connubii* irreformable? And is artificial contraception an intrinsically evil violation of the natural law? The result was no on both questions — both by 15–4 tallies. Though de Riedmatten insisted the vote was strictly provisional and not to be considered absolutely final, everyone realized its significance. A vote by this same group concerning the irreformability of *Casti Connubii* had been taken one year before during the Commission's meeting, and the result was 12–7, also against irreformability. Now three more had come over to the reformers' side. Even more significant was the vote on intrinsic evil: no distinctions about the pill — only the bold assertion that contraception as such was not something that is always forbidden under all circumstances. The four theologians who voted the other way were Ford, Visser, Zalba, and de Lestapis. De Riedmatten reminded the members that the vote count was strictly confidential, but it was reported in the Italian newspapers two days later.

The Sense of the Faithful

The minority theologians had to be further alarmed when the doctors summarized their thinking in early May. The most outspoken was

Albert Görres, a German physician and psychology professor at the University of Mainz. He said he and his colleagues were disturbed because "questions of the greatest importance for life have up until now been decided apparently without theological discussion and according to the opinions of one or two of the Holy Father's private theologians or of a curial authority."

In a scathing critique of moral theology that left Father Ford fuming, Görres claimed the centuries-old united front against contraception was in fact a sham. Those who opposed the Vatican party line found their books and opinions censored, he said, and thus the official presentation of moral doctrine was left to timid, second-rate, and overly scrupulous maintainers of the status quo who looked for evidence to bolster forgone conclusions instead of seeking truth. A large amount of moral doctrine, Görres asserted, comes out of a history scarred by Manicheism, patriarchalism, sexism, and blatantly erroneous assumptions about human biology. As a result, "moral theologians have justified with great confidence things which their successors today reject as outright immoral and unchristian: witch trials, tortures, burning of heretics, slavery, forceful violation of the consciences of unbelievers and heretics, suppression of colonial peoples, and...the castration of choirboys, this last over a period of centuries and with the approval of popes."[2]

He cited the speech by Patriarch Maximos at the Second Vatican Council in which he said the Church is suffering from a "celibate psychosis." Görres defined it as "a state of mind arising out of the psychic situation of the cleric, one that keeps him from viewing marriage and sexuality with an unprejudiced and comprehensive eye." Görres advised his colleagues not to adopt a position that leaves the present ban in place but admits of mitigating circumstances that may lessen or remove guilt. That approach is demeaning, he noted. Couples "want to know what kind of attitude God demands of them. They are unable and unwilling to claim for themselves the mitigating circumstances that apply to neurotics and psychopaths."

Görres's sharp observations were bolstered by Canon Delhaye, who had come upon an official report of the results of a poll of the world's bishops in 1964 at the request of the Pope concerning attitudes toward contraception within their jurisdictions. Delhaye said the bishops listed contraception as the leading moral problem but were stymied on how to react. All over the world, Delhaye said bishops reported, "It used to be that people talked to their confessors knowing that they were wrong.

Now they do so knowing they are right. The faithful accept other laws and see themselves as sinners when they transgress them. Here they invoke the impossibility of the law, their conscience, and God's mercy."

Appropriately enough, it was in this context that sociologist Donald Barrett presented the findings of the Crowleys' survey, along with copies of the correspondence they had received. The testimony of these CFM members, more connected to the institutional Church than average Catholics, demanded close attention, he said. The letters showed that while many took heroic measures and endured great sacrifice to obey the law, others were beginning to echo what Catholics were telling the world's bishops: an unintelligible law does not oblige. This was not presented as a theological conclusion, but, Barrett implied, it was perhaps an expression of the "sense of the faithful" that Vatican II spoke about. It was at least theoretically possible that the Holy Spirit was choosing in this instance to speak from the grass roots, from the Church's "lower-archy." And if that were true, those at the top would be the last to get the word.

The rhythm method also took a beating from Dr. André Hellegers of Baltimore, who reported that it was ineffective for many women during menopause, "precisely the time when it's most necessary."

And Dr. John Cavanagh of Washington, D.C., citing a poll of twenty-three hundred women who used the rhythm method, said 71 percent experienced their greatest sexual desire during the period of ovulation. "Rhythm is more psychologically harmful than other methods," he declared, "because it deprives a woman of the conjugal act during the time of her greatest desire."

During the 1965 meeting, Cavanagh had been a firm conservative, convinced any change would be unwise. But his own research and contact with other Commission members had made an impact.

In a note to Cardinal Heenan, he stated, "Abstinence as the only means of controlling conception has left Catholics immature emotionally and impoverished financially. It has left them insecure, rebellious and frustrated. Serious psychiatric disorders have arisen as a result. . . . When I ask myself why I changed, it seems that up to three years ago I accepted this teaching without question. Now having studied it, I find it is no longer acceptable. I am in no position to discuss the theological aspects of the problem. The position taken by the majority of the theologians . . . is very convincing. I would tend to disregard the few negative opinions, because they are held by very rigid individuals in whom change is unlikely."[3]

Witness of the Women

During the pastoral week, the rising of the laity peaked. After reading the commentary of so many wives and mothers in the Crowley survey, de Riedmatten and Hellegers (acting as his chief assistant) asked the four women members present to address the assembly and share their views on the conjugal act, rhythm, abstinence, and conception and to do so "clearly, absolutely, fearlessly."

"I was in awe," recalled Patty Crowley. "Here were all these learned men from all over the world. My inclination would have been to say little and sit down. But I had come a long way at that point. Both Pat and I had. These people needed to hear women's experiences."

The first to speak, J. F. Kulanday, a married nurse and administrator with the Public Health Department in New Delhi, India, explained a survey she had directed on the importance of intercourse in the lives of Indian women. "Women desire intercourse in marriage," she said. "It binds the husband and wife together. . . . After two or three babies it becomes possible for the woman to live her sex life in a minor key, but she still has to rise to her husband's needs; intercourse . . . keeps their love aflame."[4]

Also brief was Marie Rendu, who with her husband operated a Church-sponsored rhythm clinic in Paris. Strong advocates of the temperature method, they had lectured widely in Europe and North America. Periodic continence can and does work, she said, provided there is adequate motivation and quality instruction; in many cases it even seems to help couples' sexual relations.

Armed with a sheaf of results from the Crowley survey, Patty then spoke at length: "As a woman I am grateful for the chance to address this Commission. Neither Pat nor I consider ourselves experts. Rather we look upon ourselves as communication channels. As much as possible we hope to pass on to your our interpretation of how married people that we know feel about this subject.

"During our adult lives we have worked with married people. We have talked with them, argued with them, perhaps preached to them more than we like to recognize, worked with them, and most important have listened to them. Our work in the Christian Family Movement, which is now active in sixty-one countries, has taken us around the world several times."

Patty explained how the survey was done, then stressed the exceptional nature of the CFM respondents: "These questionnaires were not filled out by disaffected Catholics, those who may be discouraged, disillusioned or disenchanted, or whose personal problems within marriage may have caused them to drift apart from each other and from the Church. Naturally, we do not presume to judge the success or happiness of a marriage or the quality of a person's Christianity. Yet if one were to ask us to select on the basis of outward appearances men and women who are indeed happy, who are committed to pursuing Christ's work on earth, who love the Church and look to her for guidance, these are precisely the couples we would select."

She then presented her own analysis of the data. "Is there a bad psychological effect in the use of rhythm? Almost without exception, the responses were that yes, there is.

"Does rhythm serve any useful purpose at all? A few say it may be useful for developing discipline. Nobody says that it fosters married love.

"Does it contribute to married unity? No. That is the inescapable conclusion of the reports we have received.... In marriage a husband and wife pledge themselves to become one in mind, heart and affection. They are no longer two, but one flesh — and they must find mutual help and serve each other through intimate union of their persons and their actions; through an experience of their oneness with growing affection day by day.

"Some wonder whether God would have us cultivate such unity by using what seems to them an unnatural system.

"I must add that the best place for children to learn the importance of love is from the example of their parents. Yet these reports seem to indicate that instead of unity and love, rhythm tends to substitute tension, dissatisfaction, frustration and disunity.

"I feel that I would be disloyal to women if I didn't emphasize one other point: We have heard some men, married and celibate, argue that rhythm is a way to develop love. But we have heard few women who agree with them.

"Is rhythm unnatural? Yes — that's the conclusion of these reports. Over and over, directly and indirectly, men and women — and perhaps especially women — voice the conviction that the physical and psychological implications of rhythm are not adequately understood by the male Church.... Over and over, respondents pointed out that nature prepares a woman at the time of ovulation to have the greatest urge to mate with her husband. Similarly, at that time her husband wants to respond to his wife. She craves his love. Yet month after month she must say no to her husband because it is the wrong date on the calendar or the thermometer reading isn't right."

She quoted from several of the letters to illustrate aspects of the problem: " 'My husband is away on long business trips and unfortunately his company doesn't take our calendar into consideration when he has to be gone all over this country and now all over the world. He has left on trips at the wrong time of the month and arrived, all in the same month, at the wrong time of the month. This problem is detrimental to family rapport.... '

" 'Any simple psychology book tells us that people who are in a constant stricture in an area that should be open and free and loving are damaging themselves and consequently others. Any emotions that are bottled up when one does not want them to be bottled up are dangerous. And how many millions of couples live in this situation daily? Certainly far more than those who sublimate their desires or who are taught control.... '

" 'I bend over backward to avoid raising false hopes on my husband's part. This sounds ridiculous, but I stiffen at a kiss on the cheek, instantly reminded that I must be discreet. I withdraw in others ways too, afraid to be an interesting companion, gay or witty or charming, hesitant about being sympathetic or understanding, almost wishing I could be invisible.... And I wonder why I can't shake off the fear and uncertainty during the rest of the month.'

"Thus," resumed Patty, "we see the anguish expressed by some faithful Catholics. They are not alone. Some have suffered terribly and are only now asking themselves if their travail was really necessary.... Notice how these reactions contradict what in the past has been the stereotyped, conventional way of looking at the Catholic husband and wife and their large family. These fathers and mothers, surveying their children, do not sit back with pride and satisfaction. Instead they reflect a hardly muted bitterness at a condition in their lives that has forced them to stay apart from each other when their natures cried out for each other.

"Our observation and experience confirms the fact that couples the world over are consciously or unconsciously asking a question: Why then cannot the Church permit Catholics with good reason and in good conscience to select their own methods in limiting births? Is not the sex drive instilled by God a normal one? Should not husbands and wives be encouraged to express their love without adding a series of do's and don't's?"

Patty then drew her bottom-line conclusion: "We think it is time that this Commission recommend that the sacredness of conjugal love not be violated by thermometers and calendars. Marital union does lead to fruitfulness, psychologically as well as physically. Couples want children and will have them generously and love them and cherish them. We do not need the impetus of legislation to procreate. It is the very instinct of life, love and sexuality. It is in fact largely our very love for children as persons and our desire for their full development as committed Christians that leads us to realize that numbers alone and the large size of a family is by no means a Christian ideal unless parents can truly be concerned about and capable of nurturing a high quality of Christian life.

"We sincerely hope and do respectfully recommend that this Commission redefine the moral imperatives of fertility regulation with a view toward bringing them into conformity with our new and improved understanding of men and women in today's world.

"We realize that some may be scandalized: those who have no awareness of the meaning of renewal, those who disagree with the conciliar emphasis on personhood and those who do not understand that the Church is the living People of God guided by the Holy Spirit."

Those who heard this talk, Bernard Häring in particular, have commented on how powerfully it struck the audience: it was, some said, as close as they would be likely to get to the real sense of the faithful.

Colette Potvin was also moving and even more personal. "I felt like I was naked up there," she said later. "But it seemed to me we hadn't been asking the right questions at this Commission. When you die, God is going to say, 'Did you love?' He isn't going to say, 'Did you take your temperature?'"

Colette told the group she had been married seventeen years, had five children and three miscarriages, and had undergone a hysterectomy. It is important, she said, that the assembly understand "the true woman, how she thinks, how she reacts, how she suffers, how she lives." Discussion of birth control methods is taking up "too much space," she declared. "One doesn't base her conjugal life on a method."

She said it is time to "change directions, to find the true meaning of sexuality in the Christian life, to see how sex is embodied in the great commandment: Love your neighbor as yourself. To understand woman, one must stop looking at her as a defective male, an occasion of sin for man or an incarnation of the demon of depravity, but rather, as Genesis presents her, a companion for man."

For the woman, she said, the conjugal act is a total gift of body and soul to the loved one — "a gift of pleasure and of physical and psychological fulfillment that leaves the man marvelously happy. Where I come from, we marry primarily to live with a man of our choice. Children come as a normal consequence of our authentic love and not as the goal."

Colette said a woman cannot consider the conjugal act in a strictly analytical way or from an exclusively biological viewpoint, to the detriment of its other aspects: "The physiological integrity of the conjugal act is less important than the repercussions of that love on the couple and on their family. The conjugal orgasm is the result of a very strong physical attraction and a spiritual bonding which joins bodies and spirits in a union on all levels: physical, intellectual, and moral, and it carries with it a whole gamut of wonderful, sensual pleasures. The day after such a communion with her spouse, the woman is more serene.... She is more patient with her children, more loving toward everyone."

Periodic continence, said Colette, "can have a positive value if it is agreed on by both husband and wife for the good of one or the other and if it doesn't upset the tranquility of the family. But if it impedes the couple from living a serene, intimate conjugal life, one has to question its value and its affects. Must we sacrifice the psychological benefits of marital relations in order to preserve the biological integrity of an act? Is that a human way to act? Is it Christian?"

She then spoke candidly about the kind of changes she would like to see. "An excessive rigidity in our moral tradition has barred any evolution of doctrine," she declared. "In a desire to bring more children to Christ, our Holy Mother the Church has applied laws that must be obeyed without regard for character or gender or culture or maturity. As a teacher of my children, I'm unable to accept such a pedagogy." A morality that emphasizes the biology of the act in all circumstances is unfair, especially to the woman, she said. "It should be adjusted to take into account the good of the marriage, the good of the couple, the good of the children and of the whole family community."

A long silence followed. It was broken by de Riedmatten: "This," he said, "is why we wanted to have couples on our Commission." He asked Colette to repeat her talk when the bishops and cardinals arrived, and she did. Patty Crowley observed, "I'm sure those clerics never heard anything quite like that before. Colette was so intimate, so frank."

The Potvins presented the results of their survey in French Canada.

Of the 319 couples who responded, half found rhythm "an anguished and difficult task." Only 7 percent of the couples were fully satisfied with the Church's current marriage doctrine, and the great majority reported experiencing no sexual growth through the rhythm method because much of their time "is spent in the great struggle to avoid the failure of rhythm." The Rendus reported on the views of four hundred couples actively involved in promoting and teaching the temperature method of rhythm in France. Their responses were more upbeat, but even these dedicated couples spoke frequently of frustration and hoped for an "evolution" in the Church's understanding of sexuality.

Tom Burch called the extended lay testimony from across such a wide spectrum "extremely authoritative: Here was the cream of the crop, the most dedicated Catholics you could imagine. I think that had to have an effect even on the negative theologians."

The Growing Momentum

If they had been concerned before, the dissenting theologians were now near panic. The push for change was approaching avalanche proportions. The next day an angry de Lestapis told the assembly he feared a tendency to "idealize" married persons. "The couple has become a state of grace and contraception their sacrament," he said, "and the result is a sort of intoxication, a practical obliteration of the sense of God, a mystification in the psychological order, a devaluation of procreation."[5]

Others took exception to that. Said Giacomo Perico, a theologian from the University of Milan who had been quiet during the debates, "The more I hear the confessions of good Catholics on this matter, the more I feel it necessary for the Church to change. I would dare to say my own penitents have made a contribution here." Dutch philosopher Andre van Melsen said it was clear to him that if change did not come, pastoral activity would be paralyzed; confessors would lose contact with the best Catholics, and the result would be a "ghetto Church."

Pat Crowley summed up the majority view: "I think we have agreed that the sense of the faithful is for change. No arguments were presented on the side of the status quo other than the one that Rome has spoken once and to change would undermine the magisterium. I must say I heard no other argument and I don't think this is a good argument to support an otherwise objectionable position in what we like to call the pilgrim Church. The preponderance of testimony from the lay members showed that change is anticipated and great problems will arise if no change is made. If the Church fails in this, much of the progress made by the Council will be lost."

In a letter to de Riedmatten, Pat and Patty summarized their opinion at this point. Quoting philanthropist Julius Rosenwald's remark that when you have a lemon, the thing to do is to make lemonade, they suggested that in the present doctrine "we do appear to have a lemon." When a "change is proposed," they said, "the Church could make something very palatable" by "eliminating all that language of debt and duty" and "emphasizing the positive values" in the marriage relationship.

The Crowleys then took a short leave from the meeting. Three of their children, Mary Ann, twenty-two, Catherine, nineteen, and Theresa, eleven, flew to Rome and joined their parents. In a rented car they ferried across the Adriatic and spent ten days touring Greece, Yugoslavia, and Austria. Before they left on the trip, however, the Crowleys sent to the personal attention of the Holy Father copies of all the letters they had received in the survey; they were bound in white leather and tied with a white ribbon. They never learned if he read the letters or ever even received them.

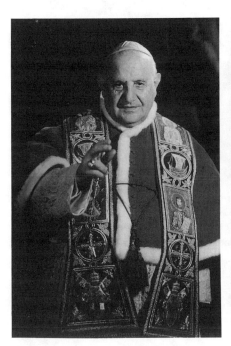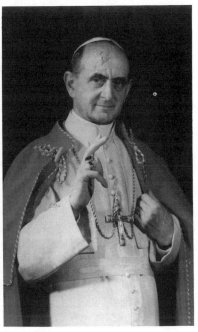

Pope John XXIII and Paul VI

Pope John XXIII created the Pontifical Commission for the Study of Population, Family and Births in March 1963 to advise on matters of world population growth and family limitation. He died three months later before the commission ever met. His successor, Paul VI, continued the Commission in existence and urged the group to make its recommendations "in complete objectivity" and "without worrying about criticism or difficulties." *Both photos courtesy of Catholic Near East Welfare Association.*

Pat and Patty Crowley

Pat and Patty Crowley, shown here in their home at about the time of their appointment to the Birth Control Commission, were then the president couple of the Christian Family Movement (CFM), which included some 150,000 married couples throughout the world. CFM members were among the most involved and concerned Catholics.

Patty Crowley and daughter Sister Patricia Crowley, O.S.B.

More than thirty years after her work on the Commission, Patty Crowley is still involved in a myriad of projects and organizations, among them Deborah's Place, a shelter for homeless Chicago women, which is under the direction of her oldest child, Sister Patricia (Patsy) Crowley (right), a Benedictine sister.

Patty Crowley in London

Patty Crowley pores over old documents in mid-1994 with author Robert Mc-Clory (center) and Dr. John Marshall, a British neurologist who was among the first six appointed to the Birth Control Commission in 1963. Patty and her husband, Pat, were appointed in late 1964. The findings of the Commission have never been officially released by the Vatican, and much of what is known about its deliberations comes from the documents and recollections of the members.

Leo Joseph Cardinal Suenens

Cardinal Leo Joseph Suenens of Malines-Brussels suggested to Pope John XXIII in 1962 that the time was ripe for the church to "reform the old idea, the more children the better" and suggested the idea of a Birth Control Commission of experts to clarify the issue. Pope John agreed. Through the course of the next four years, Suenens vigorously supported a modification of the traditional Church position on birth control at the Second Vatican Council and later as a member of the Commission itself during its final decisive meeting. *N. C. News Photo.*

Fr. Bernard Häring
The German Redemptorist and moral theologian Fr. Bernard Häring was among the first to argue before the Commission that some forms of birth control are not intrinsically evil. He later stated that the survey data presented to the Commission by the Crowleys as well as the moving testimony of its lay members had a most profound effect on the cardinals and bishops who eventually approved the Majority Report. *Herder Verlag.*

Alfredo Cardinal Ottaviani
Cardinal Ottaviani, the aged head of the Congregation for the Doctrine of the Faith, saw the Church as a "perfect society," impervious to cultural shifts, and remained firmly against any change in the Church's traditional position on birth control. It was around him and under his auspices that a small group of theologians gathered to contravene the recommendations of the Commission. *Herder Roma.*

Last Day Photos of the Commission

No photographs were permitted during the Commission meetings. These were taken with with the Crowley's Polaroid on the last day after the group formally disbanded. Shown here (from left) are: Patty Crowley, Rev. Jan Visser of Holland, Archbishop Leo Binz of St. Paul-Minneapolis, Rev. Paul Anciaux of Belgium, Cardinal Leo Suenens of Belgium, and Dr. André Hellegers of the United States. Suenens convinced Pope John XXIII to create the Commission and gave it broad support; Visser was among the four Commission members determined to scuttle its conclusions.

Shown (from left) are Commission members Rev. Giacomo Perico, Italian Jesuit; Patty and Pat Crowley; Rev. Marcelino Zalba, Spanish Jesuit; and Rev. Philip Delhaye of Belgium. Fearing the Church might lose its authority over Catholics, Zalba argued strenuously against any change or moderation of the traditional position on contraceptives.

Posing outside the Spanish College in Rome, where the Commission held its final meeting, are (from left) Rev. Joseph Fuchs, German Jesuit; Rev. Michael Labourdette, French Dominican; Archbishop Thomas Morris of Ireland; Prof. Donald Barrett of Notre Dame University; and Rev. Raymond Sigmond, French Dominican. Fuchs, an early supporter of the transitional ban on birth control, changed his mind during the Commission proceedings. Barrett, a sociologist, assisted the Crowleys in their survey of married couples' attitudes toward rhythm.

Time for Some Decision

The Final Meeting II, 1966

We should make a unanimous recommendation. That ought to impress the Pope.

— CARDINAL HEENAN

The last two weeks of May and the first week of June 1966 may have been the most productive — and the most tense — during the entire history of the Commission. It was during this time that the three most important papers were written and a final position began to jell. Tension mounted at the Spanish College and tempers flared at times. Meanwhile, subtle shifts were going on behind the scenes. Dr. John Marshall, an original Commission member who had served on its steering committee for more than two years, was told by de Riedmatten that he need not return for the final session. De Riedmatten offered no reason for the snub and Marshall didn't ask. Marshall was one of those who had begun convinced the old doctrine was irreformable, but, he openly admitted to his colleagues, the testimony and evidence of the meetings persuaded him the doctrine could be reformed and should be reformed. Also, an official of the Holy Office, not a Commission member, was assigned by Cardinal Ottaviani to sit in at all meetings of the theologians and take notes — a practice that some found a bit threatening.

De Riedmatten appointed a committee of priest theologians to draft a calm, reasoned document containing the position of the majority of the Commission. The group included Fuchs, de Locht, and Labourdette; Hungarian Dominican Raymond Sigmond of the Angelicum

College in Rome; Alfons Auer, a specialist in sexual morality from Germany; and Paul Anciaux, a seminary professor from Belgium.

On his own authority, John Ford decided to represent the opposing view. He called on Germain Grisez, a young professor of philosophy at Georgetown University, whose writings in defense of *Casti Connubii* were well known. Ford had him flown to Rome and lodged in a hotel where the two labored, apparently night and day, for more than a week. The result, signed by Ford, Visser, Zalba, and de Lestapis, was handed to de Riedmatten on May 23. It was a nine-thousand-word treatise entitled "The State of the Question: The Doctrine of the Church and Its Authority." Offered as a working paper defending the status quo on birth control in the strongest language, the document would attain prominence in the years ahead as the so-called Minority Report.

Three days later, on May 26, the theologians' committee appointed by de Riedmatten turned in their paper, which was titled "Responsible Parenthood," and, if approved by the full assembly, was intended to be the definitive word of the Commission to Pope Paul (by way of the cardinals and bishops coming at the end of June). It would be known in later years as the Commission's Majority Report.

After reading Ford's document, de Riedmatten asked Fuchs, Delhaye, and Sigmond to prepare a working paper responding to the specific issues raised by Ford. This was completed in short order and handed to de Riedmatten on May 28. Titled "Summary Document on the Morality of Birth Control," it too would attain worldwide notice later as the so-called Majority Rebuttal. Thus within a five-day period the three papers that crystallized the thinking of this body were completed and ready for discussion by the Commission members.[1]

The Minority Report

Ford's paper, passionate and aggressive in places, reviewed the Church's position on birth control over the centuries, citing authorities from St. Augustine to Pope John XXIII. He then got to the nub of the argument. "Why cannot the Church change her answer to this central question? The Church cannot change her answer because this answer is true.... It is true because the Catholic Church, instituted by Christ to show men a secure way to eternal life, could not have so wrongly erred during all those centuries of history.... The Church could not have erred... even through one century, by imposing under serious obligation very grave burdens in the name of Jesus Christ, if Jesus Christ did not actually impose those burdens....If the Church could err in such a way...the faithful could not put their trust in the magisterium's presentation of moral teaching, especially in sexual matters."

Ford's offensive was not based essentially on proofs from the natural law because, he admitted, such proofs do not exist. "If we could bring forward arguments which are clear and cogent based on reason alone, it would not be necessary for our Commission to exist, nor would the present state of affairs exist in the Church," he wrote.

Nor did he show any interest in wooing Protestants to his position: "If contraception were declared not intrinsically evil, in honesty it would have to be acknowledged that the Holy Spirit in 1930, in 1951 and 1958 assisted Protestant churches, and that for half a century Pius XI and Pius XII and a great part of the Catholic hierarchy did not protect against a very serious error, one most pernicious to souls....Therefore one must very cautiously inquire whether the change which is proposed would not bring along with it a definitive depreciation of the teaching and the moral direction of the hierarchy of the Church and whether several very grave doubts would not be opened up about the very history of Christianity." The change proposed by the majority would open the door, Ford argued, to other deviations including extramarital and premarital sex, homosexuality, masturbation, and sterilization.

Despite admitting the weakness in the natural law argument, Ford (and Grisez) presented a long and particularly dense section contending that since procreation is "a fundamental human good," any voluntary action that frustrates its intent is intrinsically evil. No exceptions are conceivable. Those who argue otherwise, they declared, display an "earthly, cultural naturalism" and a "utilitarian, exceedingly humanistic altruism," which leaves them with a "partial, transitory and vitiated vision." The non-procreative benefits sought by couples in intercourse can be achieved in ways other than contraception, said Ford: "Conjugal love is above all spiritual (if the love is genuine) and it requires no specific carnal gesture, much less its repetition in some determined frequency." Just as a father and daughter or a brother and sister can love each other intimately "without the necessity of carnal gestures," he argued, husbands and wives can learn to manage.

The Majority Rebuttal

The "Summary Document on the Morality of Birth Control" responded that Ford's argument concerning the obligation of the Holy Spirit to protect the Church from error was presumptuous since "the criteria for discerning what the Spirit could or could not permit in the Church can scarcely be determined a priori." In recent years, the authors said, a kind of creeping infallibility had tended to blur the distinction between teachings and give almost every statement an absolute authority. They categorically denied that *Casti Connubii* represented infallible doctrine since the argument from reason given in the encyclical is "vague and imprecise," and the unbroken tradition to which the Pope referred neither goes back to the apostles nor is it an expression of universal faith.

Admitting past error would not subvert the Church's position, said the writers: "Doubt and reconsideration are quite reasonable when proper reasons for doubt and reconsideration occur with regard to some specific question. This is part and parcel of the accepted teaching of fundamental theology."

The contention that the generative act is inviolable was also sharply critiqued. An unconditional respect for nature as if it were the voice of God fails to understand the call to take command of nature and shape it to human purposes, said the document: "The order of creation does not require that all things be left untouchable just as they are, but that they reach the ends to which they have been ordered.... Churchmen have been slower than the rest of the world in clearly seeing this as man's vocation."

Though marriage as a whole should be open to new life, said the authors, every marital act need not be. Non-procreative conjugal acts therefore should be judged in the context of the whole union and on whether they are "respectful of the dignity of the partner" and are accomplished "with lesser inconveniences to the subjects." Rhythm was called "deficient" because "only 60 percent of women have a regular [menstrual] cycle." The document flatly denied that approval of contraception would foster indulgent attitudes toward abortion since abortion deals with life already in existence. It was less specific about the other potential sexual deviations cited by Ford.

The Majority Report

The document "Responsible Parenthood" was far less polemical than either of the working papers. Since it was intended to convince the Pope, a serious effort was made to show how a change in Church teaching can be reconciled with tradition, especially with *Casti Connubii*: "The tradition of the Church... developed in the argument with heretics such as the Gnostics, Manicheans and later the Cathari, all of whom condemned procreation... as something evil.... Consequently, this tradition... intended to protect two fundamental values: the good of procreation and the rectitude of marital intercourse.... It is not surprising that in the course of centuries this tradition was always interpreted in expressions and formulas proper to the times.... Nor was there maintained always a right equilibrium of all the elements.... But what is of real importance is that the same values were again and again reaffirmed."

The authors then took the next step: "The facts which throw light on today's world suggest that it is not to contradict the genuine sense of this tradition and the purpose of the previous doctrinal condemnations if we speak of the regulation of conception using means, human and decent, ordered to favoring fecundity in the totality of married life and toward the realization of the authentic values of a fruitful matrimonial community."

The crucial words in the above quotation are "facts" and "totality." The relevant facts, said the document, are "social changes in matrimony and the family, especially in the role of the woman; lowering of the infant mortality rates; new bodies of knowledge in biology, psychology, sexuality and demography; a changed estimation of the value and meaning of human sexuality and of conjugal relations; most of all, a better grasp of the duty of man to humanize and to bring to greater perfection... what is given in nature."

At that point the document took special care to add among the "facts" the contribution of the Crowleys and other laypeople. "Then must be considered the sense of the faithful: according to it, condemnation of a couple to a long and often heroic abstinence as a means to regulate conception, cannot be founded on the truth."

Far from suggesting that these changed conditions open the door to sexual irresponsibility, "Responsible Parenthood" took great pains to insist that sexual activity makes sense only within the context of a chaste, permanent relationship of man and wife who are open to new life; but that does not mean that every conjugal act must be so open. "The morality of sexual acts between married people takes its meaning first of all . . . from the ordering of their actions in a fruitful married life, that is one which is practiced with responsible, generous and prudent parenthood. It does not then depend upon the direct fecundity of each and every particular act. . . . For a conscience correctly formed, a willingness to raise a family with full acceptance of the various human and Christian responsibilities is altogether distinguished from a mentality and way of married life which in its totality is egoistically and irrationally opposed to fruitfulness." It is this latter, "contraceptive" mentality which the centuries-old tradition, most emphatically in *Casti Connubii*, intended to condemn, said the authors.

The point was reiterated even more forcefully later in the document: "The true opposition is not to be sought between some material conformity to the physiological processes of nature and some artificial intervention. For it is natural to man to use his skill in order to put under human control what is given by physical nature. The opposition is really to be sought between one way of acting which is contraceptive and opposed to a prudent and generous fruitfulness, and another way which is in an ordered relationship to responsible fruitfulness and which has a concern for education and all the essential human and Christian values."

While declining to evaluate the morality of individual contraceptive acts, the document insisted there are "objective criteria" that a couple ought to follow if they decide to limit offspring: the method should not cause a loss of physical or psychic health, should be conducive to the personal dignity of the couple, and should not be carried out in an "egoistic or hedonistic" manner. Abortion was ruled out and sterilization "is generally to be excluded."

By early June this Majority Report was in the hands of Commission members and the subject of continual discussion. Since they understood this document to be the final fruit of some three years of labor, most wanted it to be logically, theologically, and pastorally intelligible for people, priests, and Pope. During this time a number of votes were taken on various aspects of the Majority Report, all indicating heavy support. But no one seems to remember if a vote by all Commission members present occurred before the report was given to the cardinals and bishops in the final week. Several published reports state such a vote of the assembly was taken and the result was 52–4 in favor of the report.[2] All other papers produced during the course of the Commission meetings, including Ford's Minority Report and the Majority Rebuttal, were viewed as working documents: background or supplementary material.

(However when all three were leaked to the press in 1967, some people assumed they were all more or less of equal weight, representing views of various segments of the Commission. In fact, only the Majority Report, "Responsible Parenthood," was intended as the official position of the overwhelming majority of the Commission.)

Cardinal Heenan Presides

Meanwhile, de Riedmatten kept the fine-tuning process alive by encouraging both minority and majority members to restate their views and by calling for occasional advisory votes. In early June, for example, he asked, "Does it seem opportune for the Church to speak on the birth control question without delay?" All forty present, theologians and others, said yes. He then polled them on the question, "Is the Church in a state of doubt concerning the received teaching on the intrinsic malice of contraception?" The response was thirty-five yes and five no — to which Dr. André Hellegers commented, "The debates have convinced me more of the intrinsic danger in irreformable statements than in the intrinsic evil of contraception."

On June 6, Cardinal John Heenan of London, much concerned about what sort of creature was about to be birthed by this group, arrived at the Spanish College, and de Riedmatten asked him to preside over the day's meeting. In a pastoral letter published in the *Catholic Herald* Heenan had already tried to prepare his people for what might come. Notions of right and wrong continually change, he wrote, noting that at the beginning of the century English law approved the death penalty for adults convicted of forgery and for children caught stealing — crimes no one today would consider deserving of capital punishment. Whatever the Pope's decision on birth control, Heenan wrote, "Nobody will be able to say that he did not listen to his priests and people. When he speaks, the Pope will have availed himself of all sources of human wisdom and knowledge."

But when the cardinal presided, he was unable to maintain such balance and calmness in the midst of this assembly contemplating recommendations of watershed proportions. He heard John Ford, representing the minority, rail against what he regarded as an imminent plunge into heresy. Ford repeated word for word sections from his Minority Report, then issued a scathing, personal attack on the leaders of the mutiny. "Among the theologians who are defending contraception are some who conceive human nature as subject to an evolution so complete that there does not exist any fixed conceptual nature," he said. "There are some who do not seem to admit that intrinsic evil is necessarily connected with the choice of any external actions. There are some who permit in certain circumstances, suicide, abortion, fornication, masturbation and adultery. There are some who defend the principle that the end specifies the means, explaining this in a way that is practically equivalent to the end justifies the means.... There are some who seem to deny that the Church can teach infallibly in matters of natural law. There are some who seem to deny that the magisterium of the Church is competent in any event to bind the consciences of the faithful to any particular behavior in any concrete case."[3]

Heenan heard Joseph Fuchs sum up in cooler language the changes that compelled the majority to reach its conclusions — new insights into biology, the institution of marriage, and the position of human beings in the created world. "As one created in the image of God, [man] should look at his responsibilities and cultivate and humanize his gifts according to their total human meaning," he said. "And so many facts have led to this deeper reflection, this more profound understanding of human nature, of sex, of marriage."

Also presented for Heenan's edification were reports from the demographic and psychological sections of the Commission. The demographers had concluded unanimously that something had to be done and that rhythm appeared to be a frail and largely ineffective remedy. At its present rate, they noted, Catholic Mexico would have the impossible population of 35 billion within two hundred years; at present, even with more than one million abortions reported in Catholic Brazil annually, the population was growing at a staggering rate.

The psychologists said birth control remains such a hang-up with the institutional Church because the belief still prevails that sex is bad; it can be humanized only when the neurotic guilt is stripped from it. Paul Anciaux of Belgium called the practice of rhythm "harmful in many cases." Echoing the findings of the Crowley report, he said, "And we are not dealing here with human weakness. We are dealing with the reaction of those who see these moral imperatives as somehow contrary to the fundamental values of marriage."

Heenan appeared upset. He said he wanted an immediate vote taken on whether the Church should change its position and, if so, what methods of birth control should be licit. "We should make a unanimous recommendation," he said. "That ought to impress the Pope." De Riedmatten and others explained that would be impossible, since a division still existed, and, at any rate, the Commission did not intend to function as a jury on birth control methods.

The cardinal's agitation only increased. How, he asked, could the Church retain its credibility with ordinary Catholics if it did not present a united front? Tom Burch, whose own fuse had been growing short during this long session, blew up. He arose and accused Heenan of "hypocrisy." It was now perfectly clear, said Burch, that what concerned the institutional Church was not the welfare of ordinary people but how it could change a position without surrendering one iota of its moral authority, without yielding an inch on its control over human behavior. With that, Burch stormed out of the session and took a long walk. "I think I slightly flipped," he said later, "but that was for me a defining moment." When he returned, his translator personally thanked him for the outburst on behalf of himself and "couples all over the world." Burch was later told he need not attend the final session of the Commission when the full array of hierarchy was present, and he therefore absented himself.

Heenan, meanwhile, continued to preside. He sat through what had to be a painful, forensic exercise, put on for his benefit. Two theologians were asked to present, as best they understood, the arguments for the position contrary to their own. Stanislas de Lestapis, a co-signer of the Ford document, attempted to argue for change, and Pierre de Locht, outspoken advocate of the majority view, tried to defend the status quo. Neither succeeded very well. At the end Heenan launched into a harangue against de Locht for failing to better uphold the ancient tradition. "Fifteen to four!" he exclaimed, citing the earlier vote of the theologians denying the intrinsic evil of contraception. "This means nothing! We have to ask ourselves about the value of the fifteen and the value of the four. How many examples do we have in history where heresies held almost unanimous sway, while only a few held fast to the truth, which finally triumphed in the end? I have read the papers you have written. They should have taken a more intelligent tack. I wonder what you were doing with your time."

With that Heenan adjourned the meetings. De Locht was so upset he told de Riedmatten he intended to cancel his talk scheduled for the following day. But the mercurial Heenan met de Locht privately, apologized for the outburst, and said he actually found himself moving toward the majority view. The next morning Heenan apologized to the entire assembly as well, and de Locht spoke as planned. So did many others, offering suggestions on how the Church could present a new face to the world concerning contraception without compromising its credibility. But Heenan was getting upset again. "The real scandal is we don't have any certain doctrine any more," he said. "We don't have the clear voice of authority."

If this was a preview of the upcoming final week, veteran Commission members wondered what chaos to expect when they were confronted with fifteen cardinals and bishops.

---------- 13 ----------

The Verdict

The Final Meeting III, 1966

Let us help the Holy Father scuttle this question so we can get on to the work of being Christ in the world.

— PATRICK CROWLEY

The fifteen cardinals and bishops who took their seats as the Commission members on June 20, 1966, were an impressive though intimidating lot. Seven were regarded as strong-willed conservatives: Cardinals Ottaviani, Lefebvre, Gracias, and Shehan, along with Bishops Colombo, Morris, and Binz. Only five were known liberals: Cardinals Suenens and Doepfner and Bishops Dupuy, Dearden, and Reuss. No one was quite sure where Cardinal Heenan stood, especially after his tempestuous debut earlier in the month. Nor could anyone predict where Bishops Pulido-Méndez from Latin America or Zoa from Africa might fit. Since Ottaviani had been appointed Commission president for this session, speculation mounted that he might try to ram through his agenda on the strength of sheer authority. But the aged head of the Congregation for the Doctrine of the Faith (the new name of the Holy Office) remained strangely distant (almost as if he knew something the others did not) and dozed through many of the discussions.

It seemed as though Bishop Colombo, a man very close to Pope Paul, had been assigned the task of carrying the banner for retention of the status quo. And he tried mightily. But a series of events during the first two days of the session served to undercut his initiative and instead direct the gathered hierarchy in the direction of change.

First was secretary de Riedmatten's carefully balanced presentation

of the Commission's history to that point. He described how the original six had been called together by Pope John and held their first
meeting in Louvain in 1963. None believed the Church was likely to
change its position, and most hoped it wouldn't. This first group saw
rhythm as the "Christian position" on population problems, praised
past papal condemnations of contraception, and hoped the Pope would
soon provide "light and order." Then in 1964 the expanded group of fifteen began to wrestle with more basic issues as they confronted the pill.
Still, the majority did not believe the pill should be approved, and the
rest were uncertain. In 1965, de Riedmatten explained, the enlarged
Commission had come to understand how the Church changed over
the centuries in its approach to sex, marriage, and procreation. The
theologians voted that *Casti Connubii* could be reformed, and everyone
began to question the benefits of the rhythm method. In their deliberations during April and May in the present year, said de Riedmatten, the
theologians had voted overwhelmingly that contraception was not intrinsically evil, and the vast majority of the Commission was now in full
agreement that the Church ought to change its ban on contraception
while upholding the overall procreative purposes of marriage.

De Riedmatten summarized the arguments concerning change,
showing how the two sides differed. The conservatives claimed the
Church had condemned contraception in its ordinary teaching from
the beginning; on the other hand, countered the liberals, there was
no Scriptural basis for such a position, and the tradition showed wide
variances, even contradictions. Conservatives then argued that marital
intercourse tended by nature toward conception, so any interference
should be seen as unnatural and evil; on the other hand, argued liberals, the Church had long approved interference with nature (though
medical operations, for example) for the greater good of the person, so
individual acts of contraception ought to be legitimate for the greater
good of the couple or the good of the human race. But permitting
contraception might start the Church down the slippery slope toward
other aberrations including abortion and sterilization, pointed out the
conservative side; on the other hand, argued the liberals, these aberrations were distinct from contraception and their immorality could be
argued on other grounds.

In his conclusion, de Riedmatten reminded these cardinals and bishops how the Vatican Council, *their council,* had extolled the "witness
of the faithful" — the ability of ordinary Christians directed by the
Holy Spirit to perceive what is true and what isn't. No longer appropri-

ate, he said, was Pius X's distinction between the Church that teaches and the Church that listens: especially in discerning the morality of contraception, married couples ought to be among the teachers.

This apparent dismissal of *Casti Connubii* bothered Bishop Colombo, who immediately sought a discussion of that encyclical. Zalba expressed deep regret that this Commission, appointed by the Holy Father himself, had abandoned the authentic doctrine of *Casti Connubii* and was seemingly determined to empty it of meaning. Cardinal Ottaviani thought it would be helpful to exhume from the Vatican archives the background papers on the old encyclical and immediately sent someone over to find them. He was unsuccessful. De Riedmatten said he too had tried to find them in vain; apparently they were lost. At that point Patty Crowley began to worry about the ultimate fate of the papers and reports from the present meeting.

That distraction out of the way, the bishops and cardinals expressed their own views on the immediate issue: Is contraception intrinsically evil or not? The immediate testimony of two cardinals provided a second thrust in the direction of change.

Cardinal Julius Doepfner, archbishop of Munich, made clear his view: "Contraception is not intrinsically evil." It is, he said, a "physical evil," which can and should be allowed for a greater good: to protect a wife from pregnancy that might endanger her health or life, or to give a couple the opportunity to care for and educate the children they already have, or to avoid the uncertainty of rhythm. Without hesitation, Doepfner declared that *Casti Connubii* is not infallible and is subject to doctrinal development — just as Vatican II approved of religious liberty without apologizing for its past assertions about "no salvation outside the Church."[1]

A Powerful Consensus

Everyone expected Doepfner to take such a stance. They were not prepared when Cardinal Gracias of Bombay arose. His long record of opposing efforts by the Indian government to control population growth was well known. At first he sounded like John Ford. "If the Church changes here," he said, "then there will be a crisis in Christendom and the Church's enemies will rejoice." But, he continued, "There is a resurrection after every death. The Church will survive. And we must find a way to help couples."[2] He said he still had personal problems with contraception but had given much thought to the pill and believed it would be a godsend for the teeming masses in his country.

Then came a third occurrence that propelled further the move for change. Bishop Colombo, alarmed by what seemed Gracias's defection from the conservative camp, interrupted the cardinal. If the Church backtracks on contraception, he warned his colleagues, they "would endanger the very indefectability of the Church, the teacher of truth in these things which pertain to salvation. Wouldn't this mean the gates of hell had in some way prevailed against the Church?"[3]

Zalba could not agree more. "What then," he asked, "with the millions we have sent to hell if these norms were not valid?"

Patty Crowley could not restrain herself. "Father Zalba," she interjected, "do you really believe God has carried out all your orders?"

A momentary stunned silence followed, then some chuckles at this intrusion of common sense in these austere deliberations. Patty seized the moment and spoke further.

"On behalf of women in general, I plead that the male Church carefully consider the plight of at least one half of its members, who are the real bearers of these burdens. Couples are generous. Christian couples want to have children. It is the very fruit of their love for each other. What is needed is to rid ourselves of this negative outlook on psychological and spiritual values. Couples can be trusted. They will accept the progress of change, and they will have increased confidence in the Church as she helps them grow in love and demonstrates her trust and confidence in them."

Gracias concurred with that, but he was still having trouble reconciling his seminary training with his pastoral instincts. He called on Fuchs, whom he knew as a careful, conscientious theologian, to explain how he had come so far in such a short time. Fuchs's candid account of his theological journey provided a fourth boon to those hoping for change. He said he, like Bernard Häring and other theologians on the Commission, had also served as experts at the Vatican Council, and they had all made this change, "some sooner, some later." His own doubts started in 1963; in 1965 they intensified and he withdrew permission from his publishers to reprint his popular textbook on Catholic morality, which presented *Casti Connubii* in glowing terms. Earlier in 1966 he had stopped teaching moral theology at the Gregorian University because he no longer wished to defend a position he did not personally accept. He had come to understand how doctrine develops, said Fuchs, how a specific condemnation must be withdrawn when the rationale behind it is no longer persuasive. "There has been an evolution in doctrine since *Casti Connubii* under Pius XII and at Vatican II," he said. "And this evolution has been moving in one direction: away from the notion that each contraceptive act is intrinsically evil."[4]

When the archbishop of Bourges, Cardinal Joseph Lefebvre, arose to address the gathering, many assumed he would try to redirect the momentum toward the right. But Colombo and Ottaviani were disappointed. He said simply, "It appears after looking at the documents given us that it wouldn't be too rash to go along with the majority." Then came Bishop Pulido-Méndez of Venezuela, whose views had not been publicized. He had problems with the word "contraception," but he agreed substantially with Doepfner and Fuchs and was ready to vote for change. Realizing that something like a tidal wave was rising, Cardinal Suenens suggested that the bishops were ready to view the edited text of the Majority Report and make a decision.

First, however, the hierarchy had to decide whether to submit one report to the Pope or two — one representing the majority position and one the minority. Monsignor Lambruschini, an Italian with long experience in the Curia, strongly advised sending just one report, and a unanimous one at that. "We don't want to embarrass the Holy Father with two views," he said in an unintentionally accurate peek into the future. "Then he would probably feel obligated to settle on the old doctrine."

However, since it seemed impossible to get a unanimous position, some bishops advocated two texts. Cardinal Heenan came up with a compromise idea: one text representing the majority position, but with "input" from Ford and the other minority holdouts. Many regarded this as a splendid idea, and the group authorized a reediting of the Majority Report. In any event, they firmly agreed that this body would submit but one official position paper to Pope Paul.

Thus after only two days, fears of a blockade by the cardinals and bishops evaporated. At least two generally assumed to be conservatives (Gracias and Lefebvre) were leaning toward change, as was at least one doubtful (Pulido-Méndez). Thus, eight of the fifteen present had aligned with the majority view. And now hope sprang up that the minority might yield a little. As it turned out, that hope was unfounded.

The Ford Holdout

On the third day, June 23, Father Ford arose and let it be known he would never compromise. With considerable oratorical flourish, he spoke of Michelangelo's painting, *The Creation of Man,* in the Sistine Chapel. "This is the moment we are talking about," he said. "This is the moment of conception. Contraception — that is, contra-ception — involves a will which is turned against new life at this moment. It is against this life, in advance, that is, against its coming to be.... Your conception is your very origin, your link to the community of living persons before you, the first of all gifts received from your parents, your first relationship with God as he stretched out his finger to touch you....

"Why did the Church always teach this doctrine? Not as a... reaction against... heresies, not because the fathers... accepted the Stoic philosophy, not because... they followed some philosophy of nature which is now obsolete, not because they were ignorant that some conjugal acts are sterile... not because they believed every conjugal act must have a procreative intent. But because, reflecting on the Scriptures and what they found there about the nature of human life and the nature of Christian chastity, they saw that contraception was a violation of human life and Christian chastity."[5]

But Ford and his colleagues, Visser, Zalba, and de Lestapis, could not turn the tide. Cardinal Shehan, assumed to be conservative, tentatively added his name to the list for change. A straw poll he authorized in Baltimore showed 70 percent of lay Catholics favoring a change on birth control. He said, "The Church develops, and the *sensus fidelium* [sense of the faithful] plays a big role in that development. The Church must recognize how marriage is lived today."

Cardinal Doepfner tried to further defuse Ford's comments. *Casti Connubii* is not infallible, he reiterated, and there would be no harm in saying for once that the Church has been wrong — even if it has taught a doctrine long, solemnly, and in the name of Jesus Christ. Having learned from married couples, especially women, Doepfner said, the Church must change "so that we do not impose on others any further sacrifices that we know in our hearts are not necessary."

Bishop Claude Dupuy and Archbishop Dearden, both liberals, concurred. Then Archbishop Zoa of Cameroon, an unknown, said he too agreed with the majority and wasn't all that worried about scandal. "The fear of scandalizing people by a change is a problem of old Christians," he said. "In our country there is no risk of scandal. We are first-generation Christians."

Doubts and Fears

Toward the end of the third day, Cardinal Heenan took the floor to say he was again having doubts about all this. He was especially hard on the theologians. "Although my heart tells me that at almost any cost we must bring relief to the magnificent Christian couples who are finding the discipline of the Church intolerable, my heart warns me against accepting too readily the arguments of converted theologians who now argue against the accepted doctrine, . . . professional theologians who until a few months ago, not twenty or thirty years ago, dogmatically taught the old doctrine. . . . I think they have changed their opinions not so much because they regard their former reasoning as false but because, like the rest of us, they are moved to compassion when they see the plight of so many married couples." That didn't mean he would oppose change, he added, only that he was struggling.

Cardinal Suenens attempted to put Heenan at ease. "For years," he explained, "theologians have had to come up with arguments on behalf of a doctrine they were not allowed to contradict. They had an obliga-tion to defend the received doctrine, but my guess is they already had many hesitations about it inside. As soon as the question was opened up a little, a whole group of moralists arrived at the position defended by the majority here. . . . The bishops defended the classical position, but it was imposed on them by authority. The bishops didn't study the pros and cons. They received directives, they bowed to them, and they tried to explain them to their congregations."

Meanwhile, Bishop Morris of Ireland had come up with an alto-gether new idea. It would be best, he proposed, that this Commission say nothing since the problem is so grave; instead the question, in the collegial spirit of Vatican II, should be put to a vote by all the bishops in the world. This thought seemed to energize Ottaviani, who called for a private session so the cardinals and bishops could consider the matter alone. Most of them regarded it as a terrible idea: the process could take years; it would dismiss as irrelevant all the work of the Com-mission; a final vote by the world's hierarchy might be seen as infallible. "And do any of us want that?" asked Cardinal Shehan. Still Ottaviani favored the concept and called for a vote. The result was 11–4 against polling the bishops. Ottaviani took the rebuke in stride.

On the fourth day, June 23, the cardinals and bishops received copies of the newly edited Majority Report and followed the text as it was read aloud. The latest version contained no input from the minority, as Heenan had suggested, because the minority wanted nothing to do with it. It was essentially the same document the Commission had received from Fuchs and his colleagues in late May. It said the world and human understanding of the world had changed, that the magisterium was in evolution, that every marital act need not be open to procreation — all couched in language reminiscent of Vatican II, supporting responsible parenthood and respect for the Church.

When the reading was over, Bishop Colombo spoke. He wanted to know if this meant the Church could not take any moral positions with the authority of Jesus Christ. Fuchs responded it can and does take such positions but added there is no simple way to tell ahead of time what the Holy Spirit, in assisting the Church, is likely to permit or not permit. Applying universal moral positions in different circumstances and different eras of history is a difficult business, said Fuchs.

Colombo then inquired if the Majority Report meant contraceptive acts might be allowed only in "extreme cases" or if they were permitted "as a norm" both for couples and for governments dealing with overpopulation. Treading carefully, Fuchs said, "The Commission is not proposing a solution only for limited application. We have tried to work out a way of reconciling . . . the duties of procreation with the needs of the couple, for the good of the couple, the children and the family as a whole. . . . The methods should be worked out by the experts in such matters. . . . I point out that rhythm is not the better method in every case." As for governments, Fuchs said, "Nothing should stop them from making birth control available," but mandatory programs should not be imposed on people against their will.

Patrick Crowley said it was time to forge ahead: "In the nineteenth century, the Church was reported to have lost many working men because it was slow in speaking on the social problem. We cannot risk the loss of married couples now by delaying a change. . . . All seem to admit that the reasons which support the teaching have lost their validity and force. This problem seems to have been escalated into a position far beyond its importance. War, peace, poverty, social justice seem more urgent. So let us help the Holy Father scuttle this question so we can get on to the work of being Christ to the world with his law of love."

The Vote at Last

Friday, June 24, was the day of decision. It came exactly two years to the day after Pope Paul had announced the existence of the Commission. De Riedmatten had three questions for the bishops to vote on. But before the tally could be taken, Ottaviani objected. He wanted a discussion of the questions. Heenan agreed, saying they were unclear. A forty-five minute discussion followed on whether there should be a discussion; the majority ruled one was not necessary.

De Riedmatten put the first and most fundamental question: Is contraception intrinsically evil? Nine bishops said no, three said yes (one of these with reservations), and three abstained. The nine were Doepfner, Suenens, Lefebvre, Dearden, Dupuy, Pulido-Méndez, Shehan, Zoa, and Reuss. The three opposing votes came from Ottaviani, Colombo, and Morris. The abstainers were Heenan, Gracias, and Binz.

The second question was then presented: Is contraception, as defined by the Majority Report, in basic continuity with tradition and the declarations of the Magisterium? The vote here was nine yes, five no, and one abstention.

The third question was: Should the magisterium speak on this question as soon as possible? Fourteen said yes, one no. How individual bishops voted on these latter two questions has never been revealed.

Later that same day the majority of the bishops and cardinals gave their formal assent to the Majority Report. It was never made clear how that vote broke down or even if there was a formal vote. Only one voice was heard in opposition. Colombo, the Pope's theologian, said, "His Holiness will never accept the proposition that contraception is not intrinsically evil." Then he added, "He [the Pope] would agree only to this: a letter to the world's bishops telling them their people are not to be disturbed. It is not necessary to disturb couples who practice contraception; close your eyes!" This seemed a bizarre proposal at that point — totally out of keeping with what the Commission had been talking about for three years and with what had just occurred.[6]

On June 25, the final day, Bishop Dupuy read a short pastoral document he had prepared as an introduction to the Majority Report. It said in part, "All this teaching . . . has in many countries produced lay and Christian family movements which have contributed powerfully to a deeper understanding of marriage and the demands of marriage union. . . . What is to be condemned is not the regulation of conception but a selfish married life, refusing creative opening out of the family circle.... As for the means that husband and wife can legitimately employ, it is their task to decide this together, without drifting into arbitrary decisions, but always taking into account the objective criteria of morality."[7] It was approved in full after some discussion.

The work of the Papal Birth Control Commission was finished at last. The experts, the married couples, the bishops, and cardinals — all appointed by the Pope — had spoken with a nearly unanimous voice. That night as everyone shared a gala dinner together, a sense of achievement, even peace, pervaded the celebration.

"I don't think there was a doubt in any of our minds that the Pope would follow the Commission report," said Patty Crowley, "after the endorsement of all those theologians and the cardinals and bishops."

"We worked so well together and in such a democratic way," said Philippine demographer Mercedes Concepción. "I was certain we had made history."

"I felt sure the problem was settled once and for all," recalled Laurent Potvin, "and I was very optimistic. "Then my wife said, 'Laurent, don't be so excited. Don't you see Cardinal Ottaviani sitting up there?'"

14

The Undoing of the Commission, 1966-68

The sovereign pontiff believes that the observations favoring a new thesis . . . do not seem sufficiently convincing.

— Cardinal Cicognani

On June 28, 1966, three days after the Commission disbanded, Cardinal Julius Doepfner and Father Henri de Riedmatten personally presented the results of the work to Pope Paul. Doepfner was acting in his capacity as the Commission's vice president during its final session, de Riedmatten as the group's executive secretary from the beginning. What they gave the Pope were the two documents representing the Commission's official legacy: the Majority Report written by the theologians and the Pastoral Introduction written by Bishop Dupuy. Both had been approved by an overwhelming majority of the membership. Also presented was a three-foot stack of background material — twelve bound volumes including summaries of all the meetings, summaries of the summaries, all the papers and reports prepared by individual members and teams, and an index with cross references to everything. Doepfner did not publicly comment on the meeting but told Bishop Reuss in a letter, "I got the impression that the Holy Father is very uncertain and hesitant in the whole question."[1]

Some observers wondered why Cardinal Ottaviani, the Commission's president at the final session, did not make the formal presentation of the material himself. The reason appears to be that Ottaviani, Father Ford, and others were already hard at work at the office of the Congregation for the Doctrine of the Faith, preparing an unauthorized, alternative report. On July 1, three days after Doepfner's audience, Ottaviani met with Pope Paul and presented him with a document repudiating what the majority had decided. It was basically Ford's so-called Minority Report, written the previous May as a working paper for the Commission and endorsed only by Ford and three other theologians. This marked the beginning of a long process that would culminate in *Humanae Vitae*.

On July 4, de Riedmatten had another audience with the Pope, who thanked him for his untiring efforts in steering the Commission through to the very end. Ever the diplomat, de Riedmatten did not share his personal views when he appeared on Italian television that evening. The Commission had agreed, he said, that husbands and wives should "consider their duties of conception with a spirit of responsibility." The "question" is now in the hands of the Holy Father, he added, whose ruling "will not be sensational — now begins the period of decision."[2]

The "Reconversion" of Pope Paul

In the mind of Ottaviani, no "question" existed. He retained as his ad hoc consultors the four co-singers of the Minority Report: Ford, Visser, Zalba, and de Lestapis. To this nucleus he added Franciscan Ermenegildo Lio, a longtime consultor to the Holy Office. It was Lio's reactionary chapter on Christian marriage prepared for the Vatican Council that so disturbed Cardinal Suenens in 1963 that he pressed for the formation of the Birth Control Commission. And it was Lio along with Ford who were the presumed authors of the so-called *modi* that attempted to insert the rigors of *Casti Connubii* into the Council's final version of the marriage chapter in 1965. Twice a loser in open, public processes, Father Lio now returned behind the scenes but with the same agenda.

According to Bernard Häring, Lio admitted to associates that Pope Paul was at first favorably impressed with the Majority Report and was attracted by its conclusions, but after two meetings with Ottaviani and Lio himself, the Pope realized his mistake and was "reconverted."[3]

In his authoritative biography of the Pope, *Paul VI: The First Modern Pope*, Peter Hebblethwaite wrote that at this point the birth control issue was entirely in the hands of Ottaviani and his closest associates. "From their point of view, it should never have been taken out of their hands in the first place: the whole experiment in consultation and let-ting non-professional theologians into the debate had already inflicted untold damage on the Church. For Ottaviani...the issue provided a test-case on the superiority of an encyclical to the Council. No matter what the chapter on marriage of *Gaudium et Spes* [the Council's doc-ument on the Church in the Modern World] said, and even though it pointed clearly in the direction of 'responsible parenthood,' the Holy Office could (and did) reply that *Gaudium et Spes* is only a pastoral text while *Casti Connubii* is the milk of pure doctrine.' "[4]

Elsewhere Hebblethwaite cited the views of two men who knew Paul intimately. Mario Rossi, former head of the Italian Student Action Coalition, "saw in him a man trapped between his Christian instincts and his role in an authoritarian institution. Said Rossi, "He served the system faithfully, while understanding the need to revolt against it. This led to a deep conflict within himself, which had the further hand-icap of a failure to understand the ordinary world, a remoteness from everyday life, and a consequent lack of balance. He was always tempted by abstraction and idealism." Cardinal Achille Silvestrini called him "the intellectual" who "saw all too clearly the infinite complexities of situations....He saw beyond the immediate day-to-day questions and tried to force reality to conform to his demands."[5] Ottaviani's influence on Paul was critical, said Hebblethwaite: "Ottaviani had the greatest hold over him because he was an old friend from the 1930s, perma-nently resident in Rome, and played on Paul's fears of undermining papal authority. By comparison Suenens and Häring were latecomers in his life; in any case, Suenens' visits were rare and Häring was de-nied access....Quietly in total secrecy, Ottaviani set about reversing the Majority Report."[6]

Paul's personal "reconversion" was not without pain, however. Throughout the summer he read the documents of the Commis-sion, anguishing over his papal duties, his pastoral instincts, and the inevitable judgment of history. In September, some two months af-ter receiving the Commission's reports, Paul held an interview with French philosopher and longtime friend Jean Guitton. Citations of the Pope's words at that meeting indicate just how edgy he had grown:

"One should not say the Church is in a state of doubt or is not sure of itself. The Church is well informed on all the latest data about contraception. Maybe something has changed? In that case, let's see what science has discovered that our ancestors didn't know. Let's see if something should change in the law. Put questions to the scientists. But having listened to them, let's listen to the voice of conscience and the law. These must make demands, raise the level. Any attenuation of the law would have the effect of calling morality into question and showing the fallibility of the Church which then, like the Jewish synagogue, would have imposed too heavy a yoke on people. Then the Church before John XXIII would appear as a Judaeo-Catholic Church, a Church of an impracticable law, from which I, a second Paul, had freed it. Theology would then become the servant of science... science's handmaid, subject to change with each new scientific discovery so that tomorrow, for example, we would have to admit procreation without a father; the whole moral edifice would collapse.... Who is to say that another scientific discovery will not come along that will subvert the discovery of the pill, showing, for example, that the pill may produce monsters in the next generation?"[7]

Less than a month later he seemed to be feeling more upbeat. In a speech celebrating the achievements of Vatican II held at Rome's Domus Mariae (where the Commission met in 1964), he indicated confidence in the voice of the Holy Spirit coming up, as it were, from below. "Theologians," he said, "are mediators between the faith of the Church and the magisterium. They are attentive to the living faith of Christian communities, their truth, their accents, their problems, the initiatives that the Holy Spirit arouses in the People of God — what the Spirit is saying to the churches."[8]

The pressure was building to say something about birth control, and he did, on October 29, in an address to the Italian Society of Obstetricians and Gynecologists. Paul praised the Birth Control Commission for the "great work" it had done but then added that its conclusions "cannot be considered definitive because of the fact that they carry grave implications... in the pastoral and social spheres, which cannot be isolated or set aside." Finding a solution, he said, requires a "supplementary study," which "we are resolutely undertaking... with great reverence for those who have already given it so much attention and tiring labor.... This is the reason why our response has been delayed and why it must be deferred for some time yet." Meanwhile, he said, everyone must abide by the traditional discipline: "The norm now taught by the Church... demands faithful and generous observance. It cannot be considered not binding, as if the magisterium of the Church were in a state of doubt at the present time, whereas it is rather in a moment of study and reflection."[9]

These comments, intended to calm the public, instead aroused only more confusion. How could the birth control teaching not be in doubt if it required so much study? And if it really was in doubt, how could Catholics be bound to obey a doubtful law? And just who was carrying on this "supplementary study?"

Paul gave no further explanation. Jesuit theologian Richard Mc-Cormick reported that the Church indeed was in doubt. "Once it is shown that there are intrinsic reasons ... why the Church may change her teaching on contraception, it would seem that the foundation for a certain obligation [to obey] has ceased to exist," he wrote.[10] English theologian Charles Davis, editor of the *Clergy Review*, was so irate over the seeming contradictions in the papal speech that he left the priesthood and eventually the Church. The statement, he said, "illustrated the subordination of truth to the prestige of authority and the sacrifice of persons to the preservation of an out-of-date institution."[11]

Cardinal Suenens tried to be more tolerant of Paul's caution. "I must say in his defense that he is concerned about the people," he said. "He thinks we are living in a dangerous time because the people are not prepared for change. I think the Pope would announce the tentative judgments of the Commission, except for one thing: there is such a great possibility of abuses."[12]

Interpretations and Reprisals

Around the world, married couples, unwilling to put their marital lives on hold, made practical decisions on the morality of contraception — more and more often with the approval of priests and bishops. In a pastoral letter to the people of the Munich archdiocese Cardinal Doepfner said those who practice contraception with reasonable motives ought not to consider themselves in sin and should continue to receive the sacraments. In the United States Charles Curran, a professor of theology at the Catholic University of America, took a similar stance in articles and speeches that were widely quoted. A consensus began to develop that, as one priest put it, "the toothpaste is out of the tube and it won't go back in."

Furthering the discussion was the surprise publication in April 1967 of three important documents from the Commission in the *National Catholic Reporter*. Like everything else associated with the Commission and its deliberations, these documents were supposed to be withheld from public view. But a priest from the Dutch Documentation Center in Rome, Leo von Geusau, obtained copies of the Majority Report ("Responsible Parenthood") and two working papers: Father Ford's Minority Report and the Majority Rebuttal of that report. At first von Geusau planned to release them to the French daily Le Monde, but was persuaded by Gary MacEoin, an American freelancer in Europe, that they would get better coverage if reprinted in full in the National Catholic Reporter. The details were worked out, and the public on April 15, 1967, got its first glimpse of Commission documents. Unaware that only the Majority Report represented the Commission's official bequest to the Pope, the editors treated all three as of more or less equal weight. They were also unaware, of course, that Ford's Minority Report was in the process of being mutated into a brand new document under the watchful eye of the nearly blind Cardinal Ottaviani. National Catholic Reporter editor Robert Hoyt called the scoop the "biggest story of the year, of the decade." And it was, at least in Catholic circles. It made the front page of the New York Times and other major newspapers worldwide.

Pope Paul was livid, since much of the evidence he was supposed to be probing over in darkest secrecy was now being discussed and debated everywhere. He ordered Cardinal Cicognani, his secretary of state, to write to the cardinals and bishops on the Commission and tell them, "The supreme pastor has grieved most heavily over the publication of these documents. The reports, scattered so imprudently, and the inept conjectures spread abroad have hardly helped bring a correct solution."[13] Efforts to identify the culprit who leaked the papers to von Geusau proved fruitless.

Two days after the National Catholic Reporter publication, the rector of the Catholic University of America in Washington, D.C., informed Father Curran that his contract would not be renewed. The obvious reason: Curran's contention that the traditional doctrine on birth control had lost its force. Curran, then thirty-three, was hardly a rabble rouser. His writings at the time were consistently calm and dispassionate. For example: "The proposal to change the present teaching of the Church on contraception is not a capitulation to situation ethics and a denial of any objectivity. Moral theology does need a more personalist approach. But the proposal for a change is based on the need for a more exhaustive, objective consideration. I do not believe that the present teaching of the Church properly reflects all the objectivity in the complex reality of marital sexuality."[14]

But the American hierarchy, some ten months after the close of the

Commission, was finding it harder to keep the lid on, and Catholic University was *their* university, and Curran made a visible target.

If the intent of the firing was to quell dissent, it backfired. Curran resolved to fight his ouster, and the issue suddenly became one of academic freedom. The theology faculty unanimously voted its support of Curran and sent telegrams to Catholic University's board, which included some of the country's most powerful bishops. Then the full faculty and the student body voted for a general strike and closed down the university for almost a week amid national publicity far exceeding that which attended the publication of the Commission documents.

On April 24, Archbishop Patrick O'Boyle of Washington, chancellor of Catholic University, begrudgingly announced that the board had abrogated its decision, though, "this decision in no way derogates from the teaching of the Church by popes and bishops on birth control."[15] Curran even got a promotion. However, in succeeding years, he would learn that his problems had only just begun.

The "Creation" of an Encyclical

Back in Rome, the task of discrediting the Commission's report continued — amid some difficulties. To oversee the writing of an acceptable text preserving the best arguments of Father Ford and protecting the doctrine of *Casti Connubii*, Ottaviani called in a French Jesuit, Gustave Martelet. He was assisted by a team of collaborators including the Ford minority from the Birth Control Commission with Bishop Colombo acting as secretary. By June 1967, a fifteen-page draft was completed. It made three major points: First, in order to uphold the magisterium, the restrictions of *Casti Connubii* cannot be reformed in any way. Second, a relaxation of traditional birth control teaching would lead to widespread hedonism and selfishness. Third, any toleration of artificial contraception would encourage governments to force family planning programs on unwilling citizens. Reportedly, this draft was so rigorous and lacking in pastoral considerations that even old-time veterans of the Holy Office found it offensive and vetoed it.

Martelet and Colombo, aided now by a staff of some twelve consultors, began working on a second draft. When this too proved excessively insensitive, two groups of experts were reportedly appointed, one operating out of the secretary of state's office and one from Ottaviani's office — each working on different sections of what would eventually become the papal encyclical on birth control.[16]

Cardinal Ottaviani was hardly able to get around due to age and infirmity but he gave himself unstintingly to the project. He finally retired in November 1967, when he was confident of the outcome of all this work. It would be his legacy for the Catholic Church.

Sensing an imminent subversion of their efforts, episcopal members of the now defunct Commission tried to intercede with Pope Paul. Cardinal Doepfner had little success. He wrote to Bishop Reuss, "I fear now . . . that the Holy Father will bring out a reaffirming document, which will at best furnish a microscopically small beginning for the crowbars of moral theologians."[17]

In an article in the magazine *Diakonia* Reuss himself begged the Pope to make public the discussions on birth control, to admit that the magisterium is in doubt about what is permitted, and to tell the faithful they must follow their consciences during this period. In a terse reply, Ottaviani quoted a paragraph from Vatican II, asserting that the Catholic Church is "the teacher of the truth." He expressed confidence that should the Pope act contrary to the advice of the Commission, Reuss would immediately abandon his own convictions and give full religious assent to the Pope.[18]

Cardinal Suenens was another who tried to get through, warning Pope Paul that if the Vatican continued on its present course, it would be confronted with more than "a credibility gap — a credibility chasm." He received from Cardinal Cicognani what appeared to be a form letter: "The sovereign pontiff believes that the observations favoring a new thesis . . . do not seem sufficiently convincing."[19]

A Call in the Night

For the most part, lay members of the Commission remained blissfully unaware of the intrigue. Thomas Burch returned to his family and work in Washington, D.C., but found it hard to throw off the pessimism that gripped him every time he thought about the Church as an institutional entity. "Even as our Commission made an honest effort to come to grips with the problem," he said, "I saw the Vatican machine moving in. I didn't like it." Burch did not try to learn what was going on in Rome during the long delay, and he preferred not to think about it.

Laurent and Colette Potvin returned to Ottawa feeling "a bit awkward" about the future of the rhythm clinic. "We were reasonably certain change was coming," said Laurent, "so it was difficult to remain convinced about the temperature method as the only Catholic form of birth control." Besides, the Crowley report had shown the awful cost of rhythm for so many people. The issue soon became moot for the Potvins; Laurent accepted a post as a clinical physician at the medical school connected with Laval University in Montreal. The whole family moved, and the Ottawa clinic continued only a short time under the direction of volunteers.

In England John Marshall kept in regular touch with Cardinal Heenan. When more than a year passed with no response from the Pope, Heenan told Marshall, "It doesn't make any difference what he says now. The people have made up their minds."

Pat and Patty Crowley were greeted with an overload of CFM business back in Chicago. Like the Potvins, they assumed it would be just a matter of time until the Holy Father accepted the Majority Report or at least a variation of it. In March 1968, Pat was contacted by campaign workers for Minnesota Senator Eugene McCarthy and asked to support McCarthy's bid for the Democratic nomination for President. Pat agreed. McCarthy had delivered a key address at the CFM convention in 1959, and Pat was greatly impressed with his honesty, forthrightness, and progressive style of politics. McCarthy was already on a roll. He came within seven percentage points of President Lyndon Johnson in the New Hampshire Democratic primary. And when Johnson announced at the end of March that he would not seek reelection, McCarthy got 56 percent of the vote in the Wisconsin primary. During the spring and summer of 1968, the entire Crowley family threw themselves into political work, with Pat as chairman of the Illinois McCarthy campaign and Patty organizing behind the scenes. It was not an easy job, since all the Chicago Democratic delegates would do the bidding of Mayor Richard Daley, and Daley was known to prefer Hubert Humphrey over McCarthy.

Thus embroiled in the campaign, the Crowleys barely noticed news reports from Rome in late July saying the Pope was about to release the long-awaited birth control encyclical; the Vatican press office repeatedly denied that anything was about to occur. Then at 4 A.M. on July 29, 1968, Pat and Patty were awakened by a telephone call from an Associated Press reporter in New York. He was contacting all the Birth Control Commission members he could find to get their reaction to Paul VI's new encyclical, which rejected the Commission's advice and reasserted the traditional ban on contraception. "We were stunned," said Patty. "Pat just said, 'I don't believe it,' and hung up. We asked ourselves why we had ever gone to Rome in the first place."

The Encyclical at Last, 1968

Ottaviani's I-told-you-so revenge was Humanae Vitae.
— PETER HEBBLETHWAITE

At the very moment the Crowleys were lying in bed trying to make sense of what they had just heard, a member of the Commission, Monsignor Ferdinando Lambruschini, was introducing *Humanae Vitae* to the world at a crowded press conference in Rome, July 29. During the Commission's final meeting Lambruschini had voted for change and had strongly recommended that only one report, not two, go to Pope Paul, lest the Holy Father feel compelled to opt for the traditional position if faced with a choice. Contrary to the Commission's intention, Paul had received two reports. Now Lambruschini was tagged with the job of explaining that the Pope had indeed chosen to reaffirm tradition.

Though he noted twice that the encyclical did not represent infallible teaching, Lambruschini said it was an authentic pronouncement of the Magisterium requiring "loyal and full assent, both interior and exterior." Those who believed in good faith that artificial contraception is permissible, he said, "must change their views and give the example by full adhesion" to its teachings.[1]

As reporters and theologians scanned the text, they learned that *Humanae Vitae* was not a mere rehash of *Casti Connubii* or Ford's Minority Report. Paul himself had labored over the final version, removing specific references to mortal sin and adding a paragraph about tolerance and charity toward sinners. The tone was similar to that of *Gaudium et Spes*, the Council's *Pastoral Constitution on the Church in the Modern World*. The document stressed the unitive characteristics of marriage, calling it "the wise institution of the Creator to realize in mankind his design of love." Conjugal love, wrote Paul, must be "fully human, that is to say, of the senses and of the spirit at the same time." It must be "total" — a "special form of personal friendship in which husband and wife generously share everything." It must be "faithful and exclusive," with a "fidelity which can sometimes be difficult but is always possible." Finally, it must be "fecund," for it is "not exhausted by the communion between husband and wife."[2]

But beneath the personalist tone, the essence of *Casti Connubii* (and of John Ford) survived intact. Paul was almost one-third of the way into the document before he became unmistakably specific. Lambruschini called this "the center, the nucleus, the apex, the heart and the key of the encyclical." Wrote Pope Paul, "The Church, calling men back to the observance of the norms of the natural law ... teaches that each and every marriage act must remain open to the transmission of life." And a little later: "Excluded is any action which either before, at the moment of, or after sexual intercourse, is specifically intended to prevent procreation, whether as an end or a means. . . . Consequently it is an error to think that a conjugal act which is deliberately rendered sterile and thus is intrinsically dishonest could be made honest by an otherwise fertile conjugal life."

The Pope did not respond to the content of the Majority Report other than to present this categorical dismissal: "The conclusions which the Commission arrived at could not be considered by us as definitive ... because within the Commission itself no full agreement of judgment ... had been reached, and above all because certain criteria ... had emerged which departed from the moral teaching on marriage proposed with constant firmness by the teaching authority of the Church."

The use of artificial contraception, the Pope predicted, would "open a wide and easy road" to conjugal infidelity; it would disrupt the marriage relationship because a man, accustomed to contraception, tends to "hold his wife in lesser esteem"; and it would place "a dangerous weapon" in the hands of public authorities bent on population control.

Humanae Vitae, said the Pope, stands not on intrinsic arguments but on the authority of the Church as the "depository and interpreter" of the moral law. "For, as you know, the pastors of the Church enjoy a special light of the Holy Spirit in teaching the truth. And this, rather than the arguments put forward, is why you are bound to such obedience."

Mostly Bad Reviews

The encyclical hit the Catholic world like a comet — all the more so because this was not the decision generally expected. At the Catholic University of America in Washington, D.C., Charles Curran and nine other theologians gathered in a basement meeting room on the afternoon of the encyclical's release, read the document slowly, and drafted a short statement. By the next morning they had the signatures of eighty-seven theologians, including Bernard Häring, on the statement, and they presented it in a press conference at the Mayflower Hotel.

Humanae Vitae, they said, "consistently assumes that the Church is identical with the hierarchical office. No real importance is afforded the witness of the life of the Church in its totality: The special witness of many Catholic couples is neglected." In addition, they said, it betrays a "narrow and positivistic notion of papal authority, as illustrated by the rejection of the majority view"; it overemphasizes the biological aspects of conjugal relations; it makes "unfounded assumptions" about the consequences of contraception, and demonstrates "no development over the teaching of Pius XI's *Casti Connubii* whose conclusions have been called into question for grave and serious reasons." Since, said the theologians, Catholics may dissent from authoritative but non-infallible teachings when sufficient reasons are present, "we conclude that spouses may responsibly decide according to their conscience that artificial contraception in some circumstances is permissible and indeed necessary to preserve and foster the values and sacredness of marriage."[3] Within a few weeks, some six hundred theologians worldwide added their signatures to the statement.

Two days later, on August 1, two members of the Birth Control Commission, Dr. André Hellegers and Thomas Burch, along with John Noonan, who had been the Commission's expert on the history of contraception, appeared at a news conference in Washington. Noonan, speaking for all three, said the encyclical suffers from "internal inconsistency" since the central teaching that every marriage act must remain "open to the transmission of life" contradicts the encyclical's parallel teaching that "the rhythm system of contraception may be used for appropriate reasons." Also, said Noonan, "it is, to say the least, surprising that what is alleged to be the design of God could only be discovered in the utmost secrecy of a military character and without subjecting the statement of the alleged design of God to the scrutiny of moral theologians ... or the comment of the faithful."[4]

Within a few days, the Crowleys had recovered sufficiently to comment briefly to the *National Catholic Reporter*. They were happy the encyclical wasn't infallible; they were distressed the Pope had based his judgment on a small minority; they were disappointed the tone was "so negative" despite the need, as the Council pointed out, for "a more positive pedagogy on marriage," and they were most unenthusiastic about the Pope's emphasis on rhythm — especially in the face of research that questioned its value "physiologically and psychologically."[5]

In October, all six of the U.S. lay members of the Commission appeared at another Washington news conference: Hellegers, Burch, Pat and Patty Crowley, Don Barrett, and John Cavanagh. Again the spokesman, Noonan said they agreed couples should follow their own consciences and were convinced the Church would someday repudiate the encyclical just as it had before buried official pronouncements condemning religious liberty and freedom of conscience.

Laurent and Colette Potvin declined to talk to the Canadian press. "We were so disappointed," said Colette. "Could there not be some trust in a Christian couple's judgment to decide what is good and what they must do?" Laurent made no further attempts to teach the rhythm method. "I decided I would not work in that field again," he said.

In England, Dr. John Marshall expressed astonishment in an open letter to the *London Times*. Even the Commission's minority, he noted, admitted "they could not demonstrate the intrinsic evil of contraception on the basis of the natural law." The majority had based its conclusions on years of study, research, and interchange, he wrote, only to see them not refuted but ignored. The Pope's claim that contraception would lead to wholesale immorality "casts a gratuitous slur" on married couples who practice contraception "and whose family life is an example to all." Marshall wondered what were the "criteria" that the Pope said the Commission had "departed" from in reaching its conclusions. The failure to specify these criteria creates a theological impasse, said Marshall, since "theology cannot advance without being in danger of falling into the same alleged errors."[6]

Dr. Hellegers made a similar point in an article in *US Catholic* magazine: "I am not among those who believe the only course open to Pope Paul would have been to accept the data and recommendations of the ... Commission. The Pope is obviously correct when he said that the conclusions which the Commission arrived at could not dispense him from a personal examination of this serious question. Moreover, it is clear that if he found the data and conclusions preferred by the Commission to be erroneous he should disagree with them. The problem of a scientist in studying *Humanae Vitae* is that nowhere does the Pope disagree with the data but in essence pronounces them irrelevant — since they lead to conclusions different from those of the past."[7] Because of this, said Hellegers, scientists "will have difficulty in seeing where the scientific method has any relevance to the Roman Catholic Church."

In *Humanae Vitae*, Thomas Burch found his gloomy forebodings about the Church justified. Years later he said, "The encyclical for me was the last straw. All that work wasted! I could see no continuity, no connection whatsoever between what the Commission did and *Humanae Vitae* — this horrible document. It was as if they found some old unpublished encyclical from the 1920s in a drawer somewhere in the Vatican, dusted it off and handed it out."

The Theologians' View

The reactions of many major Catholic theologians, though more nuanced than Burch's, were largely negative. In Belgium Philip Delhaye, a member of the Commission, published an article comparing the underlying assumptions of *Humanae Vitae* with those of the Council's document on the Church in the Modern World. "*Gaudium et Spes*," he said, "described the love of a couple in personalist terms as a mutual giving on all levels of one's individuality.... *Humanae Vitae* makes a hasty mention of 'an attempt at communion' in order to insist on its objective: procreation. Vatican II had tried to rehabilitate married love.... *Humanae Vitae* returns to the Augustinian view and justifies love only by 'finalizing' it in procreation."[8]

In Germany Karl Rahner said the encyclical "will not prove psychologically effective with many people." First, he said, it is too short to be persuasive; second, it presents a closed, static view of human nature; and third, the public is aware that it ignored the conclusions of the Pope's own Commission. Said Rahner, "The actual situation with regard to the mentality and life practice of the majority of Catholics after the encyclical will not be changed." He recommended a kind of waiting period to see how the document would be received by the faithful.[9]

Bernard Häring, himself a member of the Commission, found it remarkable that in the two years since the report was turned in, the Pope's Vatican advisors "could find no better reasons to condemn contraception than those presented in the encyclical." For practical purposes, he suggested that those who can accept the encyclical's teachings with an honest conscience do so; those couples who in good conscience cannot accept the teaching and actually use methods of birth regulation — with the exception of abortion — "need not mention it in confession"; and priests must instruct the faithful about the encyclical, but they should not be denied "the right to speak out their own opinion."[10]

In the United States, Jesuit Richard McCormick was more cautious. The encyclical failed to resolve doubts, he wrote, because it followed the same line of reasoning used in Casti Connubii. Perhaps theologians will now be moved "out of a spirit of docility" to seek other grounds for establishing the intrinsic evil in contraception, he said, though he saw the probability of success as unlikely. Meanwhile, he said, bishops would be ill advised to demand public assent from their priests, and priests should help their people form their own consciences rather than insisting on compliance with the encyclical.[11]

The Pope had supporters as well. Ironically, German philosopher Dietrich von Hildebrand, whose innovative views on the unitive nature of marital intercourse helped move theologians away from their obsession with procreation, rallied behind Paul. Yes, said von Hildebrand, in his mid-eighties, the manifestation of love is an essential characteristic of conjugal relations, but it may never be cut off from its procreative destiny. To split the two, even in an isolated act, has the same sinfulness that lies in suicide and euthanasia, because in all three individuals act as if they were the "master of life."[12]

Lawrence McReavy, chief theologian to the British hierarchy and longtime commentator on marital morality, pointed out that the Pope did not intend to base his arguments exclusively on the natural law but on the natural law "illuminated and enriched" by divine revelation. Only by focusing on humanity's supernatural destiny as collaborator in building up the Kingdom of God, he said, can one grasp the "sacredness" of human sexuality and of each conjugal act.[13]

Gustave Martelet, a major contributor to the final version of Humanae Vitae, proved — understandably — an articulate supporter. "Right and deep as married love's desire and capacity for total communion are," he wrote, "love does not become what it ought to become unless it allows the fruit of its intimacy to appear.... As soon as it systematically begins excluding this fruit, however, love immediately injures itself so that it leads to death."[14]

The Bishops' Uncertain Voice

It was to be expected that the world's bishops would line up in support of an authoritative teaching from the Holy Father. To be sure, some did so in no uncertain terms. Wrote Bishop John Wright of Pittsburgh, "Artificial contraception is objectively sinful. . . . Those who impose it, foster it, counsel it, whether they be governments, experts, or — God forgive them — spiritual directors, impose, foster, and counsel objective sin, just as if they would if they taught racism, hatred, fraud, injustice or impiety."[15]

Similarly, Bishop Robert Tracy of Baton Rouge, Louisiana, said, "There is no way now for any Catholic to continue to advance such a position in his personal life, his teaching, his preaching or in the exercise of his pastoral ministry without formally repudiating the position of the Holy Father."[16]

The hardest stance was taken by Cardinal O'Boyle of Washington. He suspended Curran and twenty-three other signers of the opposition statement, as well as some thirty parish priests who disagreed with *Humanae Vitae*. This action led to several years of appeals, hearings, and a state of very low morale in Washington.

A few bishops publicly voiced their disagreement with Pope Paul. Archbishop Denis Hurley of Durban, South Africa, spoke of the "magnificent results achieved by the Council" because "collegiality was at its finest, but "the consultation on birth control was not conducted in the same way." Bishops, he said, "cannot shrink from the issue of how they think the authority of their senior brother should be exercised."[17] One member of the U.S. episcopacy, Auxiliary Bishop James Shannon of St. Paul-Minneapolis, resigned his position as a result of his inability to accept *Humanae Vitae*. He told his superior, Archbishop Binz, a member of the Commission, "I must now . . . admit that I am ashamed of the kind of advice I have given some of these good people, ashamed because it has been bad theology, bad psychology, and because it has not been an honest reflection of my own inner reflection."[18] Shannon took a leave of absence, and eventually resigned from the priesthood and married.

The reaction of national bishops' conferences throughout the world provided an interesting contrast in styles. Some praised the document and embraced it wholeheartedly, while others issued joint statements that seemed to soften, mitigate, or, in a few cases, almost repudiate the papal word. Joseph Selling, who studied these pronouncements in great detail as part of his doctoral thesis at the University of Louvain, wrote, "Never before have so many bishops responded to a papal encyclical and never before have their responses been so varied and sometimes critical."[19] He found that eighteen episcopal conferences, including Ireland, Poland, Spain, and New Zealand, accepted *Humanae Vitae* completely and without qualification. Ten, including Austria, Belgium, Canada, and Holland, clearly mitigated the teaching. And nine, including England, Italy, and the United States, issued statements that seemed uncertain or ambiguous. Thus, concluded Selling, fewer than half of the world's bishop conferences received the encyclical with a total embrace.

In his book *Why You Can Disagree and Remain a Faithful Catholic*, Benedictine Philip Kaufman proposed that Selling's analysis may have been too conservative. The U.S. statement, he noted by way of example, "recognized the possibility that Catholics might in conscience have to reject non-infallible papal teaching." The bishops "quoted Newman's description of circumstances in which conscience could oppose the supreme, though not infallible, authority of the pope." The U.S. bishops, he said, also described themselves in their document as "witness to a spiritual tradition which accepts enlightened conscience, even when honestly mistaken, as the arbiter of moral decision."[20] Thus, concluded Kaufman, the U.S. position more accurately belongs in the clear mitigation category than with the uncertain group. So also might the Italian statement, noted Kaufman, which described the doctrine of *Humanae Vitae* as a "humble and sublime . . . ideal goal."

Kaufman found a more democratic way to look at the episcopal responses. Since some conferences like New Zealand's or Malta's represented only a few dioceses, while others like those of the United States (with 159 dioceses) or of CELAM (Conferencia Episcopal Latinoamericana, with 442 dioceses) contained many dioceses, he recalculated the breakdown into the three categories by dioceses rather than by episcopal conferences. Under that rubric, 262 dioceses (or 17 percent) fully accepted *Humanae Vitae*; 866 (or 56 percent) clearly mitigated their acceptance; and 428 (28 percent) were uncertain.

The significance of this hypothetical breakdown is critical. It suggests that only 17 percent of the world's bishops gave total approval to *Humanae Vitae*, while at least 56 percent preferred to soften or reinterpret the strong message, with the others somewhere in between. Kaufman quoted Bishop James Malone's sobering comment at a meeting of the U.S. bishops: "Teaching is not a unilateral activity. One is only teaching when someone is being taught. Teaching and learning are mutually conditional."

Polls of the laity taken after the release of the encyclical revealed large numbers of lay Catholics resisting the teaching. A September 1968 Gallup survey in the United States (two months after the encyclical's release) showed 54 percent opposed to *Humanae Vitae* teaching, while 28 percent supported it, and the rest hadn't made up their minds. A London *Sunday Times* poll registered an 80 percent disapproval rate.

A survey conducted by the University of Notre Dame showed the encyclical had not changed the minds of many American priests: 51 percent said that before the encyclical they regarded contraception as permissible in some situations; afterward 49 percent had the same view.

Pope Paul seemed not to know how to handle this avalanche of criticism. "The knowledge of our grave responsibility costs us no small suffering," he told a papal audience in late July. "We well know the heated discussion in the press. The anguish of those involved in the problem touched us also."[21] But a week later he was more cheerful in a letter to the Congress of German Catholics: "May the lively debate aroused by our encyclical lead us to a better knowledge of God's will."[22] He even yielded to a temporary indulgence in grandeur. "Don't be afraid," he reportedly told Cardinal Gagnon, "in twenty years time they'll call me a prophet."[23]

The Aftermath, 1969 - 94

Is this non-reception or disobedience or what?
— Yves Congar, O.P.

More than a quarter century has passed since *Humanae Vitae* was released, and the standoff remains. Thousands of articles and books have
been written on the encyclical and its impact. Yet the dominant theme
is rarely the theology or sacramentality of marriage. Rather, the topic is
authority: who has it and who doesn't, how it is to be used and how it's
abused, when dissent is legitimate and when it isn't. The Church remains fixed in a kind of time warp where doctrinal development seems
impossible.

During 1993, the twenty-fifth anniversary of *Humanae Vitae*, the encyclical was commemorated or commented on from all sides. A Vatican
symposium called it a bulwark against the permissiveness of a sex-
obsessed culture. An array of critics called it one of the great disasters
of Church history and a major reason why Catholics have abandoned
the Church. The arguments favoring the encyclical's position — the
long tradition of opposition to contraception, the natural law, and a
reluctance to provide any opening for wholesale sexual license — differed not a whit from those proposed in 1966. Father John Ford could
have written them all. Similarly the arguments for change — the absence of any scriptural disapproval of contraception, the inconsistency
of the Church tradition, a more holistic understanding of conjugal relations — echoed those of the mid-1960s. They restated, often using
the same terms, the propositions to be found in the Birth Control
Commission's Majority Report.

Whether *Humanae Vitae* is indeed a finger in the dike against rampant immorality or is itself a contributor to promiscuity by reason of its unbending rigor, the fact is that most Catholics show no interest in its teachings. After the first backlash of disappointment in 1968, some commentators predicted that couples would either get in line or get out of the Church. And many did leave, with a high proportion citing *Humanae Vitae* as the reason. But many more stayed, though harboring a considerable amount of anger and resentment. The dissatisfaction shows in precipitous drops in Mass attendance and Church contributions by U.S. Catholics after 1968.

In 1963, some 75 percent of Catholics between twenty and thirty-nine years of age reportedly attended Church weekly or at least several times a month. By 1990 the figure in this child-bearing category stood at 40 percent. In the 1960s, Catholic and Protestant churchgoers gave the same proportion of their income to their churches — about 2 percent. By the late 1980s, Catholic contributions had fallen to about 1 percent, while Protestant giving remained stable. The largest factor in both declines, Father Andrew Greeley discovered in a series of sociological studies, was the birth control encyclical.[1]

Polls of Catholic attitude toward birth control are boringly consistent from 1970 through the early 1990s. Variations appear largely due to differences in the way the questions are asked. A Princeton University study in 1970 reported that 66 percent of Catholic women of child-bearing age were using birth control measures condemned by the Pope, and most claimed to be doing so in good conscience. Another Princeton study in 1980 found 94 percent of Catholic women of child-bearing age using forbidden methods. A 1986 *New York Times* poll claimed almost 70 percent of adult Catholics favored the use of artificial birth control, and 80 percent said one could disagree with the Pope on this issue and still be a good Catholic. According to a 1991 Gallup poll, 87 percent of Catholics believed the Church should permit couples to make their own decisions about forms of birth control. And in a 1992 Gallup follow-up, 80 percent of Catholics disagreed with the statement: "Using artificial means of birth control is wrong."

Priests have regularly refused to support the encyclical. A 1970 National Opinion Research Center study showed only 40 percent of the U.S. clergy agreeing with the doctrine, and a mere 13 percent said they would refuse absolution to someone unwilling to avoid contraceptive practices. The 1980 Princeton poll cited above reported that less than 30 percent of the clergy agreed with the teaching of *Humanae Vitae*. Pastors rarely if ever talk about birth control from the pulpit or insist on submission to the requirements of the encyclical when counseling engaged couples.

In the United States and elsewhere the hierarchy has been less than enthusiastic. The immediate reaction to the encyclical in 1968 was tepid at best — with a mere 17 percent of bishops' conferences showing unmitigated acceptance, by Philip Kaufman's analysis.[2] Episcopal statements since have given lip service to the magisterium position on birth control but no effort is made to promote acceptance by priests or people. Although rhythm is the only officially approved method of family limitation, a 1993 survey by the National Conference of Catholic Bishops found that U.S. dioceses on the average spend less than $5,000 a year on support of natural family planning programs. Efforts to impose discipline in this area have come almost exclusively from the Vatican, not from local dioceses or national bishops' bodies. After more than twenty-five years, many bishops, it would seem, have not internalized or made their own the teaching of *Humanae Vitae* any more than their people have.

In a remarkable speech before the gathered U.S. hierarchy at their 1990 meeting in Washington, D.C., Bishop Kenneth Untener of Saginaw, Michigan, made the point as the assembly discussed a document of new guidelines on sex education: "In the text we briefly restate the teaching on birth control and say, We hope that the logic expressed here is compelling. I wonder how we can claim credibility when we make a statement like that knowing in fact that the logic is not compelling to the Catholic laity...not compelling to many priests...and not compelling to many bishops. When we know this, and don't say it, many would compare us to a dysfunctional family that is unable to talk openly about a problem everyone knows is there. We also say, it is our earnest belief that God's spirit is acting through the magisterium...in developing this doctrine.... This is true but it is not the entire truth. It is also the earnest belief of our Church that the Spirit acts through the entire people of God in developing doctrine."[3]

Such candor suggests that disagreement with *Humanae Vitae* may be quite common (though rarely spoken) at the Church's episcopal level. Could it be, theologian Yves Congar has asked, that this encyclical is the rarest of breeds — a doctrine that is "not received"? Congar and others have argued that no Church teaching has validity unless it is received and accepted by the Church. Non-reception, he explained somewhat obtusely, "does not mean the teaching is untrue, only that it doesn't call forth any living power and therefore doesn't contribute to edification." Looking at the reaction aroused in the whole Church by *Humanae Vitae*, he wondered, "Is this non-reception or disobedience or what? The facts are there."[4]

This growing development of these ideas of non-reception and of the sense of the faithful is at least one positive fruit of the encyclical. Jesuit Avery Dulles is among several moderate theologians who have written on the subject. In 1986 he noted that in past history a consensus by the people has overturned opposing belief and won full Church acceptance. One example he cited was "the real presence of Christ in the Eucharist," acclaimed by the faithful in opposition to official Church authority in the ninth century and later accepted as an absolute dogma. This sense of the faithful is more than a "head count," said Dulles; it can only be determined "in the last analysis by responsible discernment." He quoted Cardinal Newman's dictum that "infallibility does not belong either to the hierarchy alone or to the believing people alone" but to the "remarkable harmony of the Catholic bishops and the faithful." Without mentioning birth control, Dulles warned that Church officials will fail miserably if they try to force a belief or a doctrine on the faithful that doesn't make sense: "Church history affords several instances in which the 'non-reception' of devout believers or Church authorities has been a factor in overturning the teaching of popes and councils."[5]

This approach to authority as a two-way street, requiring more than a simple demand for obedience, remains still a relatively undeveloped concept in theology and one that makes Church officials quite uneasy.

The Pope Weeps

The scarcity of public dissent from the encyclical by bishops and theologians can be explained in part by developments in Rome since it was issued. Paul VI never wrote another encyclical, though he reigned for another ten years. After *Humanae Vitae* he entered "a period of dark night, of depression, of deep agonizing over his stewardship," according to his biographer Peter Hebblethwaite. "Was he a good pope or a bad pope? The answer was far from self-evident to him.... He said the rosary every day: he identified with the first sorrowful mystery — the Agony in the Garden; and on his walks in the Vatican Gardens he often paused to meditate at the shrine of St. Peter...in chains. Sometimes he had been found weeping there." The tears, said Hebblethwaite, were "over the state of the Church."[6]

Some effort was made to bring dissenting theologians into line. Bernard Häring was put through an extensive trial by the Congregation for the Doctrine of the Faith but escaped unscathed by stating somewhat ingeniously that he accepted *Humanae Vitae* "just as it was accepted... by the world's episcopal conferences in their pastoral statements."[7] As noted above, a large proportion of these episcopal statements mitigated or muted the encyclical's force.

In 1972 it was generally agreed by a planning committee that the most relevant topic for the next general synod of bishops in Rome (scheduled for 1974) would be marriage and the family. Paul at first concurred with the idea, then quickly changed his mind after a conversation with Archbishop Derek Warlock of Liverpool, England. Warlock recalled that when he suggested to Paul that the subject might lead to an escalation of distress over *Humanae Vitae*, the Pope seemed stunned, as if he hadn't realized that before. Later that day he saw Warlock again and said, "I think we ought to start looking at the world. ... Couldn't we look outward at the work the Church is engaged in such as evangelization?"[8] As it turned out, the subject for the 1974 Synod of Bishops was evangelization. Observed Hebblethwaite, "Paul's choice... was one of the most fateful of his pontificate. If he had opted for Christian marriage his whole pontificate would have gone down in history as the birth-control pontificate. Evangelization gave him a chance to look up and break out of the narrow mold."[9] It also kept the discontent festering in the Catholic world out of the limelight.

The Pope may have felt some relief in 1972 when Cardinal Suenens, the very embodiment of the progressive forces in the Church, moved out of his life. Suenens had repeatedly stirred the Vatican Council in the direction of reform and most recently had publicly criticized the Pope for not dealing with birth control in a more collegial way. But now, he told Paul, he had discovered the Charismatic Renewal Movement and was virtually pleading to leave these old battlefields to march with an altogether different (and less troublesome) army. Paul promptly responded by charging Suenens with the mission of "accompanying" the movement henceforth, almost like the Pope's personal representative, and thereby getting the energetic Belgian off his back.

During his remaining productive years, Pope Paul moved in other directions and faced other challenges, like the Traditionalist movement led by Archbishop Marcel Lefebvre, the threat of worldwide communism, and the reform of religious orders. He died in 1978 and was succeeded (after the brief reign of John Paul I) by Archbishop Karol

Wojtyla of Krakow, a man not nearly as insecure about his place in history.

The Crackdown

As Pope John Paul II, he immediately took an aggressive stance on *Humanae Vitae*, practically making it the foundation stone of his papacy. He has been greatly aided in this by a curial staff of cardinals, including Silvio Oddi of the Congregation of the Clergy (who stated that anyone disagreeing with *Humanae Vitae* is automatically out of the Church), Edouard Gagnon, head of the Committee for the Family (who has insisted the encyclical is infallible) and, Cardinal Joseph Ratzinger, prefect of the Congregation for the Doctrine of the Faith (a younger, more articulate reincarnation of Cardinal Ottaviani). Full and explicit agreement with *Humanae Vitae* (as well as opposition to women's ordination) became a prerequisite for anyone nominated to become a bishop.

In 1979 a Vatican-ordered investigation of Charles Curran began in earnest. After the unsuccessful attempt to oust him from the Catholic University of America in 1967, Curran continued to state his objections to the ban on contraception in speeches and theological journals. He broadened his critique to include questions about the traditional approach to divorce, homosexuality, and even abortion. Seeking to make an example of an American theologian (as Vatican authorities later admitted), John Paul put the finger on the very visible Curran. He was interrogated over a six-year period and apparently damaged his own case by citing statistics on negative public reactions to *Humanae Vitae*. That was just the point, argued Ratzinger: these negative reactions were largely due to the ideas spread by Curran and his sympathizers. Among these sympathizers on record were some seven hundred other U.S. theologians, the Catholic Theological Society of America and his colleagues at Catholic University.

Chicago's Cardinal Bernardin tried to work out a compromise that would leave Curran at Catholic University but outside the theology department. The effort failed when Ratzinger informed Curran in 1986 that the Congregation for the Doctrine of the Faith had ruled that "one who dissents from the Magisterium as you do is not suitable or eligible to teach Catholic theology." In the wake of that decree, no other Catholic university was willing to accept him. Curran ultimately found refuge as a professor of Christian ethics at Southern Methodist

University in Dallas, Texas; he continues to speak and write on sexual morality and Catholic doctrine. On the eve of the anniversary of *Humanae Vitae,* he wrote, "I believe that the hierarchical Magisterium can and must change its teaching on artificial contraception. I do not expect this change to come quickly or easily. But the Catholic tradition has the resources to admit its error in this case and ultimately to come up with a more adequate sexual ethic that will also avoid the dangers of the individualism so present in our society."[10]

Chastened by the Curran banishment, theologians, especially those at Catholic institutions, have been exceedingly reluctant to even raise the subject of birth control unless they support it.

In 1980, only two years after John Paul became Pope, a noteworthy attempt to open the closed subject at the top level occurred during the general synod of bishops meeting in Rome. This time the subject was "The Role of the Family in the Modern World." The Vatican had urged the 161 bishops elected to the synod to discuss beforehand with their priests and laity a position paper prepared by the Vatican on the subject. Several took the idea seriously, including the U.S. episcopal delegation. A nationwide consultation (by mail) revealed lay dissatisfaction with the paper: It exalted rhythm, failed even to mention any other form of birth control, and intimated that marriage is inferior to celibacy, said respondents.

On the first day of the synod, Archbishop John Quinn of San Francisco, head of the U.S. bishops conference, arose and said Catholics, "men and women of good will," do not "accept the intrinsic evil of each and every act of contraception....The fact that in practice the widespread non-observance of the teaching is coupled with widespread reception of the Eucharist and that in the realm of theory a notable body of theological opinion reinforces dissenting practice, means that the moral issue as such has been resolved by many."[11] Quinn also implicitly criticized *Humanae Vitae* itself by stating that in the future magisterial documents ought to be written "in a language which would be directly comprehensible to a moderately educated people in today's world." The synod, he said, must address the problem by initiating a dialogue between the Holy See and theologians including "both those who support the Church's teaching and those who do not," with the talks based on the principle that "the Church has nothing to fear from the truth."[12]

Others joined in this incipient call for action. Cardinal Basil Hume of Westminster said married people are the best theological source for

solving the dilemma, "first because they are the ministers of the sacrament of matrimony and, second, because they alone have experienced
the effects of this sacrament." These couples, he said, "cannot accept
that the use of artificial means of contraception in some circumstances
is intrinsically wrong as this matter has been generally understood."
Cardinal G. Emmett Carter of Toronto then noted that since the living Church seems to be moving away from *Humanae Vitae,* we may be
seeing here a manifestation of the sense of the faithful. Ignoring it, said
Carter, would be to "run the risk of speaking in a vacuum."[13]

The rebellion was quickly snuffed out. Quinn never explained what
happened, but the next day he told the synod, "There is no doubt
the teaching of *Humanae Vitae* on contraception is authentic teaching of the Magisterium of the Church. Neither I nor [the U.S. bishops]
are for a change in the Church's teaching on this subject."[14] Quinn
blamed the press for distorting his remarks. After that a series of bishops arose to praise the wisdom of the encyclical. But some relics of this
aborted effort survived in the propositions adopted at the end of the
synod. One said, "The Synod of Bishops cannot ignore the difficult and
painful situation of many Christian couples who, despite their sincere
good will and because of their weakness or objective difficulty, are unable to obey the moral norms of the Church. In the pastoral treatment
of the married, pastors should hold fast to the law of gradualness." In
his closing remarks at the synod, Pope John Paul took pains to make
clear that this "law of gradualness does not mean there are gradations
in the law.[15]

A Pillar of the Papacy

Through the years John Paul has seized every opportunity to extol the
doctrine of the encyclical in his speeches and audiences. Time and
again he has restated his absolute conviction that the unitive and procreative ends of marriage may not be separated for any reason. For
example: "The proper end of the sexual urge is the existence of the
species Homo, its continuation, and love between persons, between
man and woman, is shaped, channeled one might say, by that purpose
and framed from the material it provides."[16] On another occasion, he
stressed that "the union of persons in love does not necessarily have to
be realized by way of sexual relations. But when it does take this form
the personalistic value of the sexual relationship cannot be assured
without willingness for parenthood."[17] Borrowing from the teaching of

the ancient Cynics, the Pope regularly extols the notion of self-mastery and self-discipline as benefits flowing from the deliberate limitation of sexual activity. And he has often shown extreme impatience with those who do not agree. "In reality," he said on one occasion, "what is called into question by the rejection of this teaching is the very idea of the holiness of God."[18] "Because the Church's Magisterium has been instituted to enlighten the conscience," he said in another talk, "any appeal to this conscience in order to contest the truth of what has been taught by the Magisterium involves the rejection of the Catholic concept of both the Magisterium and of the moral conscience."[19]

The extent of Pope John Paul's commitment to the intrinsic evil of contraception in each and every instance can be seen in the biomedical norms issued by the Congregation for the Doctrine of the Faith in 1986. Since procreation was deemed permissible only through the natural intercourse of husband and wife, artificial insemination, even that between spouses, was ruled immoral, as were all forms of in vitro fertilization, all forms of surrogate motherhood, and the impregnation of unmarried women or widows, even with the preserved sperm of a deceased husband. One exception was allowed: couples having difficulty conceiving normally could collect the husband's sperm with a syringe after intercourse and aspirate it toward the ovum. But this could only be done morally, said the Vatican, through the use of a perforated condom that would allow some sperm to escape, so that the "integrity" of the marital act was preserved.[20]

In 1993 after six years of preparation, the Pope issued the encyclical *Splendor Veritatis*, proposed as a major legacy of his pontificate and a modern summa on moral theology. It intended to guarantee once and for all that the sort of uprising that almost happened at the 1980 bishops synod would not happen again. The Church, wrote John Paul, is no longer facing "limited and occasional dissent, but an overall and systematic calling into question...of traditional moral doctrine on the basis of certain anthropological and ethical presuppositions."[21] Quoting liberally from Scripture and tradition, he went on to state his central presupposition — that certain acts, contraception in particular, are intrinsically evil. He rejected possible objections. Appeals to conscience, he said, will not do because an uninformed conscience does not know the truth and therefore must discern the truth from legitimate authority. He refuted the argument that individual acts are not as significant as the overall moral focus of one's life by identifying even a single intrinsically evil act with mortal sin (which merits eternal damnation).

The notion that Catholic moral teaching presents an "ideal" that has to be adapted to concrete realities was dismissed as "a serious error."

John Paul addressed the encyclical not to the general public but to the bishops of the world. The Pope told them to adopt "appropriate measures to ensure that the faithful are guarded from every doctrine and theory contrary" to his teaching. That means, said John Paul, that institutions bearing the name "Catholic," including Church-related schools, universities, health care facilities, and counseling services, must accept his teaching or forfeit their "Catholic" name if they "seriously fail to live up to it."[22]

Veritatis Splendor elicited extremes of reaction. Wrote syndicated *New York Times* columnist Colman McCarthy, "This was a document the pope pondered and wrote for six years, years in which over-population worsened, poverty increased, global arms sales grew and the number of people dying daily from hunger-related diseases stayed steady at forty thousand. And the major document of John Paul's legacy is a 179-page message ordering Catholics not to use condoms."[23]

However, Germain Grisez, who some thirty-eight years before assisted John Ford in writing the so-called Minority Report during the Birth Control Commission's latter days, found the encyclical a vindication of the arguments he had been making ever since. "The rejection of the pope's interpretation is ... inconsistent with any Catholic conception of divine revelation and its transmission," he wrote. Those who take issue with the Holy Father, he said, have three choices: "To admit that they have been mistaken; to admit that they do not believe God's word; or to claim that the pope is grossly misinterpreting the Bible."[24]

Grisez, a professor of Christian ethics at Mount St. Mary's College in Maryland, is among a contingent of writers who contend *Humanae Vitae* is not only defensible but infallible and share their views in both scholarly and popular journals. Among the most articulate is Janet Smith, a professor of philosophy at the University of Dallas, whose massive volume, *Humanae Vitae: A Generation Later*, was published in 1991. Using a battery of complex arguments, she concluded that Pope Paul got it right in 1968 and that his opponents have ever since contributed to the corruption of Catholic attitudes through their contagious dissent. More recently she wrote, "Most couples who contracept undoubtedly love each other and intend their acts of sexual intercourse to be loving and bonding. ... But by using contraception, they have absorbed a view of sexuality that does not take advantage of the great love-expressing and bonding power of the baby-making ordination of the sexual act."[25]

Smith's sincerity and irenic tone make her a persuasive debater. But the argument seems to contradict itself in the face of the Church's endorsement of the rhythm method — a point Commission member André Hellegers made in 1968. If natural family planning were to become 100 percent effective (as Church officials have long hoped), a Catholic couple could practice conjugal relations in good faith and with the blessing of the Church, even though they do not intend to conceive and know there isn't the slightest possibility of doing so. They could do this because the Church would regard their conjugal acts as theoretically "open to the transmission of life" and "possessing a baby-making ordination."[26] Hellegers and most of his colleagues viewed this rationale as absurd at the time, and, despite the volumes on the library shelves, the debate hasn't moved any distance since.

On the popular front, John Paul has no better friend than Monsignor George Kelly of New York. In a series of books and articles he has lamented permissiveness in the Church and society, calling Catholics back to unquestioning submission and obedience to authority. Kelly was a member of the Birth Control Commission but attended only one meeting, and that for just one day. In Kelly's view, the Commission was the victim of a "coup" by "contraceptionists" who persuaded weaker and inept Commission members to tread where they should never have stepped. Non-theologians like the Crowleys and Potvins should not have been on the Commission in the first place, he argued, because they could have nothing to contribute to the discussion. In his book *Keeping the Church Catholic with John Paul II*, he wondered "what purpose did statisticians, social scientists, lay witnesses, even family life directors serve on this commission since they could speak only about questions irrelevant to the moral determination the original Commission was called upon to make. This mixed assortment of theological amateurs turned Paul's Commission almost immediately into a debating society arrogating to itself the function of reformulating Catholic doctrine in political caucus."[27] Thus was dismissed the experiment of Pope John — with the hope that no such attempt to broaden a discussion of doctrine will ever happen again.

In 1994 the subject of contraception seemed to come full circle when the United Nations held its fourth International Conference on Population and Development. One of the reasons for the creation of the Birth Control Commission in 1963 (and the one most widely circulated in the media) was the upcoming, first-ever UN-sponsored population conference scheduled for 1964. Now, thirty years later, the Vatican appeared just as uneasy with the idea of population limitation, though far more strident with its criticisms. Church officials lambasted the draft document for the conference as excessively "individualistic," operating out of "an ethical vacuum," endorsing "cultural imperialism," and promoting "contraceptive materialism." There should be no cause for concern, argued the Pontifical Council on the Family, since the earth can accommodate five billion more people in the next hundred years with an improved use of land. That provocative assertion angered conference delegates since it flew in the face of the best and latest research and even contradicted the findings of the Vatican's own Pontifical Academy of Sciences; that body had just reported a pressing need to contain worldwide births in order to avoid "insoluble problems" in the twenty-first century.[28]

Church officials seemed unaware how radically the tone of UN discussions on population issues had shifted since the close of the Cold War. Before there was an almost hysterical concern about unrestrained growth, with a tendency to see widespread contraceptive use and governmental controls as necessary remedies in many regions. But the 1994 proposed document, articulating worldwide priorities for the next twenty years, took a broad ethical approach, insisting on freedom from government coercion, the rights of women, the responsibility of males, educational opportunities for both sexes, a reduction in infant mortality rates, and a greater respect for cultural and religious differences.

The Vatican might well have praised these positive developments before voicing objections. Instead, its spokesmen complained repeatedly about references to contraception in the document, about encouragement of condom distribution in AIDS prevention programs, and about advocacy for safe abortions in countries where the procedure is legal. As a result, the Vatican found itself at the Cairo conference in an uncomfortable alliance with a minority of countries like Libya, Sudan, and Iran, all notorious for human rights violations and the inferior status in which women are held.

In the end, Vatican officials forced changes in a few words of the final document and then approved the text, but with serious reservations on some issues. This general approval represented some progress over previous UN population recommendations, which the Vatican had rejected totally. Still, the opposition to contraception remained as firm as it had been in the mid-1960s (and based on identical arguments). Nor did it appear any consultation with married persons or inquiry into their experiences would come during John Paul II's reign; papal commissions in the 1990s are given precious little room in which to operate. When the Pope appointed seventy scientists in early 1994 to help him formulate a response to new developments in the life sciences, the president for the Pontifical Council for Pastoral Assistance warned that any member of the commission would be instantly terminated "at the moment he or she deviates voluntarily in writing, words or actions from the teaching of the Church."

Survivors

I just can't stand the hypocrisy.
— PATTY CROWLEY

The roster of the Pontifical Birth Control Commission dwindles each year. Many of the lay members, including André Hellegers, John Cavanagh, Donald Barrett, Colin Clark, and Patrick Crowley, have passed away. So also have some of the leading clerical members, including Henri de Riedmatten, Stanislas de Lestapis, and Joseph Reuss. Others are well into their retirement years and prefer not to think about what happened so long ago. Not everyone.

Dr. John Marshall, in his seventies and semi-retired, lives with his wife in a suburb of London and volunteers his services with a British organization seeking a cure for epilepsy. After the Commission disbanded, he did no more research on the rhythm method but remained involved with the Catholic Marriage Advisory Council and is on good terms with clergy and hierarchy. Though he has avoided strident criticism, Marshall has always been candid when asked his views. "What happened shouldn't surprise anyone," he said. It's the way the Vatican runs, not like a democracy, more like a great bureaucracy. It's just the way things are — unfortunately."

In a lengthy article for the *Tablet* newspaper on the twenty-fifth anniversary of *Humanae Vitae*, Marshall wrote about the encyclical's fallout: "People formed moral judgments that the teaching was wrong and that they could practise contraception and remain in full communion with the Church. A number of surveys have shown that this is precisely how many Catholics have reacted. None of this was achieved without great anguish...which for many of the older generation still persists. This could have been avoided had the Pope listened to his commission rather than to the Curia."[1]

Thomas Burch, in his early sixties, lives in London, Ontario, and has been teaching sociology and demography at the University of Western Ontario since 1975. Scarred by his experience on the Commission, Burch left Georgetown University in 1970 to work with the Population Council in New York City. "I didn't want to work in Catholic education any more," he said. "I didn't want my career connected to the Church." He and André Hellegers conducted a study on the attitude of parish priests toward contraception in several countries; it revealed that in the United States less than half the priests considered contraception a mortal sin, while in Holland less than 1 percent considered it mortal. Burch divorced and remarried in the 1970s and has no relation with Catholicism. He considers himself an agnostic. "I have no interest whatsoever in an organized, authoritarian religion," he said.

Doctor Laurent and Colette Potvin, both in their seventies and in semi-retirement in Quebec, said their faith was not affected by what occurred in the 1960s. "No, no," said Laurent, "we always used our own good judgment in these matters." Both, however, deplored the outcome of the Commission's effort. "The Church lost an opportunity to teach some fundamental truths about generosity, the regulation of births, and the gift of love between spouses," said Laurent. "Now all we hear about is that such-and-such a technique is forbidden." The majority of the young don't go to Church or care what it says." He has not spoken out because, he admitted, "I'm not a fighter — maybe a bit of a coward on these things." Added Colette, "It will take a long time for the Church to regain the people's confidence — fifty years, maybe many more. I don't know; it's very sad."

Mercedes Concepción, in her mid-sixties, now retired from the University of the Philippines, remains active in demographic research. She never married, thus "solving the population problem my own way," she said. Concepción finds the aggressive opposition of the Church to all forms of birth regulation in the Philippine Islands "unenlightened." Surveys, she said, show 40 percent of women practicing contraception, yet the population, now at sixty-seven million, continues to spiral. If Church leaders were serious about the problem, they would at least promote natural family planning programs along with their strident disapproval of contraception, she said; but as it is, rhythm counseling is largely ignored by the Church. Her Catholic faith has remained intact through all this, she said: "I have faith and hope. There is always room for enlightenment."

The Hard Years

When Pat and Patty returned from the Commission in 1966, they shared their enthusiasm with their mentor, Monsignor Hillenbrand. But he said only, "We'll wait and see what the Pope says." After that, said Patty, Hillenbrand avoided further contact with them. In fact, it seemed to Patty that their participation in the Commission set up a kind of wall of estrangement between them and the many priests with whom they had formerly maintained warm relations.

While waiting for the Pope's decision, the Crowleys, with a grant from the Rockefeller Foundation, made plans for an international forum on the Christian Family in the World to be held in Italy in the summer of 1968. A list of important speakers from a variety of countries agreed to attend. Then in the late spring some of the most prominent, including Cardinal Suenens and Bishop Reuss, withdrew their acceptance, and the meeting was postponed. When *Humanae Vitae* was released in July, the Crowleys realized these churchmen had seen it coming and had been apparently reluctant to share their feelings at that time. The conference did take place that November at a chateau in France owned by the Little Brothers of the Poor. Commission members André Hellegers, Albert Görres, and Pierre de Locht, along with adviser John Noonan, were among the speakers.

In his talk, De Locht hoped the encyclical would stimulate a crisis of growth, not rancor. "The unity of the Church does not consist in a bland conformity in all ideas, but rather in submission to God's will and a humble but honest and ongoing search for truth," he said, quoting the statement of the Canadian bishops on *Humanae Vitae*. "This, said de Locht, "Is a call for a new type of unity, more demanding and probably more true — a concrete test of our capacity for ecumenism. How can we accept our brothers in other churches with all that distinguishes them (including their different views on contraceptives) when we are tempted to suppress the differences within our own community?"[2]

As it turned out, *Humanae Vitae* was only one of many shocks of 1968, and they all left Patty reeling: the assassination of Dr. Martin Luther King, the looting and burning that followed, the murder of Bobby Kennedy, the defeat of the Crowleys' candidate, Eugene McCarthy, at the Democratic Convention, and the police riot that accompanied the convention. Pat and Patty spent the day after the riot bailing McCarthy supporters out of the lockup at Chicago's central police headquarters. In some of the most critical sectors of life, it seemed, the wheels of progress had suddenly started moving backward.

Then in the early 1970s came the decline of the Christian Family Movement. Dissatisfaction had already shown itself in some places due to CFM's concern with "worldly" issues like race relations, politics, and international affairs. Convinced that the organization needed new leadership at the top, the Crowleys resigned as president couple (after twenty years in that position) and agreed to head the International Confederation of Christian Family Movements (ICCFM), essentially a clearing house for news and developments in CFM groups on various continents. Also in the early 1970s, CFM decided to become ecumenical, extending its programs to Protestant and Episcopal churches, thereby offending some of its veteran members, bishops, and chaplains. CFM also agreed to sponsor the Marriage Encounter movement in the United States, which, unlike CFM, had no social justice component. The new movement quickly flourished, siphoning off a sizable number of CFM leaders. Studies showed that CFM had been a powerful formative force for many years but appeared to be running out of steam: it was losing between a quarter and a third of its members every year, income was down, and only a tiny percentage of new couples were under twenty-five.

In the view of the Crowleys, the slump reflected the loss of idealism and the self-absorption that would characterize the next quarter century: John Kennedy giving way to Richard Nixon, Martin Luther King yielding to Louis Farrakhan, Pope John falling to John Paul II. *Humanae Vitae* was an integral part of all that. CFM has never recovered from the slump, subsisting in diminished form, and, under new leadership, placing great emphasis on unquestioning loyalty to the Church as conceived by John Paul II. Some CFM leaders blamed the movement's decline on the Crowleys' refusal to accept *Humanae Vitae*, but Patty argued that disillusionment with the Church after the encyclical drove far more couples out of CFM than anything she and Pat said. "I get frustrated when I see what's happened to CFM," said Patty. "I don't much like it."

A Change of Seasons

Then came the cruelest blow for Patty. In 1971 Pat was diagnosed with an illness rare among males, cancer of the breast, and he underwent surgery. He recovered for a time, and the Crowleys traveled widely on behalf of ICCFM. But in 1973 he was operated on again and the doctor suggested he put his affairs in order. "It hit me in the bottom of my heart," said Patty. "We had always been like one person."

Pat's strength was gradually diminishing, though he was able to organize and coordinate a joyous international conference in Tanzania in 1974 with a grant from the United Nations Fund for Population Activities. It was called Familia '74, co-sponsored by the World Council of Churches, and it celebrated the richness of family life around the world. On the way back, he and Patty spent a few days in London. That was the first time they had been alone, free of meetings or other business, since the start of CFM, said Patty — and it was to be the last time. Patrick Crowley died peacefully in his own home on November 20, 1974, at the age of sixty-two.

Patty declined a quiet widowhood. She continued with ICCFM for a few years, then found herself on the board of directors of many organizations dealing with social problems, minority rights, and women's issues. One was the board of the Chicago Housing Authority, which oversees the living accommodations for some two hundred thousand low-income citizens. Appointed by Mayor Harold Washington, Patty was dismissed three years later by Washington's successor when she protested the city's overruling of a majority decision by the board on hiring a new manager. "It was like the Birth Control Commission all over again," she said.

In the mid-1980s she resigned from many of the other boards because "all they do is talk and I wanted to *do* something." She and four other women conceived Deborah's Place, a shelter for women who are homeless on Chicago's near north side, and named it after a strong woman of the Old Testament. Getting it started and keeping it going required numberless calls and contacts — the kind of organizing skills she acquired in the CFM days, and she was glad she still had them.

The frustration of *Humanae Vitae* still hovered over her. "I guess I'm a little bitter," she said. No priest ever talked to me about *Humanae Vitae*. No one ever discussed what we had done or why it turned out the way it did. No one asked how we felt. We never even got a letter of thanks from the Vatican."

In 1984 when Chicago Cardinal Joseph Bernardin asked all those who had been embittered or offended by the Church in any way to send him a letter, she did. She wrote about the hard times after the encyclical was published and the silence of the clergy. "If Pat and I hadn't had each other, we could never have made it through this period," she said. "The Church was not right to publish this document. It would have been better for the Church to be silent than not to listen to the Commission it had appointed. Couples cried out for help.... Almost all are now using their own consciences on birth control. Look at the small families. Who is kidding whom?" Bernardin replied in a letter that he was not involved in the Commission's proceedings or the Pope's decision; he offered no personal comment on either. "I have deep respect for you and I greatly admire the faith that is yours and was Pat's," he said.

The Long View

Patty Crowley lives on the eighty-eighth floor of the John Hancock building in Chicago, one of the tallest in the world. This is where she has lived since 1969. The view from her three-bedroom apartment is stunning: Lake Michigan to the east, the city and suburbs to the north stretching as far as the eye can see. But she does not spend much time looking out the window. The hallway of the apartment is a veritable gallery of old photos: Pat and Patty at CFM conventions at home and abroad, Pat and Patty with important dignitaries of Church and state, Pat and Patty with their children and foster children and scores of foreign visitors. She doesn't spend a lot of time looking at the pictures either. In her early eighties, Patty Crowley is too busy.

"You cannot live your life backward," she said. "You've got to get out of the old phase and get on with the new phase. Otherwise you'll be miserable." Her new phase is still multifaceted.

She is an active volunteer at Deborah's Place, which has expanded to include a day shelter and a transitional living center. The operation has no religious affiliation but deep religious roots. "Pat and I always appreciated the Benedictine spirit," said Patty, "the idea of making people feel welcome, extending hospitality and serving a good meal without asking a lot of questions. That's what Deborah's Place does; there's a marvelous feeling there." Her oldest daughter, Patsy, a Benedictine sister, is the director.

Patty Crowley is the sole coordinator of a group of some fifty mostly

older, mostly single women who gather in her apartment monthly for
"conscience-raising" sessions. She provides a speaker on subjects ranging from foreign affairs to Christian art, from mental retardation to
Scripture study. This has been going on for twenty years, ever since
Pat died. Patty personally cooks dinner ("meat loaf or chicken, nothing
fancy") for all the guests. "It's a way to keep your mind open," she said.
"When you're alone you need that."

She is a board member of HOME (Housing Opportunities and
Maintenance for the Elderly), which manages intergenerational apartments where young and old residents assist each other. As a board
member, Patty helped HOME develop a program for volunteers, herself
included, to clean the apartments of elderly public housing residents.

Every Sunday afternoon, Patty and her daughter Patsy "go to jail" —
to the federal correctional center in Chicago to visit the women held
there. They supply yarn and plastic needles (the only kind allowed) so
the women can crochet scarves and bedspreads or clothing for their
children. "It's not a religious thing," said Patty. "We go to put some
variety in the lives of these women who have nothing to do." Lately, at
the inmates' request, she has been the organizer of bingo games.

She works three or four hours most days in the twenty-five-year-old
Space Travel agency she and Pat started, now operated by her daughter
Cathy. The office is in the Hancock building, so commuting is not a
problem. "I do what I can," she said, "pay bills, answer phones."

At her parish, Holy Name Cathedral, Patty is a Scripture reader at
Sunday Mass, a weekly minister of communion to patients at Northwestern Hospital, and a member of the Human Concerns Commission
and the Peace and Justice Committee. But the experience of the Commission and the disappointment of *Humanae Vitae* changed her attitude
toward the Church. She and Pat had thrown so much of themselves
into creating through the Christian Family Movement a more respon-
sive Catholic Church, open to all its members, open to the world —
and then this!

Remaining in the Church, she said, was a struggle for a while, but
added, "It's my Church; no one's going to kick me out." Meanwhile,
she has supported organizations trying to move the Church in the
direction of reform: the Women's Ordination Conference, Call to Action, the National Assembly of Religious Women, the Association for
the Rights of Catholics in the Church.

What bothers her most is the deeply entrenched double standard
at the Church's institutional level. "I just can't stand the hypocrisy,"

she said. However, she finds it hard to avoid. She sees it in the clergy who rant against abortion, yet never share their own views about contraception. She sees it in bishops who allow a mistake to perdure for generations rather than jeopardize their own lofty positions by honestly confronting higher authority. She sees it in official pronouncements that assume lay Catholics understand and accept the official doctrine on birth control when in fact they neither understand nor accept. Saying what you mean and doing it has always been very basic with Patty Crowley. This absence of integrity, this little secret that no one can talk about, frustrates her and probably always will.

What If?

In the end, Patty Crowley and other Commission veterans are left with questions that are as intriguing as they are unanswerable. Perhaps the most interesting is, what if?...

• What if Pope Paul VI had attended the Commission meetings, sat in the background and just listened, like all CFM chaplains were required to do? What if this man seemingly so open to the spirit of his predecessor had heard the arguments of the theologians, the findings of the scientists, and the insights of married people struggling with a doctrine that affects their most intimate moment? Instead, the Pope stayed in the Vatican, relying on second-hand accounts, abstract reports, and the concrete presence of Holy Office officials who resented the Commission's very existence.

• What if Archbishop Karol Wojtyla of Krakow had attended the Commission's last meeting in response to the Pope's invitation? What if he, who wrote so enthusiastically about the personalist aspects of marriage and who regarded the sexual union as uniquely holy, had heard the testimony of couples struggling with a doctrine that seemed irrational and contradictory? Wojtyla was only forty-six at the time, his experience limited to the hothouse Church surviving in communist Poland; there was time for him to grow. Instead, he chose to remain in Poland, the only bishop to decline the invitation.

• What if Paul on becoming Pope had dissolved the Commission and turned the matter of birth control over to the Second Vatican Council? Given the strong voices among the bishops pushing for change and the strong voices upholding the old doctrine, the debate would have been intense. But it would have been waged publicly via media coverage. The public education potential would have been enormous. Instead, the whole matter was confined to a group that met in virtual secrecy and was told to share its advice with the Pope and no one else.

• What if Father Ford, Cardinal Ottaviani, and the other minority members had decided to abide by the rules of the Commission, which had agreed to submit one report of its findings? What if they had placed their opposing papers with all the other background reports for the Pope's eventual consideration and trusted in the guidance of the Spirit? Instead, they were on the papal doorstep scarcely before the ink dried. They were there to warn and threaten and plead; unlike the rest of the Commission members, the insiders would not go away.

• What if Paul VI had accepted the Commission's Majority Report? What if he had issued an encyclical reflecting its major points: the sacredness of marriage, the dignity of sex, the importance of openness and generosity — and the recognition that there can be circumstances where a couple in good faith may join in sexual union without opening that particular union to procreation? That would surely not have brought peace. It would, in fact, have opened a Pandora's box of old fears and antagonisms and new distinctions and questions about which kinds of contraceptives are permitted and which aren't. But at least the Church would have been perceived as struggling with a deep human issue instead of shutting it up.

• What if the Pope had said, "I don't have the answer; the Church is in doubt; until we have better information, everyone will have to follow their own conscience!"? Would the world have ended? Would sexual license have overwhelmed the civilized world? Or would Catholics (and others) have respected this ancient institution for making such a refreshing admission? At the very least the Church on this issue would not be open to the charge of hypocrisy, of pretending to have answers when it doesn't.

• There remains one other perplexing question: Where was the Holy Spirit in all this? With the Commission in its decision? Or with Pope Paul and his coterie of advisers? No clear answer is possible here either. The Spirit blows where she wills. All that can be concluded, on the basis of what happened between 1963 and 1968, is that if the Holy Spirit was the inspiration of *Humanae Vitae*, then the Spirit in that case worked in and through a small minority who fervently believed the old way was the only way, who operated in nearly total secrecy, who denied the witness of the faithful could have any connection with theology, who bypassed the intent of the Committee they served on, and who achieved their goal in the end by playing on the fears and hesitancies of the Holy Father.

The answers, it appears, will be a long time coming.

"Responsible Parenthood"

Majority Report of the Birth Control Commission

This document represents the culmination of the work of the Papal Birth Control Commission. Its authors are the Rev. Joseph Fuchs, German Jesuit teaching at the Gregorian University in Rome; the Rev. Raymond Sigmond, Hungarian Dominican, president of the Institute of Social Science of the Pontifical University of St. Thomas Aquinas; the Rev. Paul Anciaux, professor at the major seminary of Malines-Brussels, Belgium; the Rev. A. Auer, specialist in sexual questions, Würzburg, Germany; the Rev. Michel Labourdette, O.P., theologian from Toulouse, France; and the Rev. Pierre de Locht of the National Family Pastoral Center, Brussels. Thirteen other theologians and several experts from other fields also signed the document. The report's final wording was worked out in the Commission's last plenary meeting, held June 4–9, 1966. Its Latin title is: "Schema Documenti de Responsabili Paternitate": "Schema for a Document on Responsible Parenthood." This translation first appeared in English in the National Catholic Reporter, *April 19, 1967.*

Introduction

The *Pastoral Constitution on the Church in the Modern World* (*Gaudium et Spes*) has not explained the question of responsible parenthood under all its aspects. To those problems as yet unresolved, a response is to be given in what follows. This response, however, can only be understood if it is grasped in an integrated way within the universal concept of salvation history.

In creating the world God gave man the power and the duty to form the world in spirit and freedom and, through his creative capacity, to actuate his own personal nature. In his Word, God himself, as the first efficient cause of the whole evolution of the world and of man, is present and active in history. The story of God and of man, therefore, should be seen as a shared work. And it should be seen that man's tremendous progress in control of matter by technical means, and the universal and total "intercommunication" that has been achieved, correspond perfectly to the divine decrees (cf. *Pastoral Constitution on the Church in the Modern World* 1, c. 3).

In the fullness of time the Word of the eternal Father entered into history and took his place within it, so that by his work humanity and the world might become sharers in salvation. After his ascension to the Father, the Lord continues to accomplish his work through the Church. As God became man, so his Church is really incarnate in the world. But because the world, to which the Church ought to represent the mystery of Christ, always undergoes changes, the Church itself necessarily and continually is in pilgrimage. Its essence and fundamental structures remain immutable always; and yet no one can say of the Church that at any time it is sufficiently understood or bounded by definition (cf. Paul VI in *Ecclesiam Suam* and in his opening speech to the second session of Vatican Council II).

The Church was constituted in the course of time by Christ, its principle of origin is the Word of creation and salvation. For this reason the Church draws understanding of its own mystery not only from the past, but, standing in the present time and looking to the future, assumes within itself, the whole progress of the human race. The Church is always being made more sure of this. What John XXIII wished to express by the word "aggiornamento," Paul VI took up, using the phrase, "dialogue with the world" and in his encyclical *Ecclesiam Suam* has the following: "The world cannot be saved from the outside. As the Word of God became man, so must a man to a certain degree identify with the forms of life of those to whom he wishes to bring the message of Christ. Without invoking privileges which would but widen the separation, without employing unintelligible terminology, he must share the common way of life — provided that it is human and honorable — especially of the most humble, if he wishes to be listened to and understood" (par. 87).

In response to the many problems posed by the changes occurring today in almost every field, the Church in Vatican Council II has entered into the way of dialogue. "The Church guards the heritage of God's Word and draws from it religious and moral principles, without always having at hand the solution to particular problems. She desires thereby to add the light of revealed truth to mankind's store of experience, so that the path which humanity has taken in recent times will not be a dark one" (*Pastoral Constitution on the Church in the Modern World*, I, c. 3, par. 33).

In fulfillment of its mission the Church must propose obligatory norms of human and Christian life from the deposit of faith in an open dialogue with the world. But since moral obligations can never be detailed in all their concrete particularities, the personal responsibility of each individual must always be called into play. This is even clearer today because of the complexity of modern life: the concrete moral norms to be followed must not be pushed to an extreme.

In the present study, dealing with problems relating to responsible parenthood, the Holy Father through his ready willingness to enter into dialogue has given it an importance unprecedented in history. After several years of study, a Commission of experts called together by him, made up for the most part of laymen from various fields of competency, has prepared material for him, which was lastly examined by a special group of bishops.

Part 1: Fundamental Principles

Chapter I: The Fundamental Values of Marriage

"The well-being of the individual person and of human and Christian society is intimately linked with the healthy condition of that community produced by marriage and family. Hence Christians and all men who hold this community in high esteem sincerely rejoice in the various ways by which men today find help in fostering this community of love and perfecting its life, and by which spouses and parents are assisted in their lofty calling. Those who rejoice in such aid look for additional benefits from them and labor to bring them about"(*Pastoral Constitution on the Church in the Modern World*, II, c. i, par. 47).

Over the course of centuries, the Church, with the authority conferred it by Christ our Lord, has constantly protected the dignity and essential values of this institution whose author is God himself who has made man to his image and raised him to share in his love. It has always taught this to its faithful and to all men. In our day it again intends to propose to those many families who are seeking a right way how they are able in the conditions of our times to live and develop fully the higher gifts of this community.

A couple [unio conjugum] ought to be considered above all a community of persons which has in itself the beginning of new human life. Therefore those things which strengthen and make more profound the union of persons within this community must never be separated from the procreative finality which specifies the conjugal community. Pius XI, in Casti Connubii already, referring to the tradition expressed in the Roman Catechism, said: "This mutual inward molding of a husband and wife, this determined effort to perfect each other, can in a very real sense be said to be the chief reason and purpose of matrimony, provided matrimony be looked at not in the restricted sense as instituted for the proper conception and education of the child, but more widely as the blending of life as a whole and the mutual interchange and sharing thereof" (AAS, XXII, 1930, p. 547).

But conjugal love, without which marriage would not be a true union of persons, is not exhausted in the simple mutual giving in which one party seeks only the other. Married people know well that they are only able to perfect each other and establish a true community if their love does not end in a merely egotistic union but according to the condition of each is made truly fruitful in the creation of new life. Nor on the other hand can the procreation and education of a child be considered a truly human fruitfulness unless it is the result of a love existing in a family community. Conjugal love and fecundity are in no way opposed, but complement one another in such a way that they constitute an almost indivisible unity.

Unfolding the natural and divine law, the Church urges all men to be true dispensers of the divine gifts, to act in conformity with their own personal nature and to shape their married life according to the dictates of the natural and divine law. God created man male and female so that, joined together in the bonds of love, they might perfect one another through a mutual, corporal and spiritual giving and that they might carefully prepare their children, the fruit of this love, for a truly human life. Let them regard one another always as persons and not as mere objects. Therefore everything should be done in marriage so that the goods conferred on this institution can be attained as perfectly as possible and so that fidelity and moral rightness can be served.

Chapter II: Responsible Parenthood and the Regulation of Conception

To cultivate and realize all the essential values of marriage, married people should become ever more deeply aware of the profundity of their vocation and the breadth of their responsibilities. In this spirit and with this awareness let married people seek how they might better be "cooperators with the love of God and Creator and be, so to speak, the interpreters of that love" for the task of procreation and education (*Pastoral Constitution on the Church in the Modern World*, II, c. 1, par. 50).

1. *Responsible parenthood* — that is, generous and prudent parenthood — is a fundamental requirement of a married couple's true mission. Illumined by faith, the spouses understand the scope of their whole task; helped by divine grace, they try to fulfill it as a true service, carried out in the name of God and Christ, oriented to the temporal and eternal good of men. To save, protect and promote the good of the offspring, and thus of the family community and of human society, the married couple will take care to consider all values and seek to realize them harmoniously in the best way they can, with proper reverence toward each other as persons and according to the concrete circumstances of their life. They will make a judgment in conscience before God about the number of children to have and educate according to the objective criteria indicated by Vatican Council II (*Pastoral Constitution on the Church in the Modern World*, 11, c. 1, par. 50; c. 5, par. 80).

This responsible, generous and prudent parenthood always carries with it new demands. In today's situation both because of new difficulties and because of new possibilities for the education of children, couples are hardly able to meet such demands unless with generosity and sincere deliberation.

With a view to the education of children let couples more and more build the community of their whole life on a true and magnanimous love, under the guidance of the spirit of Christ (1 Cor. 12:31–13:13). For this stable community between man and woman, shaped by conjugal love, is the true foundation of human fruitfulness. This community between married people through which an individual finds himself by opening himself to another, constitutes the optimum situation in which children can be educated in an integrated way. Through developing their communion and intimacy in all its aspects, a married couple is able to provide that environment of love, mutual understanding and humble acceptance which is the necessary condition of authentic human education and maturation.

Responsible parenthood — through which married persons intend to observe and cultivate the essential values of matrimony with a view to the good of persons (the good of the child to be educated, of the couples themselves and of the whole of human society) — is one of the conditions and expressions of a true conjugal chastity. For genuine love, rooted in faith, hope and charity, ought to inform the whole life and every action of a couple. By the strength of this chastity the couple tend to the actuation of that true love precisely inasmuch as it is conjugal and fruitful. They accept generously and prudently their task with all its values, combining them in the best way possible according to the particular circumstances of their life and in spite of difficulties.

Married people know well that very often they are invited to keep abstinence, and sometimes not just for a brief time, because of the habitual conditions of their life, for example, the good of one of the spouses (physical or psychic well-being), or because of what are called professional necessities. This abstinence a chaste couple know and accept as a condition of progress into a deeper mutual love, fully conscious that the grace of Christ will sustain and strengthen them for this.

Seeing their vocation in all its depth and breadth and accepting it, the couple follows Christ and tries to imitate Him in a true evangelical spirit (Mt. 5:1–12). Comforted by the spirit of Christ according to the inner man and rooted in faith and charity (Eph. 3:16–17), they try to build up a total life community, "bearing with one another charitably, in complete selflessness, gentleness and patience" (Eph. 4:2–3; cf. Col. 3:12–17). They will have the peace of Christ in their hearts and give thanks to God the Father as his holy and elected sons.

A couple then is able to ask and expect that they will be helped by all in such a way that they are progressively able to approach more and more responsible parenthood. They need the help of all in order that they can fulfil their responsibilities with full liberty and in the most favorable material, psychological, cultural and spiritual conditions. By the development of the family, then, the whole society is built up with regard to the good of all men in the whole world.

2. The *regulation of conception* appears necessary for many couples who wish to achieve a responsible, open and reasonable parenthood in today's circumstances. If they are to observe and cultivate all the essential values of marriage, married people need decent and human

means for the regulation of conception. They should be able to expect the collaboration of all, especially from men of learning and science, in order that they can have at their disposal means agreeable and worthy of man in the fulfilling of his responsible parenthood.

It is proper to man, created to the image of God, to use what is given in physical nature in a way that he may develop it to its full significance with a view to the good of the whole person. This is the cultural mission which the Creator has commissioned to men, whom he has made his cooperators. According to the exigencies of human nature and with the progress of the sciences, men should discover means more and more apt and adequate so that the "ministry which must be fulfilled in a manner which is worthy of man" (*Pastoral Constitution on the Church in the Modern World*, 11, c. 1, par. 51) can be fulfilled by married people.

This intervention of man into physiological processes, an intervention ordained to the essential values of marriage and first of all to the good of children, is to be judged according to the fundamental principles and objective criteria of morality, which will be treated below (in Chap. 4).

"Marriage and conjugal love are by their nature ordained toward the begetting and educating of children" (*Pastoral Constitution on the Church in the Modern World*, II, c. 1, par. 50). A right ordering toward the good of the child within the conjugal and familial community pertains to the essence of human sexuality. Therefore the morality of sexual acts between married people takes its meaning first of all and specifically from the ordering of their actions in a fruitful married life, that is, one which is practiced with responsible, generous and prudent parenthood. It does not then depend upon the direct fecundity of each and every particular act. Moreover the morality of every marital act depends upon the requirements of mutual love in all its aspects. In a word, the morality of sexual actions is thus to be judged by the true exigencies of the nature of human sexuality, whose meaning is maintained and promoted especially by conjugal chastity as we have said above.

More and more clearly, for a conscience correctly formed, a willingness to raise a family with full acceptance of the various human and Christian responsibilities is altogether distinguished from a mentality and way of married life which in its totality is egoistically and irrationally opposed to fruitfulness. This truly "contraceptive" mentality and practice has been condemned by the traditional doctrine of the Church and will always be condemned as gravely sinful.

Chapter III: On the Continuity of Doctrine and Its Deeper Understanding

The tradition of the Church which is concerned with the morality of conjugal relations began with the beginning of the Church. It should be observed, however, that the tradition developed in the argument and conflict with heretics such as the Gnostics, the Manicheans and later the Cathari, all of whom condemned procreation or the transmission of life as something evil, and nonetheless indulged in moral vices. Consequently this tradition always, albeit with various words, intended to protect two fundamental values: the good of procreation and the rectitude of marital intercourse. Moreover the Church always taught another truth equally fundamental, although hidden in a mystery, namely, original sin. This had wounded man in his various faculties, including sexuality. Man could only be healed of this wound by the grace of a Saviour. This is one of the reasons why Christ took marriage and raised it to a sacrament of the New Law.

It is not surprising that in the course of centuries this tradition was always interpreted in expressions and formulas proper to the times and that the words with which it was expressed and the reasons on which it was based were changed by knowledge which is now obsolete. Nor was there maintained always a right equilibrium of all the elements. Some authors even used expressions which depreciated the matrimonial state. But what is of real importance is that the same values were again and again reaffirmed. Consequently an egotistical, hedonistic and contraceptive way which turns the practice of married life in an arbitrary fashion from its ordination to a human, generous and prudent fecundity is always against the nature of man and can never be justified.

The large amount of knowledge and facts which throw light on today's world suggest that it is not to contradict the genuine sense of this tradition and the purpose of the previous doctrinal condemnations if we speak of the regulation of conception by using means, human and decent, ordered to favoring fecundity in the totality of married life and toward the realization of the authentic values of a fruitful matrimonial community.

The reasons in favor of this affirmation are of several kinds: social changes in matrimony and the family, especially in the role of the woman; lowering of the infant mortality rate; new bodies of knowledge in biology, psychology, sexuality and demography; a changed estimation of the value and meaning of human sexuality and of conjugal relations; most of all, a better grasp of the duty of man to humanize and to bring to greater perfection for the life of man what is given in nature. Then must be considered the sense of the faithful: according to it, condemnation of a couple to a long and often heroic abstinence as the means to regulate conception, cannot be founded on the truth.

A further step in the doctrinal evolution, which it seems now should be developed, is founded less on these facts than on a better, deeper and more correct understanding of conjugal life and of the conjugal act when these other changes occur. The doctrine on marriage and its essential values remains the same and whole, but it is now applied differently out of a deeper understanding.

This maturation has been prepared and has already begun. The magisterium itself is in evolution. Leo XIII spoke less explicitly in his encyclical *Arcanum* than did Pius XI in his wonderful doctrinal synthesis of *Casti Connubii* of 1930, which gave a fresh start to so many beginnings in a living conjugal spirituality. He proclaimed, using the very words of the Roman Catechism, the importance, in a true sense the primary importance, of true conjugal love for the community of matrimony. The notion of responsible parenthood which is implied in the notion of a prudent and generous regulation of conception, advanced in Vatican Council II, had already been prepared by Pius XII. The acceptance of a lawful application of the calculated sterile periods of the woman — that the application is legitimate presupposes right motives — makes a separation between the sexual act which is explicitly intended and its reproductive effect which is intentionally excluded.

The tradition has always rejected seeking this separation with a contraceptive intention for motives spoiled by egoism and hedonism, and such seeking can never be admitted. The true opposition is not to be sought between some material conformity to the physiological processes of nature and some artificial intervention. For it is natural to man to use his skill in order to put under human control of what is given by physical nature. The opposition is really to be sought between one way of acting which is contraceptive and opposed to a prudent and generous fruitfulness, and another way which is in an ordered relationship to responsible fruitfulness and which has a concern for education and all the essential, human and Christian values.

In such a conception the substance of tradition stands in continuity and is respected. The new elements which today are discerned in tradition under the influence of new knowledge and facts were found in it before; they were undifferentiated but not denied; so that the problem in today's terms is new and has not been proposed before in this way. In light of the new data these elements are being explained and made more precise. The moral obligation of following fundamental norms and fostering all the essential values in a balanced fashion is strengthened and not weakened. The virtue of chastity by which a couple positively regulates the practice of sexual relations is all the more demanded. The criteria of morality therefore which are human and Christian demand and at the same time foster a spirituality which is more profound in married life, with faith, hope and charity informed according to the spirit of the Gospel.

Chapter IV: The Objective Criteria of Morality

The question comes up which many men rightly think to be of great importance, at least practically: what are the objective criteria by which to choose a method of reconciling the needs of marital life with a right ordering of this life to fruitfulness in the procreation and education of offspring?

It is obvious that the method is not to be left to purely arbitrary decision.

1. In resolving the similar problem of responsible parenthood and the appropriate determination of the size of the family, Vatican Council II has shown the way. The objective criteria are the various values and needs duly and harmoniously evaluated. These objective criteria are to be applied by the couples, acting from a rightly formed conscience and according to their concrete situation. In the words of the Council: "Thus they will fulfill their task with human and Christian responsibility. With docile reverence toward God, they will come to the right decision by common counsel and effort. They will thoughtfully take into account both their own welfare and that of their children, those already born and those which may be foreseen. For this accounting they will reckon with both the material and spiritual conditions of the times as well as of their state in life. Finally they will consult the interests of the family community, of temporal society, and of the Church herself.... But in their manner of acting, spouses should be aware that they cannot proceed arbitrarily. They must always be governed according to a conscience dutifully conformed to the Divine Law itself, and should be submissive toward the Church's teaching office,

which authentically interprets that law in the light of the Gospel" (*Pastoral Constitution on the Church in the Modern World*, II, c. 1, par. 50; cf. c. 5, par. 87).

In other questions of conjugal life, one should proceed in the same way. There are various objective criteria which are concretely applied by couples themselves acting with a rightly formed conscience. All, for an example, know that objective criteria prohibit that the intimate acts of conjugal life, even if carried out in a way which could be called "natural," be practiced if there is a loss of physical or psychic health or if there is neglect of the personal dignity of the spouses or if they are carried out in an egoistic or hedonistic way. These objective criteria are the couples', to be applied by them to their concrete situation, avoiding pure arbitrariness in forming their judgment. It is impossible to determine exhaustively by a general judgment and ahead of time for each individual case what these objective criteria will demand in the concrete situation of a couple.

2. Likewise, there are objective criteria as to the means to be chosen of responsibly determining the size of the family: if they are rightly applied, the couples themselves will find and determine the way of proceeding.

In grave language, Vatican Council II has reaffirmed that abortion is altogether to be excluded from the means of responsibly preventing birth. Indeed, abortion is not a method of preventing conception but of eliminating offspring already conceived. This affirmation about acts which do not spare an offspring already conceived is to be repeated in regard to those interventions as to which there is serious grounds to suspect that they are abortive.

Sterilization, since it is a drastic and irreversible intervention in a matter of great importance, is generally to be excluded as a means of responsibly avoiding conceptions.

Moreover, the natural law and reason illuminated by Christian faith dictate that a couple proceed in choosing means not arbitrarily but according to objective criteria. These objective criteria for the right choice of methods are the conditions for keeping and fostering the essential values of marriage as a community of fruitful love. If these criteria are observed, then a right ordering of the human act according to its object, end and circumstances is maintained.

Among these criteria, this must be put first: the action must correspond to the nature of the person and of his acts so that the whole meaning of the mutual giving and of human procreation is kept in a context of true love (cf. *Pastoral Constitution on the Church in the Modern World*, II, c. 1, par. 51). Secondly, the means which are chosen should have an effectiveness proportionate to the degree of right or necessity of averting a new conception temporarily or permanently. Thirdly, every method of preventing conception — not excluding either periodic or absolute abstinence — carries with it some negative element or physical evil which the couple more or less seriously feels. This negative element or physical evil can arise under different aspects: account must be taken of the biological, hygienic, and psychological aspects, the personal dignity of the spouses, and the possibility of expressing sufficiently and aptly the interpersonal relation or conjugal love. The means to be chosen, where several are possible, is that which carries with it the least possible negative element, according to the concrete situation of the couple. Fourthly, then, in choosing concretely among means, much depends on what means may be available in a certain region or at a certain time or for a certain couple; and this may depend on the economic situation.

Therefore not arbitrarily, but as the law of nature and of God commands, let couples form a judgment which is objectively founded, with all the criteria considered. This they may do without major difficulty, and with peace of mind, if they take common and prudent counsel before God. They should, however, to the extent possible, be instructed about the criteria by competent persons and be educated as to the right application of the criteria. Well instructed, and prudently educated as Christians, they will prudently and serenely decide what is truly for the good of the couple and of the children, and does not neglect their own personal Christian perfection, and is, therefore, what God revealing himself through the natural law and Christian revelation, sets before them to do.

Part II: Pastoral Necessities

Chapter I: The Task and Fundamental Conditions of Educational Renewal

When sometimes a new aspect of human life obtains a special place in the area of man's responsibility, a task of educational renewal is imposed in a seriously binding way.

In order that spouses may take up the duty of responsible parenthood, they must grasp, more than in the past, the meaning of fruitfulness and experience a desire for it. In order that they may give to married life its unitive value, and do so in service of its procreative function, they must develop an increasingly purer respect for their mutual needs, the sense of community and the acceptance of their common Christian vocation.

It will not be a surprise that this conviction of a greater responsibility will come about as the effect and crown of a gradual development of the meaning of marriage and conjugal spirituality. For several generations, in an always increasing number, couples have sought to live their proper married vocation in a more profound and more conscientious way. The doctrine of the magisterium and especially the encyclical *Casti Connubii* notably contributed and strengthened this formation of conscience by giving to it its full meaning.

The more urgent the appeal is made to observe mutual love and charity in every expression of married life, the more urgent is the necessity of forming consciences, of educating spouses to a sense of responsibility and of awakening a right sense of values. This new step in the development of conjugal life cannot bear all its fruits, unless it is accompanied by an immense educational activity. No one will regret that these new demands stirred by the Holy Spirit call the entire human race to this profound moral maturity.

Couples who might think they find in the doctrine as it has just been proposed an open door to laxism or easy solutions make a grave mistake, of which they will be the first victims. The conscientious decision to be made by spouses about the number of children is not a matter of small importance. On the contrary it imposes a more conscientious fulfilling of their vocation to fruitfulness in the consideration of a whole complex of values which are involved here. The same is true of the responsibility of the spouses for the development of their common life in such a way that it will be a source of continual progress and perfection.

The God who created man male and female, in order that they might be two in one flesh, in order that they might bring the world under their control, in order that they might increase and multiply (Gen. 1–2), is the God who has elevated their union to the dignity of a sacrament and so disposed that in this world it is a special sign of His own love for His people. He Himself will gird the spouses with His strength, His light, His love and His joy in the strength of the spirit of Christ. Who then would doubt that couples, all couples, will not be able to respond to the demands of their vocation?

Chapter II: Further Consideration; Application of the Doctrine of Matrimony to Different Parts of the World

1. It seems very necessary to establish some pontifical institute or secretariat for the study of the sciences connected with married life. In this commission there could be continual collaboration in open dialogue among experts competent in various areas. The aim of this institute (or secretariat) would be among other duties, to carry further the research and reflection begun by the commission. The various studies which the commission has already done could be made public. It would be in a special way for this institute to study how the doctrine of matrimony should be applied to different parts of the world and to contribute to the formation of priests and married couples dedicated to the family apostolate by sending experts to them (cf. *Pastoral Constitution on the Church in the Modern World*, II, c. 1, par. 52).

2. Universal principles and the essential values of matrimony and married life become actual in ways which partially differ according to different cultures and different mentalities. Consequently there is a special task for episcopal conferences to institute organizations for investigation and dialogue between families, between representatives of the different sciences and pastors of souls. They would also have the task of judging which may be in practice the more apt pastoral means in each region to promote the healthy formation of consciences and education to a sense of responsibility.

Episcopal conferences should be particularly concerned that priests and married lay persons be adequately formed in a more spiritual and moral understanding of Christian matrimony. Thus they will be prepared to extend pastoral action to the renewal of families in the spirit of "aggiornamento" initiated by the *Pastoral Constitution on the Church in the Modern World*.

Under their guidance there should also be action to start in each region the genuine fostering of all families in a context of social evolution which should be truly human. The fostering of the role of woman is of special importance here.

There are many reforms and initiatives which are needed to open the way to decent and joyful living for all families. Together with all men of goodwill, Christians must approach this great work of human development, without which the elevation of families can never become actual. Christianity does not teach some ideal for a small number of elect, but the vocation of all to the essential values of human life. It cannot be that anyone would wish to elevate his own family without at the same time actively dedicating himself to opening a way for similar elevation for all families in all parts of the world.

Chapter III: Demographic Fact and Policy

The increase of inhabitants cannot in any way be said to be something evil or calamitous for the human race. As children are "the most excellent gift of matrimony" (*Pastoral Constitution on the Church in the Modern World*, II, c. 1, par. 50) and the object of the loving care of the parents, which demands from them many sacrifices, so the great number of men pertaining to a certain nation and constituting the whole human race spread over the globe is the foundation of all social sharing and cultural progress. Thus there should be afforded to it all those things which according to social justice are due to men as persons.

The Church is not ignorant of the immense difficulties and profound transformations which have arisen from the conditions of contemporary life throughout the world and especially in certain regions where there has been a rapid rise in population. That is why she again and again raises her voice to urge various nations and the whole human family to help one another in truly human progress, united in true solidarity and excluding every intention of domination. Then they might avoid all those things both in the political and in the social order which restrict or dissipate in an egotistical way the full utilization of the goods of the earth which are destined for all men.

The Church by her doctrine and by her supernatural aids intends to help all families so that they might find the right way in undertaking their generous and prudent responsibility. Governments which have the care of the common good should look with great concern on subhuman conditions of families and "beware of solutions contradicting the moral law, solutions which have been promoted publicly or privately, and sometimes actually imposed" (*Pastoral Constitution on the Church in the Modern World*, II, c. 5, par. 87). These solutions have contradicted the moral law in particular by propagating abortion or sterilization. Political demography can be called human only if the rights of parents with regard to the procreation and education of children are respected and conditions of life are fostered with all vigor so that parents are enabled to exercise their responsibilities before God and society.

Chapter IV: The Inauguration and Further Development of Means for Education of Couples and Youth

1. Couples are burdened by multiple responsibilities throughout the whole of life; they seek light and aid. With the favor of God there will develop in many regions what has already been initiated often by the married couples themselves, to sustain families in their building and continual development.

Maximum help is to be given to parents in their educational task. They strongly desire to provide the best for their children. The more parents are conscious of their office of fruitfulness, which is extended over the whole time in which the education of their children is accomplished, so much the more do they seek a way of acquiring better preparation to carry out this responsibility. Moreover, in exercising this educational office, the spouses mature more deeply in it themselves, create a unity, become rich in love, and apply themselves with the high task of giving themselves with united energies to the high task of giving life and education.

2. The building up of the conjugal and family community does not happen without thought. Therefore it is fitting everywhere to set up and work out many better means of remote and immediate preparation of youth for marriage. This requires the collaboration of everyone. Married people who are already well educated will have a great and indispensable part in this work. In these tasks providing help to spouses and to the young who are preparing to build and develop a conjugal and family community, priests and religious will cooperate closely with the families. Without this cooperation, in which each one has his own indispensable part, there will never be apt methods of education to those responsibilities of the vocation which places the sacrament in clear light so that its full and profound meaning shines forth.

The Church, which holds the deposit of the Gospel, has to bring this noble message to all men in the entire world. This announcing of the Gospel, grounded in love, illumines every aspect of married and family life. Every aspect, every task and responsibility of the conjugal and family community shines with a clear light, in love toward one's neighbor — a love which is rich with human values and is formed by the divine interpersonal love of Father, Son and Holy Spirit. May the spirit of Christ's love more and more penetrate families everywhere so that together with John, the beloved disciple of Jesus, married couples, parents and children may always understand more deeply the wonderful relation between love of God and love of one another (1 John 4:7–5:4).

Members of the
Birth Control Commission

Original members at first meeting – 1963

Rev. Stanislas de Lestapis, S.J., sociologist, Paris, France
Dr. John Marshall, neurologist, London, England
Rev. Clement Mertens, S.J., demographer, Eegenhoven, Belgium
Rev. Henri de Riedmatten, O.P., diplomat, Geneva, Switzerland
Dr. Pierre von Rossum, internist, Brussels, Belgium
Prof. Jacques Mertens de Wilmars, economist, Louvain, Belgium

Additional members appointed for second meeting – 1964

Prof. Bernard Colombo, sociologist, Padua, Italy
Prof. Thomas Burch, demographer, Washington, D.C., United States
Rev. Joseph Fuchs, S.J., theologian, Rome, Italy
Rev. Bernard Häring, C.SS.R., theologian, Rome, Italy
Rev. Pierre de Locht, theologian, Brussels, Belgium
Rev. Jan Visser, C.SS.R., theologian, Rome, Italy
Rev. Marcelino Zalba, S.J., theologian, Rome, Italy

Additional members appointed for third meeting – 1964

Rev. Tullo Goffi, parish pastor, Brescia, Italy
Msgr. Ferdinando Lambruschini, theologian, Rome, Italy

Additional members appointed for fourth meeting – 1965

Rev. Paul Anciaux, seminary rector, Malines, Belgium

Rev. Alfons Auer, theologian, Würzburg, Germany

Prof. Donald Barrett, sociologist, Notre Dame, Ind., United States

Dr. J. R. Bartolus, psychiatrist, Paris, France

Most. Rev. Leo Binz, archbishop, St. Paul, Minn., United States

Dr. John Cavanagh, psychiatrist, Washington, D.C., United States

Prof. Colin Clark, economist, Oxford, England

Prof. Mercedes Concepción, demographer, Manila, Philippines

Mrs. Patricia Crowley, co-founder, Christian Family Movement, Wilmette, III., United States

Mr. Patrick Crowley, co-founder, Christian Family Movement, Wilmette, Ill., United States

Rev. Philip Delhaye, theologian, Namur, Belgium

Mr. Michael Dembélé, governmental administrator, Senegal, Africa

Prof. Manuel Diegues, sociologist, Rio de Janeiro, Brazil

Prof. Anthony Feanny, economist, Kingston, Jamaica

Dr. Jacques Ferin, gynecologist, Louvain, Belgium

Rev. John Ford, S.J., theologian, Washington, D.C., United States

Dr. Marcel Gaudefroy, gynecologist, Lille, France

Dr. Albert Görres, internist-psychologist, Frankfurt, Germany

Dr. André Hellegers, gynecologist, Baltimore, Md., United States

Msgr. George Kelly, diocesan administrator, New York, N.Y., United States

Mrs. J.F. Kulanday, governmental administrator, New Delhi, India

Rev. Michel Labourdette, O.P., theologian, Toulouse, France

Rev. Louis Lebret, sociologist, Paris, France

Msgr. George Lemaitre, scientist, Louvain, Belgium

Dr. Juan José López-Ibor, psychiatrist, Madrid, Spain

Msgr. Jean Margeot, diocesan administrator, Isle of Mauritius, France

Prof. Armand Mattelart, sociologist, Santiago, Chile

Prof. Andre van Melsen, philosopher, Nijmegen, Holland

Dr. Henri Moins, gynecologist, Tunis, Tunisia

Dr. Paul Moriguchi, psychiatrist, Tokyo, Japan

Rev. Giacomo Perico, S.J., Rome, Italy

Mrs. Colette Potvin, lay representative, Ottawa, Canada

Dr. Laurent Potvin, internist, Ottawa, Canada

Mr. Remy Rabary, diocesan administrator, Tananrive, Madagascar

Ambassador Jules Razafimbahiny, Indian diplomat, London, England

Dr. Charles Rendu, gynecologist, Paris, France

Mrs. Marie Rendu, lay representative, Paris, France

Most Rev. Joseph Reuss, bishop, Mainz, Germany

Prof. John Ryan, demographer, Bangalore, India

Rev. John Sasaki, demographer, Kobe, Japan
Rev. Raymond Sigmond, O.P., sociologist, Rome, Italy
Prof. Marcel Thibault, zoologist, Paris, France
Rev. Francesco Vito, university rector, Milan, Italy

Cardinals and bishops appointed as the official Commission members for the fifth and final meeting – 1966

Most Rev. Carlo Colombo, papal theologian, Rome, Italy
Most Rev. John Dearden, archbishop, Detroit, Mich., United States
His Eminence Julius Doepfner, archbishop, Munich, Germany
Most Rev. Claude Dupuy, archbishop, Albi, France
His Eminence Valerian Gracias, archbishop, Bombay, India
His Eminence John Heenan, archbishop, Westminster, England
His Eminence Joseph Lefebvre, archbishop, Bourges, France
Most Rev. Thomas Morris, archbishop, Tipperary, Ireland
His Eminence Alfredo Ottaviani, president of the Holy Office, Rome, Italy
His Eminence Lawrence Shehan, archbishop, Baltimore, Md., United States
His Eminence Leo Joseph Suenens, archbishop, Brussels, Belgium
Most Rev. José Rafael Pulido-Méndez, archbishop, Mérida, Venezuela
Most Rev. Karol Wojtyla, archbishop, Krakow, Poland (did not attend)
Most Rev. Jean Baptiste Zoa, archbishop, Cameroon
(Archbishop Binz and Bishop Reuss had been appointed to the Commission for the
    fourth meeting and continued as members of this select group.)

Notes

Chapter 2: The Doctrine

1. The quotations and citations in this chapter are from John T. Noonan, Jr., *Contraception: A History of Its Treatment by the Catholic Theologians and Canonists*, enlarged ed. (Cambridge: Harvard University Press, 1986).

Chapter 3: The Challenge

1. Cited in William H. Shannon, *The Lively Debate: Response to Humanae Vitae* (New York: Sheed & Ward, 1970), 6.

2. Cited in John T. Noonan, Jr., *Contraception: A History of Its Treatment by the Catholic Theologians and Canonists* enlarged ed. (Cambridge: Harvard University Press, 1986), 423.

3. Except where otherwise noted, the quotations in this section are from Noonan, *Contraception*, 492–98.

4. Cited in Shannon, *The Lively Debate*, 17–22.

5. Ibid.

6. Ibid., 8

7. Ibid.

8. Quotations from *Casti Connubii* are from *Social Wellsprings*, vol. 2 (Milwaukee: Bruce Publishing Co., 1942).

9. Gerald Kelly, "Notes on Moral Theology," *Theological Studies* 7 (1946).

10. Pius XII, "Apostolate of the Midwife," *Catholic Mind* (January 1952).

11. Cited in Noonan, *Contraception*, 518.

12. Ibid., 461.

13. John Rock, *The Time Has Come* (New York: Alfred A. Knopf, 1963), 149.

14. The citations that follow in this section are from Shannon, *The Lively Debate*, 48–50.

Chapter 4: The Awakening

1. Cited in Jay Dolan, *The American Catholic Experience* (New York: Doubleday, 1985), 37.
2. Dolan, *The American Catholic Experience,* 40.
3. John N. Kotre, *Simple Gifts: The Lives of Pat and Patty Crowley* (Kansas City: Andrews and McMeel, 1979), 13.
4. Ibid., 33.
5. The quotations in this section are from Kotre, *Simple Gifts,* 35–43.
6. Ibid., 55.
7. Ibid., 78.
8. Ibid., 64.
9. Ibid., 54.
10. Ibid., 68.

Chapter 5: The Commission Created: The First Meeting, 1963

1. Cited in John T. Noonan, *Contraception: A History of Its Treatment by the Catholic Theologians and Canonists,* enlarged ed. (Cambridge, Mass.: Harvard University Press, 1986), 522.
2. A full account of this meeting is in Peter Hebblethwaite, *Paul VI: The First Modern Pope* (New York: Paulist Press, 1993), 298–301.
3. Cited in Robert Blair Kaiser, *The Politics of Sex and Religion* (Kansas City: Leaven Press, 1985), 39.
4. The quotations in this section are from Kaiser, *The Politics of Sex and Religion,* 18–34.
5. William Bekkers, "Birth Control: Viewpoint of a European Bishop," ACT (June 1963).

Chapter 6: Confronting Fundamental Issues: The Second and Third Meetings, 1964

1. Cited in Robert Blair Kaiser, *The Politics of Sex and Religion* (Kansas City: Leaven Press, 1985), 43.
2. Cited in William H. Shannon, *The Lively Debate: Response to Humanae Vitae* (New York: Sheed & Ward, 1970), 57.
3. Cited in John T. Noonan, Jr., *Contraception: A History of Its Treatment by the Catholic Theologians and Canonists,* enlarged ed. (Cambridge, Mass.: Harvard University Press, 1986), 512.
4. Cited in Kaiser, *The Politics of Sex and Religion,* 49.
5. Kaiser, *The Politics of Sex and Religion,* 51.
6. Cited in "Bishops' Statement," *Catholic Herald,* May 8, 1964.
7. ACT (March 1964).
8. ACT (May 1964).
9. Kaiser, *The Politics of Sex and Religion,* 55.

Chapter 7: An Expanding Dialogue: The Council and Commission, 1964

1. Cited in Robert Blair Kaiser, *The Politics of Sex and Religion* (Kansas City: Leaven Press, 1985), 57.

2. Ibid., 62.

3. The quotations of the bishops in this section are from the *National Catholic Reporter,* November 11, 1964.

4. Cited in Philip Kaufman, *Why You Can Disagree and Remain a Faithful Catholic* (New York: Crossroad, 1991), 35.

5. Cited in Kaiser, *The Politics of Sex and Religion,* 67.

6. Kaufman, *Why You Can Disagree,* 35.

7. Cited in Rev. Ralph M. Wiltgen, S.V.D., *The Rhine Flows into the Tiber: The Unknown Council* (New York: Hawthorn Books, 1967), 269.

8. A full account of the NCCM television cancellation can be found in Kaiser, *The Politics of Sex and Religion,* 72–74.

Chapter 8: Seeking "Immediate Action": The Fourth Meeting, 1965

1. The quotations of Ford, Labourdette, and de Locht in this section are cited in Robert Blair Kaiser, *The Politics of Sex and Religion* (Kansas City: Leaven Press, 1985), 88–90.

2. Ibid., 88.

Chapter 9: Dodging the Bullet: The Council, 1965

1. Alberto Cavallari, *The Changing Vatican* (New York: Doubleday, 1967), 186–87.

2. Cited in Robert Blair Kaiser, *The Politics of Sex and Religion* (Kansas City: Leaven Press, 1985), 101.

3. Ibid., 104.

4. Cited in Xavier Rynne, *The Fourth Session: The Debates and Decrees of Vatican Council II* (New York: Farrar, Straus and Giroux, 1966), 215.

5. Cited in Peter Hebblethwaite, *Paul VI: The First Modern Pope* (New York: Paulist Press, 1993), 439.

6. *The Documents of Vatican II,* "Pastoral Constitution on the Church in the Modern World," para. 49 (New York: Guild Press, 1966), 252–54.

7. A full account of Ford's efforts is in Kaiser, *The Politics of Sex and Religion,* 114–22.

8. A full account of the *modi* affair is in Rynne, *The Fourth Session,* 211–20.

9. Ibid., 224.

Chapter 10: The Survey, 1965–66

1. Walter Imbiorski, "What We Should Ask Ourselves," *ACT* (July 1964).

2. *ACT* (August–October 1964).

3. The survey report and the letters and responses are in the Crowley collection in the archives of the University of Notre Dame.

Chapter 11: The Rise of the Laity: The Final Meeting I, 1966

1. The quotations of individual Commission members in this section are from Robert Blair Kaiser, *The Politics of Sex and Religion* (Kansas City: Leaven Press, 1985), 131–33.

2. The quotations of Görres, de Locht and Cavanagh in this section are cited in Kaiser, *The Politics of Sex and Religion*, 138–39.

3. William H. Shannon, *The Lively Debate: Response to Humanae Vitae* (New York: Sheed & Ward, 1970), 89.

4. Cited in Kaiser, *The Politics of Sex and Religion*, 40.

5. The quotations from de Lestapis, Perico, and van Melsen in this section are cited in Kaiser, *The Politics of Sex and Religion*, 142.

Chapter 12: Time for Some Decision: The Final Meeting II, 1966

1. Quotations from all three reports are from the *National Catholic Reporter*, April 19, 1967.

2. William H. Shannon, *The Lively Debate: Response to Humanae Vitae* (New York: Sheed & Ward, 1970), 103.

3. The quotations from Commission members in this section are cited in Robert Blair Kaiser, *The Politics of Sex and Religion* (Kansas City: Leaven Press, 1985), 147–54.

Chapter 13: The Verdict: The Final Meeting III, 1966

1. Cited in Robert Blair Kaiser, *The Politics of Sex and Religion* (Kansas City: Leaven Press, 1985), 160.

2. Except where otherwise noted, quotations of Commission members in this section are cited in ibid., 159–62.

3. Cited in Bernard Häring, *My Witness for the Church* (New York: Paulist Press, 1992), 74.

4. The quotations of Fuchs, Lefebvre, Pulido-Méndez, and Lambruschini in this section are cited in Kaiser, *The Politics of Sex and Religion*, 159–62.

5. Ford's speech and the quotations of Commission members in this and the following sections are cited in ibid., 163–73.

6. Ibid., 175.

7. Quoted in Daniel Callahan, ed., *The Catholic Case for Contraception* (London: Macmillan, 1969), 150–52.

Chapter 14: The Undoing of the Commission, 1966–68

1. Cited in Robert Blair Kaiser, *The Politics of Sex and Religion* (Kansas City: Leaven Press, 1985), 178.
2. *National Catholic Reporter*, July 16, 1966.
3. Bernard Häring, *My Witness for the Church* (New York: Paulist Press, 1992), 79.
4. Peter Hebblethwaite, *Paul VI: The First Modern Pope* (New York: Paulist Press, 1993), 470.
5. *National Catholic Reporter*, July 19, 1993.
6. Hebblethwaite, *Paul VI: the First Modern Pope*, 471.
7. Ibid., 472.
8. Ibid., 476.
9. William H. Shannon, *The Lively Debate: Response to Humanae Vitae* (New York: Sheed & Ward, 1970), 99–100.
10. Cited in Kaiser, *The Politics of Sex and Religion*, 181.
11. Cited in ibid., 182.
12. Cited in ibid., 127.
13. Cited in Hebblethwaite, *Paul VI: The First Modern Pope*, 487.
14. Charles Curran, "Personal Reflections on Birth Control," in Daniel Callahan, ed., *The Catholic Case for Contraception* (London: Macmillan, 1969), 27.
15. *National Catholic Reporter*, May 13, 1967.
16. Hebblethwaite, *Paul VI: The First Modern Pope*, 488.
17. Cited in Kaiser, *The Politics of Sex and Religion*, 192.
18. Ibid.
19. Ibid., 193.

Chapter 15: The Encyclical at Last, 1968

1. National Catholic News Service, August 8, 1968.
2. Quotations from *Humanae Vitae* are from the U.S. Catholic Conference translation, 1968.
3. Cited in Daniel Callahan, ed., *The Catholic Case for Contraception* (London: Macmillan, 1969), 70.
4. *National Catholic Reporter*, August 7, 1968.
5. Ibid.
6. *The Tablet*, September 21, 1968.
7. *US Catholic*, April 1969.
8. Cited in Robert Blair Kaiser, *The Politics of Sex and Religion* (Kansas City: Leaven Press, 1985), 206.
9. *National Catholic Reporter*, September 18, 1968.
10. Cited in Callahan, *The Catholic Case for Contraception*, 90.
11. Cited in William H. Shannon, *The Lively Debate: Response to Humanae Vitae* (New York: Sheed & Ward, 1970), 163.
12. Dietrich von Hildebrand, *The Encyclical Humanae Vitae: A Sign of Contradiction* (Chicago: Franciscan Herald Press, 1969), 80.
13. Cited in Shannon, *The Lively Debate*, 155.

14. Cited in Kaiser, *The Politics of Sex and Religion*, 200.

15. Cited in ibid., 201.

16. Cited in ibid., 203.

17. Cited in Shannon, *The Lively Debate*, 195.

18. Cited in Kaiser, *The Politics of Sex and Religion*, 213.

19. Joseph A. Selling, *The Reaction to Humanae Vitae: A Study in Social and Fundamental Theology* (Ann Arbor: University Microfilms International, 1979), 31.

20. A full of analysis of the reactions of the world's bishops' conferences is to be found in Philip Kaufman, *Why You Can Disagree and Remain a Faithful Catholic* (New York: Crossroad, 1991), 72–83.

21. Cited in Kaiser, *The Politics of Sex and Religion*, 190.

22. Cited in Shannon, *The Lively Debate*, 193.

23. *National Catholic Reporter*, August 7, 1968.

Chapter 16: The Aftermath, 1969–94

1. Full analyses of the causes and extent of Catholic decline can be found in Andrew M. Greeley, William C. McCready, and Kathleen McCourt, *Catholic Schools in a Declining Church* (Kansas City: Sheed and Ward, 1976); Andrew M. Greeley, *American Catholics since the Council: An Unauthorized Report* (Chicago: Thomas More, 1985); and Andrew M. Greeley, *The Catholic Myth: The Behavior and Beliefs of American Catholics* (New York: Charles Scribner's Sons, 1990).

2. Philip Kaufman, *Why You Can Disagree and Remain a Faithful Catholic* (New York: Crossroad, 1991), 77.

3. Kenneth Untener, "*Humanae Vitae*: What Has It Done to Us?" *America*, June 18, 1993.

4. Yves M. Congar, "Reception as an Ecclesiastical Reality," *Concilium 77* (New York: Herder and Herder, 1972), 57–76.

5. Avery Dulles, "The Question of Non-Reception," *America*, November 1986.

6. Peter Hebblethwaite, *Paul VI: The First Modern Pope* (New York: Paulist Press, 1993), 594.

7. Bernard Häring, *My Witness for the Church* (New York: Paulist Press, 1992), 131.

8. Hebblethwaite, *Paul VI: The First Modern Pope*, 597.

9. Ibid., 598.

10. Charles Curran, "Encyclical Left Church Credibility Stillborn," *National Catholic Reporter*, July 16, 1993.

11. Cited in Robert Blair Kaiser, *The Politics of Sex and Religion* (Kansas City: Leaven Press, 1985), 233.

12. Peter Hebblethwaite, "Echoes of Old Showdown Haunt New Encyclical," *National Catholic Reporter*, August 27, 1993.

13. Ibid.

14. Kaiser, *The Politics of Sex and Religion*, 232.

15. Hebblethwaite, "Echoes of Old Showdown."

16. Cited in Janet E. Smith, *Humanae Vitae: A Generation Later* (Washington: Catholic University of America Press, 1991), 240.

17. Ibid., 241.

18. Ibid., 253.

19. Ibid., 228.

20. Cited in Kenneth A. Briggs, *Holy Siege: the Year That Shook Catholic America* (San Francisco: Harper, 1992), 224–25.

21. *National Catholic Reporter*, October 8, 1993.

22. Ibid.

23. *New York Times*, October 16, 1993.

24. Cited in *National Catholic Reporter*, July 23, 1993.

25. Janet E. Smith, "Barnyard Morality," *America*, August 13, 1994.

26. William H. Shannon, *The Lively Debate: Response to Humanae Vitae* (New York: Sheed & Ward, 1970), 188.

27. Msgr. George A. Kelly, *Keeping the Church Catholic with John Paul II* (New York: Doubleday, 1990), 36.

28. David Toolan, "The Tempest over Cairo," *America*, August 27, 1994.

Chapter 17: Survivors

1. John Marshall, "Inside the Commission," *The Tablet*, July 7, 1993.

2. Pierre de Locht, "Four Theological Considerations," *The Christian Family in Today's World* (Chicago: Foundation for International Cooperation, 1968).

Index of Names

199